# Pointed thoughts for people on the go.

A good devotional is essential for organizing the daily quiet time you need for spiritual fulfillment. Yet many busy people don't have time for lengthy, structured devotionals. *Every Single Day* consists of promises, instructions, and affirmations from Scripture, designed to help you find daily enrichment and fulfillment in just a few moments. Unlike other devotionals, the pages in *Every Single Day* are numbered — not dated. This allows you to start at the beginning and proceed in order, regardless of the day, or time of year. Though each message takes only a short time to read, its impact will provide you with spiritual energy throughout the entire day. If you're looking for power-packed devotions without a lot of time-consuming structure, *Every Single Day* is written just for you.

BY JIM SMOKE

Suddenly Single
Every Single Day

# Jim Smoke

# Every Single Day

Fleming H. Revell Company
Old Tappan, New Jersey

Scripture quotations identified NIV are from Holy Bible, New International Version, copyright © 1978, New York International Bible Society. Used by permission.

Scripture quotations identified TEV are from the *Good News Bible*—Old Testament: Copyright © American Bible Society 1976: New Testament: Copyright © American Bible Society 1966, 1971, 1976.

Scripture quotations identified TLB are taken from The Living Bible, copyright © 1971 by Tyndale House Publishers, Wheaton, IL. Used by permission.

Scripture quotations identified PHILLIPS are from THE NEW TESTAMENT IN MODERN ENGLISH (Revised Edition), translated by J.B. Phillips. © J.B. Phillips 1958, 1960, 1972. Used by permission of Macmillan Publishing Co., Inc.

Scripture quotations identified RSV are from the Revised Standard Version of the Bible, copyrighted 1946, 1952, © 1971 and 1973.

Scripture quotations identified NAS are from the New American Standard Bible, © The Lockman Foundation 1960, 1962, 1963, 1968, 1971, 1972, 1973, 1975, 1977.

Scripture quotations identified NEB are from The New English Bible. © The Delegates of the Oxford University Press and the Syndics of the Cambridge University Press 1961 and 1970. Reprinted by permission.

**Library of Congress Cataloging in Publication Data**
Smoke, Jim
 Every single day.

 1. Single people—Prayer-books and devotions—
English. 2. Devotional calendars. I. Title.
BV4596.S5S627   1983     242'.2     82-23021
ISBN 0-8007-5120-5

TO Todd, Tori, and Timi Jo,
our children . . . every single day!

Special thanks

To Eve Craig, my secretary, for her typing skills and critical eye

To Lloyd John Ogilvie, Senior Pastor at Hollywood Presbyterian Church, for his inspiration

# How to Use Every Single Day

What do you feel you need as you start today or end it—a promise from God—some instructions in your Christian walk—an affirmation of God's love for you?

*Every Single Day* is not designed with a day and date on every page. Life's struggles are not that easily lined up. It is designed to be read any way you want to read it.

You can read a promise one day, an instruction the next, and an affirmation the third. You can read "Promises" for a week or a month, then switch to "Instructions" or "Affirmations." Your heart will tell you what you are in need of.

As you read a page for the day, put a little check mark up in the right-hand corner. Let's call it a growth mark. It will help you know what you have read and what remains unread, as you journey through *Every Single Day*.

# *Promises*

Has anyone ever made a promise to you and broken it? Most of us have had that experience more often than we care to remember. As a result, we tend to lose confidence in people, and ultimately in ourselves.

One of the richest treasures God has for us is the many promises found in Scripture.

At the beginning of a new day or the end of a long day, it is good to know that the promises of God to us will not be broken. They are there for eternity.

It is important to know just what God promises us. In this first section of *Every Single Day,* I want to plant the foundation of God's promises deep in your life.

Strength comes from storing up promises! Endurance comes from living them out—every single day.

# Every Single Day

## *Promise:* God Has Not Deserted You

*"I know the plans I have for you," declares the Lord, "plans to prosper you and not harm you, plans to give you hope and a future."*

Jeremiah 29:11 NIV

The picture looked pretty bleak for Israel. They were in captivity in Babylon when Jeremiah sent them a letter of encouragement. His letter was a clear promise that God had not deserted them. Even though they were to live through tough times in a foreign land, God was still going to work through them. His promise to them was that He had a plan in mind. That plan contained four elements.

First, He would prosper them even in oppressive surroundings. Second, He would protect them from any harm that might come their way. Third, He would give them a hope that would take them through each day. And fourth, He had a future in mind for them. Babylon was not the end of the road. It was merely a challenge on the journey.

When all your well-laid plans seem to go off track, do you find yourself feeling deserted by God? Wouldn't it be great to get a letter in the mail like the one Jeremiah sent to the captives? The same promise that God sent through Jeremiah to Israel is His promise for you today. He hasn't abandoned you. He still has the blueprint for your life in His hand. Claim today's promise for yourself. Begin to live today, knowing that God has these same four things in mind for you as He had for His children many years ago.

## *Promise:* God Will Keep You Safe

*When I lie down, I go to sleep in peace; you alone, O Lord, keep me perfectly safe.*
Psalms 4:8 TEV

If the many manufacturers of sleeping pills and muscle relaxants believed the above promise, they would be out of business. If you believed that promise, you would help put them out of business. The truth is that millions of dollars are spent each year on varied assortments of sleeping aids for the American public.

We lie down to rest after a busy day and find that we can't sleep. Our minds are crowded with the thoughts of the day just lived, and overcrowded with the thoughts of the day about to come. We roll and toss and finally fall into a fitful form of sleep.

Why? What did David, the Psalmist, know that we don't know today?

David discovered that his source of peace in sleeping was in knowing that God was protecting him. He was able to release all of his anxieties and problems to God. He knew that all of the fears that seem to grow larger in the night are really God's problem. His safety and protection was in God's hands. Knowing that, he was able to relax and let the peace of God flood over him at night.

Are you carrying your daily agenda to bed with you every night? Are you reaching for the chemicals rather than the promises?

God will surround you with a safe refuge and a release from your daily cares if you ask Him.

## *Promise:* The Best Kind of Fruit Comes From God's Market

*When the Holy Spirit controls our lives he will produce this kind of fruit in us: love, joy, peace, patience, kindness, goodness, faithfulness, gentleness and self-control. . . .*                                     Galatians 5:22, 23 TLB

I grew up on a farm that produced about twenty different varieties of fruit. I could go and pick the best fruit at any time and enjoy it. That kind of early freedom makes it difficult for me to buy fruit in today's supermarkets. The quality is often poor and the price high. But I recently discovered a small fruit market where the fruit is much as it was on my farm, first quality and very tasty—also very expensive. It sort of reminds me of the fruit that comes from God's market.

Paul told the Early Christians at Galatia that God dispenses first-quality fruit when the Holy Spirit controls our lives. His kind of fruit in our lives gives us a nutritional balance that leads to good, sound spiritual growth. The fruit of the Spirit showing in our lives is a slow process. There is no speeding it up. It takes cultivating and care, just as growing the fruit on my farm did.

Which of the above nine fruits that Paul talks about do you feel most in need of today? They are all important. Just pick out one today and allow the Holy Spirit the freedom to cultivate and nourish that fruit in your life.

## *Promise:* **God's Word Lights Your Pathway**

*Your word is a lamp to guide me and a light for my path.*

Psalms 119:105 TEV

A recent article in the *Los Angeles Times* told of the phasing out of the many lighthouses along the California coast. It spoke of the new sophisticated technology that has outdated the usefulness of the old lighthouses. Some are abandoned and some are up for sale, while others have been converted to guest lodges and private homes. I thought about the many sea captains over the years who must have looked through the fog for the welcome light.

God's Word can be compared to a lighthouse. It sends out a strong, clear beacon to those who enter its pages. It gives guidance in the situations we all face daily. It illuminates things in our lives and shows them as they really are. It warns us when we are getting too close to the edge of a disaster. It cuts through the haziness that sometimes clouds our lives.

The Psalmist suggests two kinds of light in this verse. The lamp is used for seeing things that are close to us. The light is for seeing things more distant.

The Scriptures have a way of giving us direction in the situations that are closest to us. For many of us, this gets uncomfortable. We want to use the light to look way down the road and deal with what's there sometime in the future.

What are God's lamp and light showing you today?

## *Promise:* **God Is the Conductor**

*We should make plans—counting on God to direct us.*     Proverbs 16:9 TLB

I'm a list maker. If I can't plan it and write it down, I won't get it done. If I lose my list, my plan is shot. At the end of the day, I know whether I have accomplished anything by the lines through my listed items.

I meet many people in my travels who never make lists and never have plans. They just seem to float along, but they never get very much done. Their plan is to get organized tomorrow. Sadly, their tomorrows are as disorganized as their todays.

I believe we should prayerfully make plans each day and expect God to direct us as we pursue those plans. The miracle of order and design in the universe clearly tells us that God knew how to make a plan and follow it through. His creation is not put together with tape and string.

Pressure usually comes when we have no plan. We are like the man who got on his horse and rode off in all directions.

What's your plan for today? What needs to be done? What's a priority? Where's that list where you just wrote everything down?

God can only bless your plan and direct you in accomplishing it if you have one.

## *Promise:* God Doesn't Shortchange You in Life

> *". . . My purpose is to give life in all its fullness."*                 John 10:10 TLB

There are many people today who feel that they are missing out in some of the areas of what life has to offer. If we are to believe the media pursuit of materialism, we are all missing out on something or other that can add meaning to our lives.

Many of us feel that we need just one more thing and our lives will be full. We get that one thing and we still have a void.

John tells us that Jesus intended for you and me to have everything that life has to offer. He did not intend for us to be shortchanged in any department. The problem that most of us have is knowing how to fill our lives with the right things.

In the first part of verse 10, John talks about the purpose of the thief. He tells us this thief comes with the intention of stealing, killing, and destroying our fullness. Jesus, in marked contrast, comes to reverse the intentions of the thief. He is the giver of life. The thief is the taker.

Are the things that you are after in life ultimately going to rob you of God's fullness? Is God trying to put His things of meaning in your life?

God wants us to live life to the hilt. It is His gift to you and me. Don't be robbed of real life by phony pursuits.

## *Promise:* There Will Be a Sunrise

> *His anger lasts a moment; his favor lasts for life! Weeping may go on all night, but in the morning there is joy.*                 Psalms 30:5 TLB

David, the Psalmist, was an optimist. So am I. How about you?

David was always able to get a clear picture of what was going on in his life and around him. He was able to feel the depths of despair and tell us about it. He was also able to look beyond the edge of despair and view the goodness of God. He was the original survivor.

David's eye on optimism did not deny the weeping that takes place in life. It is a part of the struggle. But he didn't dwell there permanently. He said that there is a certain kind of joy in surviving the weeping.

Perhaps the question you are asking is, "When does my morning come? I want some joy!" I wish I could answer that in hours and days for you, but only God is holding the timetable for your life. His promise is that He will not leave you stuck in the night, lost in your tears. There will be a morning, and with it a sunrise. With that sunrise will come the quiet sound of joy.

Have you locked yourself into the night and lost hope of the morning sunrise? Let God sink this promise into your very soul as you look toward catching His joy in the morning.

## *Promise:* **God Is Constant**

*"I the Lord do not change. . . ."*                                  Malachi 3:6 NIV

Yesterday I went to my favorite bookstore. As I parked, I looked over to my left and thought I was lost. Almost overnight, a giant new supermarket had replaced the upper reaches of the bookstore parking lot. Changes! Blink twice, and someone puts up a new building.

Changes are coming thick and fast in our world and in our lives. They can be both frightening and exhilarating, stretching us or stunting us in our growth.

God is constant in a world of change. For the Old Testament prophets like Malachi, it meant that God was an anchor in a world suddenly adrift. His nature, His personality, His properties did not change. His principles were still solid. People changed but God did not.

The changes in today's world are coming more rapidly than ever. New advances in technology make yesterday's inventions obsolete overnight.

Some people would like to change God. They would like to update Him and give Him a twentieth-century look—maybe some racing stripes and mag wheels! They would like to give Him a contemporary cloak and make Him more acceptable in a changing world.

God may be the only thing today that is not undergoing society's overhaul. He remains constant, solid, certain, secure. He is our rock! Aren't you glad?

## *Promise:* Leave That to God

*Dear friends, never avenge yourselves. Leave that to God, for he has said that he will repay those who deserve it.*                    Romans 12:19 TLB

Have you ever wanted to get even with someone for what they have done to you? We all have. The desire for personal justice runs strong in most of us.

We deal with retribution on three levels. The first level is emotional. We spend a great deal of time thinking about what we would like to do or say to the person who has wronged us. We can get so wrapped up in this, we think of little else.

The second level is actually doing something to that person. We may verbally tell him or her off or even physically attack him. By our act we are telling him that he can't get away with what he has done to us.

The third level is dealing with retribution on a spiritual plane. The Roman Christians were just like you and me. They wanted to get even when wronged. Paul suggested a better way to defuse their anger: leave it to God to take care of. In the end, He is the judge of us all anyhow.

Tough advice! Are you carrying around a desire for revenge on someone, spending a lot of mental and emotional energy for naught?

Leave it to God. Trust Him with the whole situation and claim His promise that He will take care of any repayment. Today's load will be lighter if you do!

## *Promise:* Give Generously

*Give generously, for your gifts will return to you later. Divide your gifts among many, for in the days ahead you yourself may need much help.*
                    Ecclesiastes 11:1, 2 TLB

Are you a giver or a receiver? Recently I asked a large audience of singles that question. More than 80 percent of those in the room indicated by raised hands that they were givers and felt uncomfortable receiving. The truth is that if 80 percent are givers, there has to be an 80 percent somewhere who receive. In reality, most people would rather give because it creates a feeling of control over a person or situation.

Solomon tries to put giving into perspective for us with the above words of promise. He states that gifts given in a right spirit will bring dividends to us later. That doesn't mean that we are to give with the objective of storing up a landslide of gifts for ourselves. We are always recipients when we give with a right spirit.

The mood in our society is usually the reverse of Solomon's urging. Our society says, "Look out for number one." Get all you can while it's being passed around. Store and hoard for a rainy day. Our homes and garages are full to overflowing with our getting.

In sharp contrast, God's person is to be a giver with a generous spirit.

Do you have some gifts to give away today? How long has it been since you knew the joy of giving with no expected returns?

## *Promise:* **Good-bye to the Old**

*If anyone is in Christ, he is a new creation; the old has gone, the new has come!*                                              2 Corinthians 5:17 NIV

Have you ever looked back over your life and wished you could start all over again? Probably most of us have. Usually it's when things are not going too well or we have just put together a whole string of defeats. All of us have learned that you can't go backward, you can only go ahead.

Paul knew this. Looking back over his life, he saw a few things he wasn't too proud of—like helping cheer on the crowd that stoned Stephen to death.

Paul also knew firsthand what it was like to have his life changed from the inside out. When God interrupted his journey on the Damascus road, he became a changed person. He was invaded by the love of Christ, and God began to change him from within. Paul's old nature began to dissolve, and a new nature took its place. God wrapped His arms around him and wouldn't let him go!

Have you been changed by Christ's love? It's not an overnight process. It happens when you invite Christ into your life by an act of the will. The decision only takes an instant. The conversion takes the rest of your life.

God promises to help you say good-bye to the old you and hello to the new you!

## *Promise:* **Giving It All to God**

*Commit everything you do to the Lord. Trust him to help you do it and he will.*
                                                           Psalms 37:5 TLB

Is God interested in the little things in your life?

Some of us have two lists. One is the big, long list of hard-to-do, next-to-impossible things we try giving to God to solve. The shorter list contains the I-can-do-it-myself-without-God's-help items. The funny thing is that we seem to stumble the most over the little things we try to do ourselves.

God is not a "some things" God. He is an "everything" God. He wants us to give Him both lists, however short or long. After we present Him with the list, our trust factor shifts into gear and we can await the results.

It's hard. We keep wanting to withhold some things for our own solving. Sometimes we feel that we are bothering the Creator of the universe with things He has no interest in. Yet Matthew says the hairs of our head are numbered. Hairs are pretty small.

Commit, trust, and watch the results. Turn God loose on your agenda for today and see what He will do.

What would you like to give to Him today? What are you trying to solve yourself that He would do so much better?

You can trust the Creator.

## *Promise:* **Practice Loving**

*"My command is this: Love each other as I have loved you."*

John 15:12 NIV

In a high-level strategy session, Jesus speaks to the disciples on the Mount of Olives. He is issuing their marching orders for the rest of their lives on earth. He is also equipping them with His plan to win and make disciples of all men.

No involved militant plans here. No coups or takeovers. No guerilla warfare. Just a simple command for the disciples to demonstrate to the world how much they love each other.

Love always begins with the person closest to you. It does not begin with nameless and faceless people. It begins with those you sweat and struggle with—those who frequently disagree with you and put you down. That's why it is so hard.

It is easier to love the world than your closest relative. The world is general. Your relative is specific. The world is vague. Your relative has a character.

I am sure the disciples looked at each other when Jesus spoke these words and just waited for Him to get on to the real business at hand. He kept coming back to this command because He knew it was the source of changed lives. He shared His love and was about to share it even more deeply on Calvary. He simply wanted it demonstrated among those closest to Him.

Whom will you love today? Can you love him or her in the way Christ loves you? It won't be easy. Love is never an option!

## *Promise:* **Knock—Somebody's Home**

*"Ask and it will be given to you. Search and you will find. Knock and the door
will be opened for you. The one who asks will always receive; the one who is
searching will always find, and the door is opened to the man who knocks."*
                                                    Matthew 7:7, 8 PHILLIPS

There are two kinds of people in life. One kind is a settler while the
other is an explorer.

Settlers just kind of sit with arms folded and watch the world rush by
around them. Explorers are people who are always climbing the next hill
to see what is on the other side. Which one of the two groups would you
place yourself in today?

In Matthew's Gospel, we read Jesus' long discourse to the disciples and
the people gathered around Him. He cautions them, exhorts them, challenges them, and affirms them. In the above verse, He strongly encourages us to become door-knocking explorers. His word is to ask, search,
and knock. His promise is that we will receive, find, and go through open
doors.

Many of us expect things to happen in our lives with little or no effort
expended on our part. Jesus constantly urged the people around Him to
be adventurers and explorers. He did not send them blindly into these
new experiences. He sent them with a promise. They were to do the work
and He would provide the blessing and reward.

Are you asking, searching, and knocking in new areas of your life? God
is at home to you. He wants to answer your knock!

## *Promise:* **A Day at a Time**

*"So don't be anxious about tomorrow. God will take care of your tomorrow
too. Live one day at a time."*                    Matthew 6:34 TLB

Someone has said, "Today is the tomorrow you worried about yesterday." Most of us have that problem at least once a week. We tend to
hurry through today as we build a mountain of worry about tomorrow.
When that tomorrow comes, we just push all our worries a day ahead.
Following this pattern, we could spend the rest of our lives worrying.

Jesus knew that our human tendency would be to be anxious and
worry about things, people, problems, events. Notice that His word about
worry and being anxious is authoritative. He simply says not to do it. If
that were all He said, it would be of little help, but He backs up His command with a promise. He says that He will take care of your tomorrows

and my tomorrows. That means living our lives in trust that tomorrow, as well as today, is really God's problem. He owns all our tomorrows. We don't.

Jesus offers us a command, a promise, and a solution as we live the days of our lives. The solution is found in centering on today—living it, embracing it, affirming it, enjoying it.

What's on your "tomorrow" agenda? Is it ruining your "today" as it tumbles through your mind? Give it to God and start living in *today!*

## Promise: **God Will Not Overload Us**

> *No temptation has come your way that is too hard for flesh and blood to bear. But God can be trusted not to allow you to suffer any temptation beyond your powers of endurance. He will see to it that every temptation has its way out, so that it will be possible for you to bear it.*    1 Corinthians 10:13 PHILLIPS

*"I can't take it anymore!"*

If you are a normal human being, you have probably echoed these words more than once. It is usually an indication that we have reached the bottom line of our endurance in a situation. We want out or we want breathing space.

Paul's statement to the Corinthian church members could be in part a response to their human feelings. He tells them that God will not overload them and push them beyond their ability to endure.

However, he doesn't leave them with just a positive note of divine optimism. He tells them that God will provide the way out when they feel there is no way out.

Part of our problem is that it seems easier to see closed doors than open doors. Our frustrations, temptations, and confrontations seem to seal all the escape routes. Our problems become walls instead of bridges.

God promises a way out. Are you looking past your problems for God's open doors?

## Promise: **God Loves Gray Hair**

> *"I will be your God through all your lifetime, yes, even when your hair is white with age. I made you and I will care for you. I will carry you along and be your Savior."*                                                        Isaiah 46:4 TLB

Have you seen the television commercial for the miracle solution you comb into your hair each day and within two weeks, all the gray hair is gone? The whole premise of the commercial is that gray hair is to be avoided at all costs if you want to appear youthful and successful. Gray hair means you are getting old in a world where the emphasis is on youth.

Isaiah gives us a promise that tells us God is still with us even as our hair turns to gray and then to white. The world may write us off and retire us to Wrinkle City. God promises us four things.

First, He will be our God through our entire lifetime. We don't retire from Him and He doesn't retire us. Second, He promises that He will care for us. Our primary care will always come from God. Third, He promises to carry us along. At one time or another, we all need a lift. God promises He will carry us when we are too tired to carry ourselves. Fourth, He promises to be our Savior. The dictionary says *savior* means one who saves, rescues, or delivers. God does all of that for you and for me, whether our hair is graying, falling out, or growing in.

Are you worrying about growing older and getting grayer? No matter how hard we try to prevent it, that's our destiny. It's all right. God loves gray hair!

## *Promise:* God Is Not Confused

> *God is not a God of confusion but of peace.*          1 Corinthians 14:33 RSV

Several weeks ago I was standing outside the lost-and-found area at a ski lodge. As I looked at the human jam of skiers coming and going, I noticed a sobbing little girl being guided toward the lost-and-found desk by a woman. She cried out her bewilderment at not being able to find her father and mother in the crowd of skiers, ski poles, ski tows, and general confusion. I empathized with her as I felt her sense of confusion and lostness. After an announcement on the public-address system, her parents appeared to claim her. Her comment was, "Daddy, you were lost and I was confused!"

Who was lost and who was confused—the little girl, her father, the rest of the skiers?

That Saturday at the ski lodge was a microcosm of life. There is a lot of confusion around all of us every day—sounds, people, activity. Some days we wonder where God is in relation to all this confusion. Is He as disorganized and disoriented as we are?

God is not confused by the things that confuse us. God's design is one of peace. The gift He brings to you and me is one of order, organization, and calm.

We buy into the order of confusion in life only when we forget what God is about.

What have you ordered up for your life today—a little more confusion than yesterday? Why not place an order with God for a little peace today?

## *Promise:* **A Home for the Lonely**

*He gives the lonely a home to live in and leads prisoners out into happy freedom....*                                                                                     Psalms 68:6 TEV

There are many prisons in life that people place themselves in. One of the worst is the prison of loneliness. It is a place of inner and outer desolation. It is often surrounded by the four walls of self-pity, depression, guilt, and anger.

I meet many lonely people in my travels. Most blame their loneliness on others. Too few are willing to take the blame.

David, the writer of the Psalms, knew about the loneliness that comes from being cut off from a vital relationship. In David's situation, much of his loneliness came as a result of being cut off from God. He knew the joy of his friendship with God and the loneliness of his isolation from God. He knew what it was like to be the prisoner of his own loneliness and to find the ultimate happiness in being set free.

God's new home for the lonely is found beyond the walls of self-imprisonment. In this new place there is a happy freedom—a freedom to grow, to stretch, to bury yesterday and its self-indicting thoughts.

Everyone feels a little lonely now and then. That's normal. If loneliness persists in your life, take a look at who built the walls, and then think about God's offer to lead you out into a new home of happy freedom.

## *Promise:* **The Good Stuff and the Bad Stuff**

*And we know that God causes all things to work together for good to those who love God, to those who are the called according to His purpose.*
                                                                                     Romans 8:28 NAS

Have you had any bad things happen to you lately? If you are a part of the real world, your answer will be yes.

When the bad things happen, most of us see them as bad and often wish they had happened to someone else or not at all. Human vision seldom gives us the long look into how the bad can work out to any good.

God has given us a marvelous promise to claim in the midst of bad happenings. He tells us that He can weave all the bad things into a tapestry in our lives that will bring about good. Our common question with this promise is, "How?" or perhaps even, "When?"

Fortunately, that's God's mystery. He works over the broad span of time and is not limited to our tunnel vision. Our commitment to the fulfillment of this promise in our lives is to trust and wait and see. God's requirement for the fulfilling of this promise is to love Him and be called to His purposes in life.

Love, trust, wait and see! Don't short-circuit the returns from God on your problems. Let Him sort, shift, shuffle, rearrange, and direct them. He knows what to do with them and where to take them.

Have you given the bad stuff to God and entrusted the results to Him?

## Promise: God Isn't Afraid of Anything

*For God has not given us a spirit of timidity, but of power and love and discipline.*                                    2 Timothy 1:7 NAS

*Agoraphobia* is sometimes defined as the fear of everything. Many people spend their days and nights sealed in their homes for fear of what might happen when they leave. Fear is a readily available commodity in our society. Each of us has our public and private lists of fears. We fear the things we have to do and the things we ought not to do. Walls, gates, burglar alarms, insurance—all are to protect us from inevitable fears that can rob our peace of mind.

Timothy tells us that timidity (*fear* is the word used in other translations) does not come from God. He did not originate it nor does He sanction it. Fear is simply our distrust of God.

In the place once occupied by fear in our lives, God wants to put three strong antidotes: power, love, and discipline. (Another translation uses the words *sound mind* for discipline.)

These three are gifts that God places into our intellect and our being to help us kick the fear habit. God's power will release us from the immobilizing effect that fear brings. His love will surround us and overwhelm any fears that we have. He will bring order and discipline into our lives. Discipline always squelches fear, for fear thrives best in disorganization. A sound mind is having a mind set at peace while we live in a world filled with fears of every kind.

Have you kicked the fear habit? Are fears squeezing the joy and vitality out of your life? Turn your fears over to God today and allow Him to bring peace into your life.

## *Promise:* **God Holds Hands**

*"I, the Lord, have called you in righteousness; I will take hold of your hand. I will keep you. . . ."*                    Isaiah 42:6 NIV

Have you ever noticed how many people hold hands in public? It seems to me that there are two predominant groups: the young and the very old. The young often do it to express their love and affection for each other. Old people do it to solidify and affirm a love that has stood the test of time and perhaps also to physically support one another.

Did you ever wish you had someone to hold your hand at a given moment? Have you ever tried to hold a hand that did not want to be held? Both can be frustrating experiences.

Having someone hold your hand can give you a feeling of support, of being loved, of being important, of being comforted, and being protected.

Isaiah affirms the fact that God is into holding hands! He has a firm, secure, and loving grip when we reach out to Him. This Scripture tells us that He will not only take hold of our hands but that He will keep us as well.

Take a moment right now and close your eyes. As you do, reach your hand out as if someone were coming forward to take it. Visualize in your mind that God is reaching out with His strong hand of love to take hold of yours. Feel His strength and support.

He is always there to take hold of our hands. He simply waits for us to reach out!

## *Promise:* **God Keeps His Promises**

*The God who made both earth and heaven, the seas and everything in them. He is the God who keeps every promise.*                    Psalms 146:6 TLB

We live in an age of failing promises. Great businesses and financial institutions are folding around us overnight. Those who worked in them felt secure because the company promised if they did their jobs, they would be treated fairly and have job security. An employee's response to a folding company is usually one of anger and disappointment. The larger the company, the bigger the promise and the greater the disappointment. Inner feelings say, *Whom can I really trust?*

David sensed a certain security in being able to affirm that God made both earth and heaven. Both are God's companies and He is in charge. There will be no failure and no looming unemployment with God—no broken promises!

How many broken promises have you been the recipient of in your life? Hundreds, even thousands, perhaps? All of us have been at the place of the shattered promise.

There are more than seven thousand promises in the Word of God. None of them have ever been broken. God keeps His promises.

Every broken promise that you experience in life can be a reminder that God stands solidly behind all that He has promised to you and me. What He says, He will do. You can trust God.

## *Promise:* God Approves Your Plans

*Commit to the Lord whatever you do, and your plans will succeed.*

Proverbs 16:3 NIV

Have you ever planned that perfect outing, prayed for sunshine, and had it rain all day? Frustrating, isn't it? You wonder whether you should blame yourself, the local weatherman, or God. The truth is that our best-laid plans don't always meet our expectations.

What was Solomon, the wisest man who ever lived, talking about in this promise? Was he telling us to simply inform God what we wanted to do, and everything would always work out to our satisfaction? I don't think so.

Solomon starts this promise with a huge request: Commit everything you are about to do to the Lord. If you are about to do something wrong by God's standard, you will have a hard time committing it to Him. If your desire is to please God in everything you do, it will be easy to commit those plans to Him. Notice the big word in this promise is *whatever.* That is pretty inclusive, isn't it?

If you commit to God what He can joyfully bless, then your plans will succeed. God wants you to succeed, but within the framework of what He knows is best for you.

Sometimes I try to outguess God. I think I know what is best for me in making my plans. I am sure God sadly shakes His head many times and rejects my game plan. Back to square one to check out my plans.

Give God your set of plans for today. Then give Him the freedom to make any alterations.

## *Promise:* God's Pick-Me-Up

*He gives power to the tired and worn out, and strength to the weak.*
                                                                Isaiah 40:29 TLB

A recent statistic in a local newspaper stated that there were more auto accidents on Los Angeles freeways when people were coming home from work than when they were going to work. Why? It seems people were rested, relaxed, and alert in the morning and weary, uptight, and upset in the evening.

Tired emotions put us on edge. We become simmering volcanoes, ready to erupt at the slightest provocation. Sometimes I feel we live in a tired world where everyone is ready to pop off on cue.

God promises us a second wind when we are tired and worn-out. His pick-me-up is to give power and strength in the midst of our weariness. Isaiah does not intimate that we are not spiritual or are out of touch with God because we are tired and worn-out. He seems to accept it as a natural human condition. He knows it, God knows it, and it is all right. God will simply move to meet the need by giving a power boost. Isaiah does not even condemn weakness. He recognizes it as a part of life's struggle and affirms God's promise for renewed strength in our weakened state.

Are you feeling wiped out today—simply out of gas? Ask God for a supply of His power and strength for your life right now!

## *Promise:* The Patient Receive the Promises

*You need to be patient, in order to do the will of God and receive what He promises.*                                               *See* Hebrews 10:36

I remember when I couldn't wait for Christmas to come. Every day I would ask my parents how much longer it would be. Their response became standard year after year: "Be patient. Christmas came last year and it will come again this year." I crossed off days on the calendar in an effort to exercise patience. Other things were tried and abandoned. Nothing worked. I was simply an impatient person, and even remain tinged with impatience today.

Apparently the Hebrew Christians were impatient, too. It's not a new disease. Paul set before them the rewards of being patient. They would be much better at doing the will of God if they were patient, and they would also receive His promises. Paul seemed to be telling them that God was not in any hurry.

Most of us live life in one big hurry. We even wish God would hurry things up in our lives. We don't want to wait for anything that we know will be good. If we know it's going to be bad, however, we hope it never comes.

Patience is enjoying the distance between promises. It is knowing that the will of God is only revealed in the space of time.

Are you moving too fast today to smell the flowers or to know God's will or to receive what He has promised you? Slow down! You might run by it all!

## *Promise:* **Thank You, God**

> *Give thanks to the Lord, for he is good; his love endures forever.*
> Psalms 107:1 NIV

Most of us send more mental thank-you cards to our friends than we send of the Hallmark variety. A friend does something extraspecial for us and we think, "I must send a thank-you card." We get busy, forget, and the thought is canceled. Sometimes it takes the death of a friend for us to catch up with our thank-yous. We say it through flowers or words, but the friend never receives the message.

Life should be a series of thank-yous for all of us. It takes time and thought and sometimes even a postage stamp. The affirmation helps others grow.

David had much to be thankful for as he penned this promise. He was thankful for the expressed nature of God toward him. He tells us that God is good and His love endures forever. This is no conditional thanks. It is unconditional because that's what God's love is. No matter what our performance record with God is, His goodness and love still come through.

God has been good to you. You just may not have added up the many ways His goodness has come through lately. His goodness is wrapped in His enduring love for you. Take a minute right now and thank Him. Maybe you need to say it out loud. Thanksgiving is not relegated to one day a year. Thanksgiving is today!

# *Promise:* **A Not-So-Fragile Gift**

*"I am leaving you with a gift—peace of mind and heart! And the peace I give isn't fragile like the peace the world gives. So don't be troubled or afraid."*
John 14:27 TLB

What kind of peace does the world promise us? Peace of mind if we buy the right product, peace of soul if we have the right insurance plan, peace and productivity in daily living if we have the right career with the right company. Society's cry is to do a certain thing and be assured of peace. Even in a world situation, we are told we must have more arms than anyone else in order to keep the balance of power and have peace among nations.

In a conversation with His disciples, Jesus got into the topic of what real peace is all about. The disciples knew what it was like to live in a troubled world. They thought Jesus would set up His own kingdom, appoint them to the ruling class, and they would know peace.

The real gift that Jesus wanted to give the disciples and the world was an inner peace that no exterior circumstances could shake. Peace of mind is a quiet confidence of really knowing who is at the controls of the universe. Peace of heart is putting us at rest with our list of desires and wants. Jesus told the disciples that this is a strong peace. It is not fragile. It is enduring. When it is at the center of your life, you will not be troubled and afraid.

You have this same gift-wrapped promise today! It is offered to you with no strings attached. Claim it and experience a new peace from God.

# *Promise:* **Get to Know Him Better**

*For as you know him better, he will give you, through his great power, everything you need for living a truly good life: he even shares his own glory and his own goodness with us.*                                                                 2 Peter 1:3 TLB

How do you get to know someone better? You spend time with that person. The greater the investment of your time, the more you will receive from the friendship.

Many of us are shortchanged on good friendships because we will not invest the amount of time it takes to cultivate the relationship.

Peter tells us that the same principle is true in our relationship with God. If we refuse to take the time to get to know Him, we will be robbed of the things we need to live a good life. If we spend time getting to know God better, we will be the recipients of His power and His gifts. Peter even adds that this friendship holds nothing back. God adds to it a share of His own glory and His own goodness.

True friendship is always one of deep sharing. As we give depth to a friendship, we receive depth in return. As we spend time knowing and enjoying God, we will find it easier to give the required time for the deepening of the relationship. It eventually becomes a joy rather than a ritual.

Real friendships are spontaneous and casual. There is no pretense and no fear. A close friendship with God should be a natural part of our lives.

Do you know God well enough to receive the blessings of your friendship with Him?

## *Promise:* It's So Simple to Ask

*If you want to know what God wants you to do, ask him, and he will gladly tell you, for he is always ready to give a bountiful supply of wisdom to all who ask him; he will not resent it.*                                              James 1:5 TLB

Have you ever been stumped when trying to decide what God wanted you to do in a situation? We all have. What do you normally do in that kind of situation—ask everyone around you what you should do? When you follow this route, you generally become more confused.

You can find direction by simply asking God. Perhaps you have a fear of asking. The fear might be that God will tell you to do something you don't want to do.

God is in the business of giving good directions. He can be trusted to get us from one point in decision making to another. He has the whole road map in His hands. We usually see only the roads immediately around us.

James tells us that God gladly gives us directions. He is happy that we want to know. His response is to equip us with a bountiful supply of wisdom. God is no miser in the wisdom department. He does not resent our asking Him for directions.

What are you facing right now that you need direction and wisdom in—little things, big things? Have you placed them before the Lord? He is anxious to respond to your needs. He is just waiting for you to ask!

# *Promise:* God Is Your Protector

*The Lord will protect you from all danger; he will keep you safe. He will protect you as you come and go now and forever.*

Psalms 121:7, 8 TEV

The private-bodyguard business is booming in today's world. The rich and famous hire these people to protect them from being mobbed, attacked, robbed, adored, kidnapped, and killed. Bodyguards are equipped to protect their employers from any and every danger that life can hold.

Every Christian has his own private bodyguard, and it doesn't cost a penny. The Psalmist tells us that we will be protected from all danger, not just some dangers. Added to that protection is the knowledge that we will be kept safe. God's security system for the believer is the finest available today.

David goes one step further with God's promise to us. He lets us know that God's protection system is in operation twenty-four hours a day, seven days a week. He is with us as we come to and go from situations. He is with us right now, and He will be with us forever. We are totally surrounded by His protection.

Are you worrying about some of the dangers you will face today or later this week? Are you taking steps to protect yourself or are you willing to let God do the protecting? If we really belong to Him, we are His responsibility.

# *Promise:* God Helps Us Do Greater Things

*"I tell you the truth, anyone who has faith in me will do what I have been doing. He will do even greater things than these, because I am going to the Father."*

John 14:12 NIV

What do you wish you could do that Jesus did when He was on earth? Miracles! That's what most of us would say. People would believe in God if they could just witness His miraculous power.

Isn't it amazing that many who witnessed the miracles of Jesus still did not believe? Philip seemed to be on the edge of this skeptical group. He wasn't too sure about Jesus, His miracles, His destination, or His power. He was a little like all of us, uncertain and wanting to be convinced.

Jesus gave Philip a promise that would make his faith become operative rather than stagnant. He offered him the baton of miracle-working power if Philip would only put his faith in Him. Then Jesus went one step beyond by telling Philip that he would do greater things once Jesus had gone to the Father.

One would have expected Philip to say, "Wow!" God expects us to say, "Wow!" because the same promise that was given to Philip is given to us today. The Scripture says, "anyone."

God wants to enable us to do even greater things than we are doing. We plug in the faith and He generates the power.

Are you ready to go to the Source for the power you need in your life today?

## *Promise:* **Branded By God**

> *He has put his brand upon us—his mark of ownership—and given us his Holy Spirit in our hearts as guarantee that we belong to him, and as the first installment of all that he is going to give us.*
>
> 2 Corinthians 1:22 TLB

In the ranching areas of our country, cattle are branded to show ownership. No matter where they roam to feed, their brand identifies the owner. The cattle may not know to whom they belong, but the owner knows.

When we receive Christ into our lives by faith, we become part of His family. He places His brand upon us. We now belong to Him. From time to time we may forget that we have a special place in His family, but He doesn't.

God does not label us externally with some identifying mark. He puts the Holy Spirit within us in order that good things will come from us. As those good gifts are drawn from us, people will identify us as owned by God. It will not matter where we go. Our identification will not change.

This promise tells us that the gift of the Holy Spirit within us is only the first installment of what is to come. There is more. As the Holy Spirit moves within us and we continue to grow in Christ, greater gifts for ministry and growth will become a part of our lives.

God's brand is internal. It starts from the heart. Do you know to whom you belong? Is His brand readable in your life-style?

## *Promise:* **Stick to the Book**

*This book of the law shall not depart out of your mouth, but you shall medi-*
*tate on it day and night, that you may be careful to do according to all that is*
*written in it; for then you shall make your way prosperous, and then you shall*
*have good success.* Joshua 1:8 RSV

Joshua was assuming the reins of leadership of Israel after Moses' death. He probably wondered how he could follow in the footsteps of a leader like Moses. The Israelites probably wondered, too. God removed the wondering on Joshua's side by giving him the formula for successful leadership and living.

Stick to the book! Keep your heart, head, and nose in the laws of God day and night. Translate the laws into living, and you will be prosperous and successful.

Sounds like a simple plan, doesn't it? Just do what God tells you to do and things will turn out fine. You won't even have to emulate Moses or worry about people saying, "But Moses did it *that* way!" Forget about Moses and follow God.

God is always bringing us back to basics, just as He did in Joshua's situation. We try to create our own success formulas, but God keeps calling us back to His. Ours are so complicated and His are so simple.

Would you like a little prosperity and success in your life? Join Joshua and get with God's simple plan. Stick to the book!

## *Promise:* **One Step at a Time**

*A man's steps are ordered by the Lord. . . .* Proverbs 20:24 RSV

Our journey through life is marked by the footprints we leave behind. Some of these footprints we would like cast in bronze and immortalized. These are the signposts of our good deeds. Other footprints we would like to erase, much as the incoming tide does during a walk down the beach.

Solomon tells us that the footprints of the Christian are ordered and directed by the Lord. They are not left by the steps of chance but by divine planning. There is a beginning and an end. It is not a haphazard trip but a carefully plotted course.

Sometimes our steps through life are much clearer as we look back upon them. While we were taking them, we were a little uncertain about our direction. As we look back, we can see why we were allowed to work and walk in certain areas.

Confidence in taking new steps and leaving our footprints behind

comes as we grow in Christ. When we walk with Christ, we gain a new
sense that our steps are being directed by Him. We stay on course more
easily. We don't get sidetracked. Our goals become clearer and more defined.

Are your steps today being ordered by the Lord? Are you willing to
take them one at a time? Are you leaving footprints in life that count?

## *Promise:* God's Love Is Like Glue

> *I am convinced that nothing can ever separate us from his love. Death can't,*
> *and life can't. The angels won't, and all the powers of hell itself cannot keep*
> *God's love away. Our fears for today, our worries about tomorrow, or where*
> *we are—high above the sky, or in the deepest ocean—nothing will ever be able*
> *to separate us from the love of God demonstrated by our Lord Jesus Christ*
> *when he died for us.*                                    Romans 8:38, 39 TLB

Have you ever been separated from one you love? Did the few or many
miles between you cause your love to die? Probably not. In fact, the bond
of love usually grows stronger when greater barriers exist. Memories are
stirred and the power of love experienced when you were close is released. Love is a survivor!

Paul wanted the Roman Christians to know about God's promise of
love. He painted a graphic picture of the potential destroyers of love:
death, life, angels, the powers of hell, fears, worries, location—none of
these things has the power to separate us from the love of God. Paul's
model of love was found in what Christ did when He died for us. Love
was not silenced on the cross. It was amplified so loudly that the entire
world could hear it. The reverberations of that love have never died
down.

Are there some things in your life today that will try to separate you
from God's love? The world is full of the destroyers of love. Recognize
them when they appear, and don't let them move into your life.

## *Promise:* God Has a Big Family

> *For his Holy Spirit speaks to us deep in our hearts, and tells us that we really*
> *are God's children.*                                    Romans 8:16 TLB

How old were you before you realized who your parents were? For me,
this knowledge came slowly. Constant care and recognition helped me
identify them. Later I realized we had the same last name. This had to
mean I belonged to them. For years I wanted to belong to them and be

identified with them. Then those adolescent years descended and I wanted to be known for myself. Forty-eight years later, even though my parents have passed away, I am still one of their children. I have their name and I am part of their family. That will never change.

Today, I also belong to God's family. I became a member by my new birth. It's been a long time since I joined God's forever family, and I am as much a member today as I was when I joined as a child.

In a world where everyone is trying to belong somewhere, it is important to have our place. There is a security and peace that comes from belonging. Most of us need constant reassurance that we fit or belong.

God's promise today tells us that the quiet voice of the Holy Spirit that resides in our hearts reminds us that we belong to God. We are His children—we are vital and important members of His family. Even if we feel unconnected in life, we are connected to Him.

God has a big family. I belong!

## *Promise:* Look What You Did—Look What God Did

*I am the God who forgives your sins, and I do this because of who I am. I will not hold your sins against you.*                     Isaiah 43:25 TEV

Has anyone ever held your mistakes against you? Every chance he got, he brought them up before you. You began to wonder if the record could ever be erased or changed. It didn't matter how sorry you were, he simply would never let you forget.

It's a good thing God isn't like that. God's record in forgiving is equal to our record in wrongdoing. He is a specialist in forgiveness because that is His nature.

Isaiah wanted to correct an impression that some people had about God. Some people in his time were so beleaguered with the sins they had committed that they doubted God could ever forgive them. Perhaps they had the image of God some of us got as children. We sinned and God kept the record book. We sinned and He wrote them all down. I wondered when He was going to run out of paper on me.

God's assurance is that He will not hold our sins against us. He won't even hold out the big ones while He dismisses the little ones. He treats them all alike, big ones and small ones.

Love is forgiveness. Forgiveness is love.

Are you holding some things against some people in your life—long lists, short lists? It takes more energy to remember than to forgive and forget. If God is willing to throw your list away, shouldn't you be willing to get rid of your list against others?

## *Promise:* **What a Victory**

*Overwhelming victory is ours through Christ who loved us enough to die for us.*                                                            Romans 8:37 TLB

Have you ever been on a winning team? Have you ever won by a wide margin of points? How did you feel?

It's one thing to win a contest by a narrow margin. It's quite another to win by overwhelming your opponent. Winning is fun, but winning by a wide margin is more fun. It says we really were better, superior, magnificent.

God has promised us the greatest victory we will ever know in life. It does not come by outclassing our opponents in a game. It comes through Christ, who loved us enough to die for us. His ultimate victory was the victory over death and sin. The world at that time thought they had turned Christ into a loser. His life seemed to end abruptly in a defeat. Even His own disciples had worked and hoped for a different ending.

When it seemed to all that death had won the final victory over life, God's power turned it all around on a Resurrection morning almost two thousand years ago.

The overwhelming victory that was the Resurrection then is our victory in living today. The promise remains the same.

Are you living with defeat today? God promises you a big victory.

## *Promise:* **Don't Stop Doing Good**

*Let us not become weary in doing good, for at the proper time we will reap a harvest if we do not give up. Therefore, as we have opportunity, let us do good to all people....*                                    Galatians 6:9, 10 NIV

Helping others is hard work. There are usually two kinds of people who need our help: those who have needs because of temporary problems they can't solve alone, and those who will always have needs because they don't want to solve their problems. One group is independent but needy, while the other is dependent and needy.

Helping others is tiring. It is tiring both physically and emotionally. It is sometimes easier to give up than to give on.

Helping others is rewarding. There is a joy that comes from being there when others have needs. There is a happiness that comes from making the difference between a problem and a solution.

Helping others is an opportunity for us to grow. We learn caring, patience, loving, and giving by helping others.

The harvest the above promise talks about is usually slow in coming when you are a people helper. It only comes if we persist in helping and do not give up.

Love is a helping spirit that knows no inconvenience. How long has it been since you rolled up your sleeves and became a helper? You will not have to look far to invest your efforts.

## Promise: God Is in the Rescue Business

*The Lord can rescue you and me from the temptations that surround us....*
2 Peter 2:9 TLB

Most of us joke about temptations. We talk of working too much, eating too much, talking too much, spending too much. We feel that these are more deterrents than temptations in our lives.

The dictionary says that temptation is something that entices or allures us. It draws us away from an intended discipline or goal.

The struggle with temptations in our spiritual lives is a very real one. Satan actively works at distracting us from the direction that God would have us pursue. His temptation offerings often appear enjoyable, perhaps more enjoyable than God's disciplines. How do you survive Satan's temptations?

Peter tells us that God's promise regarding temptation is that He will rescue us. But the promise does not say that He will prevent all temptations. In order to experience God's grace and love, we have to be allowed to struggle. The victory is in knowing that God is our rescuer. He will not allow us to drown in the swirling sea of temptations. He will get us out!

This promise is for all of us. We struggle with temptations in community. God's promise is a corporate one. As we help one another with temptations, God helps all of us.

We all face temptations. We need God's rescue squad to free us as we seek to grow through temptations. Ask Him!

## *Promise:* **God Doesn't Take Vacations**

*God is always at work in you to make you willing and able to obey his own purpose.*                                    Philippians 2:13 TEV

Did you ever feel that God had gone on a vacation and left you all alone to wrestle with life's problems? Or that God was still around but not very much was happening in your life?

We all go through periods of feeling very alone and very deserted by God and by our friends. We indulge in a little self-pity and feel that no one loves us.

Paul was in prison when he wrote these promising words to the band of struggling Christians at Philippi. He took the opportunity to assure them that they would keep growing and God would keep working even though Paul couldn't spend time with them any longer.

Paul was concerned that the Philippians might feel abandoned in his absence. He did not want them to think that God only functioned through Paul. He let them know that God, not Paul, was at work in their lives.

In the gray days of our lives, we need the affirmation that God is always at work in us. We may not feel His presence very strongly, or perhaps we may not feel it at all. That does not mean He is on vacation.

God works in us to give us a willingness to obey His purpose in and through our lives. Sometimes that is a slow and silent process.

Do you sense and feel God at work in you today? He is!

## *Promise:* **God Is at the Controls**

*To be controlled by human nature results in death; to be controlled by the Spirit results in life and peace.*                                    Romans 8:6 TEV

When was the last time you flew on a commercial airliner? As you boarded the plane, the stewardess smiled at you, took your ticket, and pointed you toward your seat. You probably settled down, buckled up, and prepared for a smooth flight. As your DC-10 rumbled down the runway in takeoff, did you have any desire to run to the cockpit and see who was flying your plane? I doubt it! You had the confidence to know that the airline would not allow some student pilot to sit at the controls of your plane. Knowing that you were in good hands allowed you to relax and enjoy your flight.

God knows that there are two ways you can take your journey through life. One way is to let your human nature sit at the controls and give directions. This is about as effective as letting the student pilot fly your DC-10.

The other way is to allow the Holy Spirit to sit at the controls. Our promise for today tells us that life and peace will be our gift when we allow this to happen.

It is not an easy process to turn the controls of your life over to the Holy Spirit. It will mean that we can no longer use our own flight plan but must rely on His.

Who is at the controls of your life today—you or the Holy Spirit?

## *Promise:* God Is a Superb Gardener

*He has made everything beautiful in its time. . . .*
                                          Ecclesiastes 3:11 RSV

Last fall my wife and I planted some bulbs in our flower garden. Our nurseryman told us we would have some very beautiful flowers along about March.

Week after week I waited for the first green shoots to break through the ground. I became so impatient that I wanted to dig down toward the bulbs and see if they were sprouting. Finally, they broke through the ground but seemed to be going nowhere as the days passed. After a few good winter rains, they really took off in growth.

Today, our garden is in full bloom. The dry bulbs of last fall are now a brilliant array of spring flowers of every color. It took time and proper conditions for our flower garden to bloom.

God makes things beautiful but He is never in a hurry. Only you and I are impatient. God works from eternity to eternity. He does things right and you never find Him racing toward the end of a day.

Beautiful creations are gifts from God made in time. You and I are His creative work. He knows that we will eventually bloom. To prepare us, He works silently in our lives.

Many people around you and me today are in a great hurry. They may miss being His creations and enjoying His creations. Don't let that happen to you. Take time to smell the flowers today!

## *Promise:* **God Is a Healer**

*[Jesus] healed all who were sick. This was to fulfil what was spoken by the
prophet Isaiah, "He took our infirmities and bore our diseases."*
Matthew 8:16, 17 RSV

Visiting people in hospitals has always been difficult for me. I never
quite know what to say or do when I get there. The nurses and doctors are
really running the show, and I feel I come in with a very small prayer
Band-Aid for the sick person. I want to do more than just pray for, encourage, and affirm the patient. I find myself wishing I could whistle for
Jesus to duck into the room and totally heal the sick person.

Jesus was really in the healing business as He walked through the society of His time. He healed everyone who was sick, whether they came to
Him as individuals or as groups. He healed people physically and emotionally. He never left anyone as He found him.

Our lives are a collection of hurts and healings. Situations, people, and
diseases bring many hurts into our lives. God wants to move through
those hurts and bring His healing power to bear in us. God is still in the
healing business today. He meets and heals physical needs. He heals the
inner wounds that have scarred our emotions.

Do you need His healing touch in your life today? Ask Him!

## *Promise:* **God Gives Us Super Stength**

*I have strength for anything through him who gives me power.*
Philippians 4:13 NEB

Niagara Falls is an awesome sight. No matter how many times I have
seen it, I am still struck by its size, its roar, and the tremendous volume of
water that daily crashes over its cliffs. As a child, I wondered when it
would dry up. But it never did. A few miles below the falls is the power-
generating station. The water that energizes those huge turbines brings
electricity to millions of homes in the New York and Ontario areas.

Without the falls, the power center would be useless. Without the
power center, the falls would only be another scenic wonder of the world.
Both are needed to create the product of electricity.

God is the river of power that flows through your life and mine. Without Him, we would be powerless. With Him, we have an endless supply
of power that enables us to live.

God's power is not just a trickle that helps us accomplish small things.

It is a power that helps us accomplish anything. There is nothing so great that we cannot do it with God's power flowing through us.

What do you need His power for today? If you are wise, you know that you need it for everything in your life.

God is the source of our strength. He gives us His resources to equip us for anything that might come our way. That's His promise!

## *Promise:* Have a Seat With God

*"Come to me, all you who are weary and burdened, and I will give you rest."*
Matthew 11:28 NIV

Johnny Appleseed was a character who walked through the country planting apple seeds. The supposed results of his labors were apple trees everywhere.

If I could walk through our country, I would plant park benches everywhere. It seems to me that we need more restful places to stop and sit awhile. The first place I would plant my benches would be around churchyards and church patios. People are always in such a hurry to get in church and get away from church. Church should be a place where we have a chance to rest awhile in an informal setting, and in something more comfortable than pews.

A bright-green park bench always seems to be an invitation for me to rest and enjoy God's creation. I feel Jesus would have enjoyed dotting His countryside with benches so that people who were weary could rest with fellow travelers.

God promises us rest if we will take the time to come to Him. We all get weary with the responsibilities we carry. Our burdens can wear us down to the place where we are barely able to keep going.

Have you sat on a bench with God lately? Have you taken the time to unload all your cares on Him? He promises rest!

## *Promise:* God's Love Is Warm

*We are able to hold our heads high no matter what happens and know that all is well, for we know how dearly God loves us, and we feel this warm love everywhere within us because God has given us the Holy Spirit to fill our hearts with his love.* Romans 5:5 TLB

Do you remember when you were a child and a thunder-and-lightning storm awakened you in the middle of the night? If you were really small, you ran to your parents' room for protection. If you were a little older, you probably pulled the pillow over your head, closed your eyes tightly, and stuck a finger in each ear. Somehow you felt if you could just hide your head, the storm would go away.

Years later, some of us are still trying to hide our heads from the storms of life. This attitude stands in direct contrast to what Paul tells the Roman Christians. He tells them that the love of God will enable them to hold their heads high and not hide, no matter what happens. When we are surrounded by His love, we have no fear and we know that all is well.

Paul adds that we will feel surrounded and penetrated by the warmth of God's love for us. His love will form a protective shield about us. The center of that love is found in the Holy Spirit's ability to fill our hearts.

Would you like to hide your head from some of the things you fear most today? Hold your head high and let God's warm love wash over you. You will be amazed at how quickly the fear passes away when you know how much God loves you.

## *Promise:* **The Happy Hearers**

*"How happy are those who hear the word of God and obey it!"*
Luke 11:28 TEV

What makes you happy? You probably could fill several pages with the answer to that question. Some of us would list the small, unnoticed things in life that makes us happy—double-dip ice-cream cones on a hot summer day, the smell of freshly mowed hay, the dusty scent of a fireplace on an early-autumn evening. Perhaps others would list the big things in life that make them happy—things such as a new home, a new career, a promotion, a new car, or a trip around the world.

All of us have a mental "happy" list. Luke, physician and disciple of Jesus, tells us that those who hear the Word of God and obey it are happy. This doesn't mean that the Word of God is some magical book that brings instant happiness when we read it. Luke suggests that the Word of God has to be integrated into our lives in order to bring happiness to us. As we study Scripture and find ways to live out its teachings, a new kind of happiness comes into our lives.

God's kind of happiness is not based on things. His happiness for us comes in doing His will and conforming to His plans for our lives.

How much happiness is filtering into your life as a result of hearing God's Word and following its teachings? God's plan for a new kind of happiness in your life works!

## *Promise:* **Help With Our Daily Problems**

*And in the same way—by our faith—the Holy Spirit helps us with our daily problems and in our praying. For we don't even know what we should pray for, nor how to pray as we should; but the Holy Spirit prays for us with such feeling that it cannot be expressed in words. And the Father who knows all hearts knows, of course, what the Spirit is saying as he pleads for us in harmony with God's own will.* Romans 8:26, 27 TLB

Did you ever fall asleep while praying? I've done it numerous times. Did you ever try to pray and simply find yourself at a loss for the right words? That happens to all of us. We wind up by just asking God to do something, to do anything.

Today's promise tells us that God understands when we don't know what to pray for or how to express our prayer thoughts. Even more than understanding us, the Scripture says that the Holy Spirit will take over for us and take our hearts' cry right to God's presence. In effect, the Holy Spirit becomes our interpreter of prayer.

This promise also tells us that the Holy Spirit helps us with our daily problems. Most of us have a long list of those.

The Holy Spirit is able to help us process our problems into a prayer that touches the heart of God with our needs. God's promise is that He will hear and act.

Are your prayer requests stuck in your heart right now? Do you find it difficult to express them to God? Ask the Holy Spirit to move through you in power and take your inexpressible needs to God. He will do it if you ask!

## *Promise:* **A New You**

*[He] satisfies you with good as long as you live so that your youth is renewed like the eagle's.* Psalms 103:5 RSV

Ponce de León became famous as an explorer in his dauntless search for the Fountain of Youth. He never found it, yet hundreds of years later, we seem to believe it exists in various forms. Plastic surgery, tummy tucks, nose jobs, hair coloring, exercise gyms, vitamin concoctions—all oppose the natural process of aging. Our goal is to be fifty and look like thirty. Some people even achieve it for a time.

The clock never runs in reverse, despite our attempts at resurfacing our physical bodies.

The Psalmist offers us a formula for renewal that is not found in a health-food store or gym. David's promise tells us about a satisfaction with good things in our lives. The "real" good things in life come from God, and they bring a permanent satisfaction. Inner peace would be one of the main things. The fruit of the Spirit found in Galatians would continue the list.

Satisfaction in life leads to a renewed spirit. It gives us a zest for living and gives wings to our optimism. A renewed spirit knows no aging process.

Wouldn't it be great to soar above the struggles of life for a day instead of being caught in them? You can't turn back the clock, but you can let God renew your spirit!

## *Promise:* Laugh With God

> *"God has brought me joy and laughter. Everyone who hears about it will laugh with me."*                                   Genesis 21:6 TEV

Try an experiment today. Listen all day long and see how many people around you are laughing. How many times today will you be laughing?

God enjoys a good laugh. I think He even enjoys a good joke. He had both in Sarah's case, back in the Book of Genesis.

Abraham was one hundred years old and Sarah was close behind. God promised them a child and forgot about the fact that this wasn't supposed to happen at their age. After Isaac was born, Sarah made the statement of the year: "Everyone who hears about this will laugh with me." And I imagine many did for a long time.

A few verses later in this scriptural account, we read that Abraham gave a party to really celebrate the occasion. Can you imagine all the laughing and joking and celebrating that must have gone on? Don't you wish for a moment that you could have been there?

Joy and laughter are often lost ingredients in today's world. We have so many big problems to solve that there is no time to see humor and laughter in anything.

Is it time you had a good laugh? God injects His humor into many of life's situations. God enjoys a good laugh. Ask Him for the opportunity today to celebrate your life and your laughter.

## *Promise:* Healing Comes Through Sharing

*Therefore, confess your sins to one another, and pray for one another, so that you may be healed. The effective prayer of a righteous man can accomplish much.* James 5:16 NAS

When was the last time you spent an evening with your friends confessing your sins? I don't mean the small, insignificant sins like kicking the dog or running a red light. I mean the soul sins that lodge deep inside us, the kind that frequently hinder our relationship with God and one another.

Risky business, this sharing of sins. Most of us would rather pay a therapist seventy-five dollars an hour to deal with them.

James doesn't recommend a random confession of sins to just anyone. There has to be a trusted hearer to a confession, and the hearer has to pray for the confessor in order for any healing to take place. Any sharing of our sins without prayer attached will turn them into food for gossip. When gossip starts, healing ends!

James further adds that effective prayer speeds up the healing process.

All of us are in various stages of being healed. The beginning of this process starts by sharing with a trusted person those things that have hindered our growth.

Confession is an act of humility and honesty. It is soul therapy. It releases us and unbinds us. If this need is unmet in your life, ask God to send someone to you who can share in your healing and growing process.

## *Promise:* God Is Your Consultant

*I will instruct you (says the Lord) and guide you along the best pathway for your life; I will advise you and watch your progress.* Psalms 32:8 TLB

We are living in the age of consultants and experts. Corporations and industries hire them to explore ways they can become more efficient and make larger profits. Usually, when a consultant walks in the door of a company, the employees get very nervous. One word of recommendation can often close an entire department and send employees to the unemployment line.

God offers to take your life into His consultation service. He makes some promises that are far different from the ones made in our secular society. He is not concerned with profit. He is concerned with progress—yours and mine.

The first thing He offers us is instruction. He even presents us with an instruction manual, the Bible.

The second part of the promise says that He will guide us along the *best* pathway for our lives. We usually find two pathways: ours and God's. His is always the best, and we will be happiest when we follow His choice.

The third part of the promise tells us that He will be our adviser and monitor our progress. God doesn't give advice and run. He stays around to observe our progress and our growth.

God offers to be your daily consultant in life. All you need to do is allow Him to take over the controls of your life.

## *Promise:* God Stands Close

*The Lord is close to the brokenhearted and saves those who are crushed in spirit.*                                                    Psalms 34:18 NIV

How did you feel about God the last time your heart was broken and your spirit was crushed? If you are counted among the normal Christians on earth, you probably felt that you had been deserted by God and had to face your struggle all by yourself.

It is easy to feel that God stands outside of our hurting places and doesn't understand how we really feel. If He did, He would wipe it all away immediately and we would be fine.

Throughout Scripture we constantly see God moving into lives that are demoralized, dcfcated, and on the edge of despair. David understood God's watchfulness because he suffered from a broken heart and a bruised spirit. Yet he did not get mad at God or blame God, as many of us do. He felt the very closeness of God at the time of his greatest isolation from God.

How does God save us in this kind of situation? Sometimes He has to save us from ourselves and our self-inflicted wounds. It is easy to blame ourselves when we are down, and lock our spirits inside the prison of self-pity.

At other times, He has to rescue us from those around us who appear to help but in reality hinder. He brings us back to a basic trust in Him alone.

In the last area, God saves us from situations that can damage us further. He moves us into new and safer places.

God stands close! Can you feel that closeness today?

## *Promise:* God Renews Your Mind

*Don't let the world around you squeeze you into its own mould, but let God re-make you so that your whole attitude of mind is changed. Thus you will prove in practice that the will of God's good, acceptable to him and perfect.*
Romans 12:2 PHILLIPS

Have you ever felt that hundreds of outside forces were trying to gain control over your mind? We are deluged with the sounds of a world seeking to make indelible impressions on our minds. Sounds and thoughts bombard us from every direction. The battle for the control of our minds is a daily thing.

The Early Christians living in Rome had the same problem that you and I have today. As they tried to center their thoughts and minds on Christ, their world seemed to push in with its agenda and desire to control their thinking. Paul told them that they were in a battle for their minds. His note of hope was that the only way they could win this battle was to have God remake or remold their minds from the inside out. The world will try to win by battling from the outside in.

Paul added that when God controls your mind, you will know that His plan for you is best and will keep you on the true road to spiritual growth and maturity.

Is your world putting the squeeze on you today? Are its pressures, thoughts, motives, controls, and demands vying against what God wants for you?

Perhaps a good prayer for today would be, "God, begin a remolding of my mind from the inside out. Plant Your thoughts, dreams, and ideals there."

## *Promise:* A Bunch of Blessings

*God is able to provide you with every blessing in abundance, so that you may always have enough of everything and may provide in abundance for every good work.* 2 Corinthians 9:8 RSV

God is no miser when it comes to providing blessings in our lives. His giving knows no limits.

God's purpose in giving to us is not so that we will consume His blessings and gifts, or that we will store His blessings for a more barren time of our lives. God gives to us in abundance so that our basic needs will be met, but also so that we can become channels to others of what He gives us.

The Christian really owns nothing in this life. All that he has is given in trust from God. His responsibility is utilization, not self-indulgence.

It is easy to become an "I" specialist in life. Our focus turns quickly from needs to wants. Wants can create an insatiable appetite.

God's formula for us is very simple: He provides and we distribute. The distribution process never comes to an end and the supplies are never exhausted.

How many things have you asked for in life and received? How did you use them once you obtained them?

God is in the blessing business. But those blessings are only blessings when they are shared with others. Don't be afraid to pass along some of the things God has blessed you with today.

## *Promise:* God Keeps You From the Banana Peels

*... he is able to keep you from slipping and falling away, and to bring you, sinless and perfect, into his glorious presence with mighty shouts of everlasting joy. Amen.*                                                    Jude 1:24, 25 TLB

The other day I was about to climb several steps of a platform to speak to an audience. As I hit the first step, I slipped and fell. I caught myself as the audience gasped. I collected my arms and legs, feeling rather awkward and embarrassed as I moved to the podium. It was a memorable entrance, to be sure.

No matter how hard we try, we all slip and fall in front of people once in a while. We can laugh it off or turn red with embarrassment.

God's promise to us today is that He will bring us through the hard places in life and keep us from slipping and falling. The pathway of spiritual growth and progress is not a freeway. It is a rutted, bumpy, potholed road. If we try to navigate it on our own strength, we will slip and fall. If we walk with the hand of God in our hands, His support will stabilize us.

His promise is not only for navigation but also for improving everything about our journey and getting us to the goal of someday standing in His presence. Jude tells us that there will be a mighty celebration of joy when we arrive. But that's at the end of the journey. We are still in progress.

How is your journey going this week? Are you slipping and sliding along, spending all your energies climbing out of potholes? Grab hold of God's hand and let Him direct your walk through today!

## *Promise:* **Standing on Solid Ground in a Shaky World**

*I waited patiently for the Lord; he turned to me and heard my cry. He lifted me out of the slimy pit, out of the mud and mire; he set my feet on a rock and gave me a firm place to stand.* Psalms 40:1, 2 NIV

How do you pray when you are in a hurry to have God get you out of a mess in your life? If you are like me, you want God to get the rescue crew underway *right now!* The hurt, frustration, fear, danger, or anxiety of the situation demands instant attention. You want to get from hurt to help in the snap of God's fingers.

We learn, as David learned, that rescue demands patience. Perhaps God wants us to learn something about the situation we are in. An instant rescue would rob us of the learning revelation. Rescue comes in God's time.

David sets forth the pattern of God's plan for a rescue. First we wait, then God turns and hears us. His next step is lifting us out of the struggle. He doesn't just sit us down in another struggle but puts us in a safe, secure place where we can stand for a while. The rock symbolizes for me a place to renew my strength and gain my footing before other struggles come along.

We live in a pretty shaky world. As it trembles and moves around and under us, we look for a secure place to stand. God's promise is to keep us on solid ground. He knows we will be up to our ears in the mud and mire from time to time. But He is there with lifting and stabilizing power.

Do you need a lift from God today? Ask Him! He will put some solid ground under your shaky feet!

## *Promise:* **Real Freedom**

*"If the Son sets you free, you will be free indeed."* John 8:36 NIV

Summer vacation, when you are in grade school, is the most fantastic time of your life. I think my best memories are of the last day of school before summer. I couldn't wait to get out and enjoy those long, warm, fun-filled days. I remember running down the school steps with my classmates and yelling at the top of my lungs, "I'm free!" Free from school and free for the summer. No homework, no tests, no restrictive schedules. It was a real freedom back in those days.

Most of us still yearn for that kind of freedom, but as we grow, we grow 'nto responsibilities.

John tells us that Jesus Christ came to earth to reacquaint us with freedom. His initial freedom for us was to free us from the sin that kept us from fellowship with Him. Once those shackles had been broken, we were to continue with Him into a growing freedom in all areas of our lives. Because of Christ's setting us free, we are free to grow, free to struggle, free to fail, free to succeed, free to be ourselves—the list could go on and on.

Even with Christ's freedom in our lives, some of us still stay bound and restricted. People, places, things, and fears keep us from Christ's intended freedom to live.

God's promise is that He *really* sets us free in all areas of our lives. But with that freedom comes a responsibility to use it and enjoy it.

How free are you in your spirit today? Does Christ need to touch your life in a new way, and cut you loose from some growth-inhibiting things? Ask Him. He will set you free!

## *Promise:* **God at Work**

*For I am confident of this very thing, that He who began a good work in you will perfect it until the day of Christ Jesus.*          Philippians 1:6 NAS

Have you ever felt that your Christian life was on hold? Nothing much seemed to be happening and you wondered if God had gone on a sabbatical. Sometimes when the fireworks of our faith seem to be reduced to a fizzle and a pop, we feel that God has moved to another area of the country.

Apparently the Philippian Christians had the same feeling. They knew Paul had left them, and perhaps they felt as though God had gone along with Paul and they were on their own.

Paul's answer to them contained a promise of the assurance that when God begins something, He keeps it going. He never leaves a person to plod along by himself.

We often watch a new Christian filled with the joy and excitement of his or her faith. Everything in this new life is an adventure to him. It is easy to look on and wonder what happened to us or to our joy. Perhaps a tragedy befalls us, and we wonder how God could allow it to happen. We feel deserted by God.

Paul exuded a personal confidence even while in prison. He knew he was on a shelf, but God was on the shelf with him. He had not been deserted.

God's work in you and me keeps going on regardless of feelings, situations, and problems. He is with us and He is directing us!

## *Promise:* Needs and Wants

*And my God shall supply all your needs according to His riches in glory in Christ Jesus.* Philippians 4:19 NAS

Have you ever planned and plotted to get some desired item? You just knew you couldn't live without it. Then, after you acquired it, it sat around and you hardly ever used it. That's why we have so many garage sales in our country. We have garages full of things we had to have but seldom use.

There is a vast difference between what we want and what we need in life. Our want list is usually taken from the merchandisers who really want our money for their products. Our need list is more geared to what we really need to keep alive and well.

On the nonmaterial side, we need love, affirmation, friendship, meaning and purpose in our lives. And that's just a small part of the list of intangibles.

Paul tells us that God promises to meet each of us on the "need" level of our lives. God's riches are so vast that He can just tap into His inexhaustible supply and distribute them freely to us.

Have you been moping recently over the things you don't have instead of thanking God for what you do have? God always knows what will be good for us, and those are the things He sends our way. God is in the business of meeting our needs—even the most gigantic ones. Trust Him today for yours!

## *Promise:* Confession Is God's Detergent

*If we confess our sins, He is faithful and righteous to forgive us our sins and to cleanse us from all unrighteousness.* 1 John 1:9 NAS

Have you ever struggled with admitting you were wrong in a certain situation or discussion? Remember how hard it was? Wouldn't it be great to always be right and never have to confess that you were wrong?

God created us to be very human. Along with our humanness comes the conflict of right and wrong. God seemed to know that we would make mistakes, so He provided a way to help us take care of them. His formula is, confession equals cleansing and forgiveness. It's not an easy formula to live with, but it is the only one that helps us keep a right relationship with both God and man.

Perhaps you have noticed that this promise begins with an *if.* That might prompt you to ask what happens if we don't confess wrongs or sins.

From my experience, lack of confession leads to the guilt trap, the anger syndrome, and the pits of depression.

Many of us cart around things that need to be confessed to God. Only when we confess them, admit them, and own up to them can God do anything with them. His promise becomes a cleansing therapy that will keep us whole.

Are you living with a big stack of unconfessed things that you need to take to God? God will take them from you if you allow Him to. He will set you free. Tell Him about them right now, and experience the release and freedom He can give you.

## *Promise:* **God Has a Secret Plan**

> *... For God's secret plan, now at last made known, is Christ himself. In him lie hidden all the mighty, untapped treasures of wisdom and knowledge.*
> Colossians 2:2, 3 TLB

"If you buy the map, you can find the treasure." As she talked, the gift-shop clerk held the map depicting the locations of sunken Spanish galleons off the coast of Florida. I had visions of buying the map, taking off on my expedition, and becoming rich and famous as a successful treasure hunter. Instead I went waterskiing and left the treasure hunt in the far reaches of my mind.

I imagine the Early Christians at Colossae were excited when Paul wrote and told them what God's treasure cache held in store for them. They didn't have to buy a map and go on an expedition to obtain God's treasure. God's direction to finding the treasures of wisdom and knowledge was in knowing Jesus Christ and growing through Him.

God's treasure for us is not the kind that corrodes and rusts and lies at the bottom of the ocean. God wants us to have two of the most valuable treasures on earth: wisdom and knowledge. They are the gifts that equip us to face the daily questions and assaults that life makes on us. They equip us to make the right decisions.

God's direction for our lives comes from the relationship we establish with Jesus Christ. His resources are largely untapped and He waits to make them readily available to us.

Could you use a little wisdom and knowledge in your life today? Go to the well of His Word and He will supply those needs!

## *Promise:* **God Is a Generous Problem Solver**

> *And if, in the process, any of you does not know how to meet any particular problem he has only to ask God—who gives generously to all men without making them feel guilty—and he may be quite sure that the necessary wisdom will be given him.* James 1:5 PHILLIPS

A problem is an opportunity that needs resolution. Our daily lives are filled with a never-ending succession of these opportunities. In some, the solutions are quite clear and we enact them. In others, we remain puzzled and distraught for days, weeks, or months.

James shares some simple thoughts about finding solutions to our opportunities. Quite directly, he tells us to just "ask God."

I think many of us don't want to bother God with the things we think we can take care of ourselves. We might feel that our concerns are too small, and we would feel foolish taking them to God.

This promise tells us that God will not make us feel foolish or guilty, odd or unusual. We can freely bring any assortment of frustrations that we have to God. He will not laugh at us or make fun of our concerns.

God's promise is that we will be given wisdom in order to find resolution to our problems. We can count on it—if we will only be honest with God.

What particular problem-opportunities are stumping you today? You may have some that have been around for a long time. Take a moment right now and ask God for His help. In His time, He will answer.

## *Promise:* **Listen for God's Voice**

> *"My sheep hear my voice, and I know them, and they follow me; and I give them eternal life, and they shall never perish, and no one shall snatch them out of my hand ... no one is able to snatch them out of the Father's hand."* John 10:27–29 RSV

There is nothing more important than hearing the voice of a loved one during a critical or lonely time in your life. That voice, perhaps miles distant on a telephone line, can bring comfort, reassurance, hope, or joy. The telephone company seems to know the importance of that when they tell us to "reach out and touch someone." The touch of a voice is only one step removed from physical touch.

Jesus knew the importance of His voice to His followers. It helped form an identity-discipleship bond to those who belonged to Him. Hearing, knowing, and following became the steps in a new walk with Him.

The promise to those who walked with Him was that they would have eternal life and never perish, and that no one would be able to steal them away from the heavenly Father. There was to be security in being a part of the family of God.

A follower of Jesus Christ has to listen for and to His voice. It takes more effort to be a listener than a talker. Are you listening today? Do you recognize the voice of God when it speaks to you about your life?

## *Promise:* **God Is a Provider**

*The Lord is my shepherd, I shall lack nothing.*                    Psalms 23:1 NIV

The Twenty-third Psalm is the best known of all David's writings. It is generally known as the psalm of comfort. It is probably recited at more funeral services than any other psalm. I don't think David had funerals in mind, however, when he wrote it.

David's message in this psalm is that God is the one and only provider of the needs of our lives. There is no other source, not even our paychecks, social security, or unemployment benefits.

David viewed God as a shepherd would be viewed by his sheep. The shepherd was responsible in both biblical times and even today to provide good pasture for the sheep. Without good grazing land, a sheep would die. After the proper food supply, the shepherd provided protection from the elements, wild animals, and thieves.

A sheep that followed the shepherd's leading would lack nothing. David could well have written this psalm as he tended his own flock of sheep. As God was the provider to David, so He is our provider today. There is nothing that we will lack if the Lord is the shepherd of our lives.

Many of us look for someone to take care of us as we journey through life. If we put all our needs in a human basket, we will be disappointed. God is the only total-care facility for the Christian.

Whom are you trusting to shepherd your life today? What are you lacking because of an improper trust? When God is your shepherd, you will have everything you need!

## *Promise:* God's Love Is World-Sized

*"God loved the world so much that He gave His only Son, that everyone who has faith in him may not die but have eternal life."*     John 3:16 NEB

Have you ever wished you could love all the people you come across in your life? The people at your church, at your job, on your street, on the freeway! Perhaps you are thinking, *Only God can love some of the people I have to contend with.* And He does!

John recorded the greatest statement ever made about God's love. He tells us that God's love is world-sized and totally comprehensive. It is nonselective and nondiscriminatory. It is all-inclusive.

That's hard for most of us to understand, when we look at the extremes of God's kind of love. The only way it can make sense to us is when it is personalized by the word *everyone.* That brings it down to you and me, to where we live. In order for God to love the world, He had to love *me.* Even if I might not love myself, God still loves me.

Love is God's statement to us. Eternal life is His promise to us. His love is wrapped up with His promise that we will never die but live forever.

Our responsibility in all of this is simply to believe that God means what He says. We accept who He was, why He loved us, and why He sent His son, Jesus, to earth.

God's love is individualized in *you* and *me.* God loved us and He gave His son as proof. I accept His love and He keeps on giving to me! Fill your life with a chunk of God's love today!

## *Promise:* God Dispenses Power

*He gives power to the faint, and to him who has no might he increases strength.*     Isaiah 40:29 RSV

Have you ever wished you could get a prescription from your doctor for power pills? Whenever you felt weak, tired, or out of emotional or physical gas, you could simply pop one and bounce back with new strength.

We have become a pill-popping culture in search of the ultimate ingredients that will give us more power than we have. We are willing to try anything that someone else says works. The problem is that the ultimate power pill doesn't exist and never will.

Isaiah wrote a prescription for power in the form of a promise. He tells us that God is the only source of power and that He dispenses it to those who are ready to faint. That description probably fits all of us at one time or another.

Isaiah further states that God increases our strength. This part of the promise suggests a staying power rather than just a short burst of power that will keep us from the brink of passing out.

If you have ever watched a weight lifter, you know he lifts with spurts and sustained power. There is a definite place for both.

We operate the same way, and God knows this. He is our power source when we need that quick lift, and He is a supplier of the power that sustains us over the long haul.

Are both kinds of His power operating in your life today? He is ready to supply you with what you need.

## *Promise:* **Mountain-Moving Faith**

*"For if you had faith even as small as a tiny mustard seed you could say to this mountain, 'Move!' and it would go far away. Nothing would be impossible."*
Matthew 17:20 TLB

Look out for the mountains! You may get hit by one going by. Has your faith in what God can do rearranged any mountain ranges lately? You are probably thinking, *Don't I wish.*

We would all like to have mountain-moving faith. We all have a few craggy peaks in our lives that we would like to see removed. How does it happen? Why doesn't it happen?

Many of us simply dismiss our lack of mountain-removal ability by saying we lack the faith. If our faith could be larger, than we would be in business.

Maybe our problem is that we are not allowing our faith to grow to the place where we can start removing anthills before we concentrate on the larger variety. We fail to read between the lines of Scripture to understand how God operates in and through us. His program is to always start where we are, to attempt the little things so that our faith can be exercised and strengthened.

If I were to go into training to run a marathon, I would not run 26.2 miles the first day. I would not even run that the first month. I would slowly work up to that over many months of training. If I am willing to submit to the process, I eventually will be able to run the distance.

Are you trying to push mountains around without building up your "faith strength"? Get in training! Let the mustard seed grow. Start with the little hills first!

## *Promise:* God's Awesome Power

*... how tremendous is the power available to us who believe in God.*
Ephesians 1:19, 20 PHILLIPS

How much power does God have? How much of God's power is available to us?

Most of us would say that God has *all* the power. Three of His most awesome displays of power are the power displayed in the creation of the world, the power displayed in the maintaining of creation, and the power exercised in the Resurrection.

Paul's prayer when he wrote to the Philippian Christians was that he would know the power of the Resurrection. Resurrection power is the power of new life, the power to rebuild, renew, or change.

In writing to the Christians at Ephesus, Paul wanted them to know two things about God. The first was that His power is tremendous. It is not some puny power but an awesome power that no one else in the universe possesses. Second, Paul wanted every Christian to know that God's power is available to anyone who believes in God.

Knowing God's power is ready for us to claim in all situations gives us the strength to face life's daily conflicts and problems. It does not do us any good, however, if we never use it. It is like being a millionaire and living in poverty. You have to use what is available to you or it will do you no good.

All of God's power is ready for us to plug into: power to live, power to meet frustrations, power to know the right decisions, power to make the necessary changes in our lives that will help us grow.

Are you tapping into God's power in your daily life? Try it today. You will be surprised at the results!

## *Promise:* God Puts Distance Between Our Wrongs

*As far as the east is from the west, So far has He removed our transgressions from us.* Psalms 103:12 NAS

Have you ever felt as though you were walking around with a huge garbage bag full of your wrongdoings tied to your neck? We seem to collect our mistakes much more quickly than our good memories. We spend our time wishing we had not done this or that or said certain things to people or made certain decisions. Like most people, we have excellent hindsight.

I meet many people who are walking guilt collectors. All they can talk about are their wrongdoings. The joy of living today is choked out by the mistakes of yesterday.

God never intended for us to live with our sins tied to us. He knew that they would only deform us and ultimately render us useless. He provided many promises in the Scriptures to help us deal with our sins.

David knew what it meant to have a load of sins lifted. When he was released from his, he was able to write the words of today's promise. David's point was that God didn't just take the sins from his back and mind and drop them beside him on the road of life. God cast them so far away that they would never have to be dealt with again.

What God did for David, He does for you and me. Are you walking around with your sins strangling you? God wants to get them away from you and out of your sight. Prayerfully give them all to God today, and feel His release as you begin to walk tall again.

## *Promise:* You Belong to God

> *"Fear not, for I have redeemed you; I have called you by name; you are mine."*                                           Isaiah 43:1 NIV

Have you ever experienced the fear of not belonging? You meet a new group of people and you wonder if you will fit in. Living is one long process of belonging. We know we won't belong everywhere and to everyone, but our deep desire is to belong somewhere to someone.

Isaiah's word today was given to Israel. They wandered from country to country and people to people. They seldom felt settled or that they belonged anywhere or to anyone. Isaiah tried to put words of hope into their lives. He affirmed them by telling them that they had been redeemed by God and personally called by God. In wrapping God's promise around them, he told them that they belonged to Him.

I am sure that the Israelites had to go back to this promise many times. When life threw its discouragements at them, they found it easy to feel that God did not care and that they did not belong anywhere. Many new immigrants in our country feel that way today. They feel dispossessed, anxious, lost. It takes the hand of another in theirs to help them feel at home.

God's promise to Israel is His promise to us today. He has redeemed us and He calls us His children. We belong to Him. The next time you feel as if you don't belong, just say softly to yourself, "I'm the child of the King!" You will feel your fears fade away and a pride of belonging move into your life.

## *Promise:* **The Giving Boomerang**

*"If you give, you will get! Your gift will return to you in full and overflowing measure, pressed down, shaken together to make room for more, and running over. Whatever measure you use to give—large or small—will be used to measure what is given back to you."*                                Luke 6:38 TLB

Have you ever thrown a boomerang? It takes a great degree of skill to get it to come back to you. Anyone can get it out there somewhere, but only the talented can get it back.

Giving has a boomerang effect. You cannot give without receiving. The more you give, the more you will receive. This does not always mean you will get the same thing in return, but it does mean that you will receive *something* in return.

Luke's promise tells us that if we give little, we will get little back. If we give much, much will be returned.

Many people are cautious givers. They feel the world is full of takers and all they will get for their efforts will be empty hands. God does not intend for us to give *only* so we can receive. He wants us to give because it brings special joy and blessing into our lives. God wants us to share the joy and the blessing that can be ours.

God's concept for giving is to give abundantly. He is not a guarded giver, nor does He expect us to be. God wants you and me to be extravagant givers.

If you give, you will get! Have you been involved in any "fun" giving lately? Try it. It could change the way you live.

## *Promise:* **God Says to Relax**

*A relaxed attitude lengthens a man's life; jealousy rots it away.*
Proverbs 14:30 TLB

The seminar ad said, "Relax and learn how to deal with stress!" For the sum of one hundred dollars and the investment of three days' time, the seminar leader promised that all of your stress would either be gone or become manageable. The interesting thing I noticed was that he gave the answer to stress for free in the title of the seminar: *Relax!* A person who has learned to relax will not be bothered by stress.

Have you noticed that the people in your life are getting more uptight? We seem to have lost our ability to relax and go with the flow of life and its events.

Solomon must have felt that the people in his day had the same problems we have today. His words were to have a relaxed attitude toward all the things around us. Don't be driven into a corner or up the wall.

Solomon further adds the promise that our lives will be lengthened if our anxiety level comes down. Medical science even tells us this. It seems that someone has wound all of us up and we are desperately trying to find ways to wind down.

The last part of this promise is a warning. It seems to be thrown in as an afterthought. Jealousy will rot your life away! Jealousy causes stress in our lives. A jealous attitude says that I will not rest until I have what you have, do what you do, or do better than you do.

How relaxed are you today? Cool it—you will live longer!

## *Promise:* **God Loves Parents**

*"Honor your father and your mother, that your days may be long in the land which the Lord your God gives you."*                    Exodus 20:12 RSV

The Exodus for the Israelites was a time of transition. They were between places in their lives. It was at this critical time that God gave them the Ten Commandments. Mingled in with the many "thou shalt nots" was a strange command accompanied by a promise.

The command had to do with parents and their children's attitude toward them. *Honor* means to hold in a place of high esteem and respect. Some of us would say that this is a lost ingredient in today's society. Perhaps it was in Moses' time, also.

The promise part of this verse simply says that God would allow those who followed His command to live a long time in the Promised Land.

Perhaps a part of God's motivation for this commandment was to reaffirm the relationship between parents and children. A new closeness and feeling was to be established that would give strength and security in the land that Israel would someday enter.

Honor, respect, love! They are not easy words to say. Sometimes there is no continuing relationship between parents and children, and these words have little meaning.

How long has it been since you told your parents you loved them? Love knows no distance and no boundaries!

## *Promise:* God's Good Right Hand

*Fear not, for I am with you. Do not be dismayed. I am your God. I will strengthen you; I will help you; I will uphold you with my victorious right hand.* Isaiah 41:10 TLB

How strong is your right hand? If you are right-handed, it is stronger than your left. I notice when I lift weights that I can lift a lot more with my right hand than with my left. Most of us have strong right hands developed through constant use.

God has a strong right hand! Isaiah describes it as being victorious and capable of stabilizing us when we feel drained of our own strength.

God's promise today is fourfold. He promises us that He will be with us when fearful and nervous times come. He does not just stand quietly by, but He infuses us with His strength when we have little or none of our own.

God does not merely promise us that we will feel strong but He also takes a course of action, telling us that He will help us. He will not leave us helpless. Finally, He promises that He will uphold us or raise us above the sea of problems that we often find ourselves swimming in.

God's good right hand stands ready to pick us up when we feel knocked down or knocked out. He gives us an injection of His power. He personalizes Himself to us by telling us that He is *our* God. Because He is personally involved with our lives, He will work through us and help us.

Do you need God's strong right hand to give you a lift today? Claim this promise and feel your fears and frustrations slip away.

## *Promise:* God Is Your Healer

*". . . I am the Lord, your healer."* Exodus 15:26 RSV

The Red Sea was behind them and the wilderness of Shur was ahead of them. After three days of travel, the Israelites were discouraged to find the drinking water of Marah bitter. Through God's miracle, the water became sweet and the Israelites drank. It was there that God challenged them with a requirement for healing their diseases.

God asked the Israelites for three things. First, they were to listen to His voice. Second, they were to obey what He said. Third, they were to do what was right. Their promise after meeting God's conditions was that they would not suffer the diseases of their former captors, the Egyptians, for God would heal them.

God's healing touch sometimes has conditions attached to it. These conditions can be designed to test our faith and commitment. They can give us a yielded spirit and an openness to what God wants to do in our lives.

If you cut your hand, the conditions for healing would include washing the cut, putting medication on it, and covering it with a Band-Aid. If the conditions are not followed, the cut can become infected, and ultimately a hand could be lost.

God tries to get our attention focused on Him and what He would like to do for us. His conditions are to finely tune us to His will. His requirements are not restrictive but restorative in nature.

Many years after the Israelites' test, God's conditions are still in effect. Healing comes by reading God's directions. Are you following His prescription today?

## *Promise:* God Rolls Away the Clouds

*". . . I will turn their mourning into gladness; I will give them comfort and joy instead of sorrow."*                                    Jeremiah 31:13 NIV

Have you ever watched parents trying to quiet crying children? They usually use two methods. The first is to hug and hold them until the crying ceases. The second is to try and distract them from their crying by giving them something or diverting their attention by telling them to look at something or someone.

When God sees us in tears, He does not use the above tactics to get us to stop crying. Instead, He gives us a promise that He will change our attitude and even our condition. He does not say exactly how He will do this. He simply says He will turn our mourning into gladness. Along with His gift of gladness, He promises comfort and joy.

Comfort means that God understands our tears and sorrow. His gentle spirit hugs our spirit, and we receive His gift of comfort.

God's gift of joy in the wake of our sorrow means that we are able to look beyond the situation to the many joys in life that are still ours. We can celebrate in all situations because God is really in charge, even though our spirit may be saddened due to our situation.

God promises us His presence in the midst of our sorrow. He doesn't offer a string of condolences. He offers us His person.

We all have moments of mourning. Maybe you have had some recently. God stands with you today to help you go from sorrow to joy!

## *Promise:* What to Expect in the World

*". . . In this world you will have trouble. But take heart! I have overcome the world."* John 16:33 NIV

Most of us identify closely with the words of the old Negro spiritual, "Nobody knows the trouble I see." This song can easily be echoed by all of us. We live in a world full of troubles of various sizes and descriptions.

John seemed to be pretty sure that all of us would experience trouble in living in this world. Apparently, he did not want the people in his day to get so heavenly minded that they lived above their troubles.

What John did want to convey was the promise that God is in charge of the trouble department in the world. He specializes in overcoming troubles and therefore is uniquely equipped to help us overcome ours.

It is easy to feel that we will someday get all our troubles behind us and live a trouble-free existence. That will not happen in this life. Part of life is taking care of the daily flow of problems. As we solve them, we grow.

Our strength in problem solving is in knowing that we are connected to the Problem Solver. God stands ready to help us with both big and little problems. He tells us to "take heart." Taking heart is having courage. How is your courage level today? Don't spend all your time listing your problems. Start letting go of them by giving them to God to solve.

## *Promise:* Getting Close to God

*Come close to God and he will come close to you.* James 4:8 PHILLIPS

I saw a bumper sticker the other day that said, IF YOU ARE NOT CLOSE TO GOD, GUESS WHO MOVED? That slogan tells a lot about our relationship with God on a day-to-day basis.

I meet many people who expect God to do all the work. They want to be close to God and have a good relationship with Him, but they expect God to put forth all the effort. That's not how God works.

Any relationship starts with two people investing an equal amount of time in each other. If one person lets down on the relationship, it will lose strength and closeness.

The same is true in our relationship with God. James cements this fact with a promise to us. He puts a strong emphasis on our responsibility to direct our relationship to God by pulling toward Him. As we do that, the distance between us and God is eliminated and a closeness takes over.

How does a person draw close to God? Three of the strongest ways are through time spent in prayer, time spent in meditation, and time spent in studying His Word. These are the ways that the nature of God is revealed to us. They help us develop a new closeness with Him.

All of these ways mean an investment of our time. We are busy, but we have to realize that there are no instant relationships in life or in knowing God.

Are you drawing a little closer to Him today?

## *Promise:* God Gives Success

*"I myself will go with you and give you success."*          Exodus 33:14 TLB

Everyone wants to be successful. Bookstores are overflowing with books that tell us how to succeed in every area of life. Everybody seems to be preoccupied with the struggle to achieve a level of success that will mean wealth and recognition.

There is nothing wrong with wanting to be successful. The big struggle is how we get it, who it comes from, and what it can do to us once we have it.

Moses was trying to be successful as God's leader over Israel. Some days the Israelites didn't seem to cooperate, and other days God didn't seem too involved in the whole struggle. Moses felt alone and frustrated.

In today's promise, God gives Moses the guarantee that he will not have to lead alone and that God will cause him to be successful in his leadership.

Sometimes leadership is lonely. It means making unpopular decisions, not being able to please everyone, and often being misunderstood. God understands that, and His promise is that He will be with us in all those times. We will not be left alone to wander aimlessly down our leadership path. His affirming presence will be with us.

God's pattern for success with Moses was in having the people follow Moses willingly. As Moses walked with God, the people would walk with Moses. Successful leadership is having followers.

Are you willing to walk with God today? You can lead others if God is walking with you!

## *Promise:* **God's Love Is Warm**

*We are able to hold our heads high no matter what happens and know that all is well, for we know how dearly God loves us, and we feel this warm love everywhere within us because God has given us the Holy Spirit to fill our hearts with his love.*                                                    Romans 5:5 TLB

Have you ever watched how people walk? Some walk with their heads held high and seem to be looking over everything around them. Others walk and look straight ahead as if in a trance. Still others walk with their heads down as though they were counting the cracks in the sidewalk.

How do you walk as a member of God's family?

Today's promise starts with an instruction for walking. Paul tells us we are to hold our heads high no matter what is going on around us. Now that's not easy unless we know that we are surrounded by the love of God.

Sometimes life seems to conspire against us to cause us to look down rather than up. Paul tells us that we don't just feel God's love on the outside. We feel it *within* us and it enables us to know that all is well even when it appears not to be.

You can only walk through life with your head held high if you are saturated with the love of God. God's love becomes the lifter of our spirits as well as our heads.

God has filled your heart today with His love. He has given you a reason to walk tall and smile broadly!

## *Promise:* **God Cheers for Me**

*. . . If God is for us, who can be against us?*                          Romans 8:31 NIV

Have you ever had anyone cheer for you? Perhaps you played sports and tossed in the winning basket, or made a home run as the crowd cheered for you. There is a feeling of exhilaration and joy that comes from being the hero of the game. The affirmation of the spectators is the capstone of that experience. Winning and being affirmed is fun. Losing and being a scapegoat is pure misery.

The reality is that we don't always have people cheering for us. We don't always win and, more often, we are not the heroes.

Paul's words to the Roman Christians seem to be directed to those slow days in life when no one is cheering for us. He asks the question, "Who is against us?" On some days you and I would probably reply, "Almost everyone."

Paul says that it doesn't matter how many people are against you. It doesn't matter how many problems you have stacked on your head. God is for you and is your constant cheerleading squad of *one!*

Paul is concerned with letting us know that God is always our head cheerleader. He never stops cheering for us. He never stops affirming us. He never stops loving us. Even when we feel we are losing in the game of life, God stands by with His ever-present support for us.

How many things are piled up against you today? How many people are leaning on your life? It doesn't matter. God is in the majority and He is cheering for you!

## *Promise:* **God Has a Purpose**

*The Lord will fulfill his purpose for me; your love, O Lord, endures forever. . . .*

Psalms 138:8 NIV

When I get to heaven, I'm going to have a long talk with God. I have a very long list of "whys" that I want God to answer. You may have an even longer list as you look back at the events that happened to you but seemed to make little sense at the time.

Perhaps that's why eternity will be so long. It will take that long to have our questions answered.

David probably had his own list of "whys." Somehow, he was able to put them on the back burner and affirm the fact that God was daily about the business of fulfilling His purpose in David's life. David seemed to understand that God had the whole road map to life while he, David, had only one day's portion to look at.

The second part of this promise tells us that God loves us with an enduring love. We can trust God's purpose if we can accept His promise. If He loves us, He will not allow anything to happen to us that will ruin His plan for our lives.

God views things that happen to us differently than we do. We question, wonder, doubt, and distrust the daily events of our lives. God takes them in stride and fits them into His ongoing plan for each of us.

God has a purpose for me today. I claim His love and lift my life to Him for this day's direction!

# *Promise:* A Day at a Time

*Just as you trusted Christ to save you, trust him, too, for each day's problems;*
*live in vital union with him.* Colossians 2:6 TLB

Can God be trusted in everything? Most of us would answer a re-sounding "Yes!" Then we would quietly retreat into some of our own private areas of doubt and questioning. Our fear of trusting God in everything is usually centered in the concern that He might do something that will cause us discomfort or unhappiness.

How much trust did you place in Christ to help you become a new person in Him? You probably gave all there was of you to all you knew of Him. It took a giant step of faith on your part. You trusted Him to do ex-actly as He promised.

Salvation is the first step of the Christian walk. Trust brought you into that new relationship. The second step is to live out that trust on a daily basis. It means you give *all* your daily problems to God and trust Him for guidance and direction as well as solutions. Some of us want to keep some things back from God and try to solve them ourselves. That doesn't work. God wants us to bring the whole load to Him and trust Him with the results.

At the end of this promise, Paul issues a directive. We are to live in union or close fellowship with Him. The only way you can develop a growing trust in God is to live close to Him. Trust is the natural out-growth of a close relationship.

Did you trust Christ to save you? Are you trusting Him with the prob-lems of today? Are you living close to Him?

# *Promise:* God Makes the Going Easier

*And I will lead the blind in a way that they know not, in paths that they have*
*not known I will guide them. I will turn the darkness before them into light,*
*the rough places into level ground. These are the things I will do, and I will*
*not forsake them.* Isaiah 42:16 RSV

Have you ever felt as though you did not know where you were going? Sometimes that happens to us as we seek direction for our lives. We know that we are on the journey, but all the directional signs seem to be ob-scured from our vision. We get confused and filled with doubt, and some-times hesitate to make any decisions.

Our greatest danger at a time like this is listening to the voices in the crowd around us. We may ask people for directions or they may simply offer them to us. We tend to collect, sort, file, and feel even more frustrated. Some tell us to stop while others tell us to go.

What does God want you to do in a situation like this? Ask Him for directions and trust Him when He points out the way. It may not look like the direction you would choose, but you have to trust Him.

Today's promise tells us that God will lead us and guide us. He will bring His light to shine on our pathway, and He will smooth out the rough spots in the roadway. Finally, He promises that He will not forsake us.

If we turn our journey over to God, He promises to become involved in the twists and turns, the bumps and detours, and the stopping and starting. God is a master road builder and is able to help us navigate, even when we wonder where we are headed!

## *Promise:* **The Joy of the Lord**

*Always be full of joy in the Lord; I say it again, rejoice! Let everyone see that you are unselfish and considerate in all you do. Remember that the Lord is coming soon.*                                    Philippians 4:4, 5 TLB

These words written by Paul while he was in prison could be subtitled, "How to Be Happy in Jail!" If you and I had been in Paul's situation, we probably would have been crying the blues and asking for some pity. Paul used his prison experience to tell the Early Christians what the joy of the Lord was all about.

Real joy is not tied to circumstances. It does not go up and down, depending on whether things are good or bad. Real joy is constant and comes from within, not without.

Notice that Paul does not say that we should be half-full of joy. He does not recommend a dab a day. He want us to be full to overflowing. If your life is full of joy, there will be no room for unhappiness.

Joy is contagious. You catch it from the Lord and spread it to your friends.

Paul knew that people would be attracted to faith in Christ if they could just witness the joy in the lives of those who already knew Him.

How full of the joy of the Lord are you today? Life's situations and problems will always try to rob you of the joy that the Lord gives. Ask God to fill you with an overflowing joy today. He is the source and supplier!

# *Promise:* We Ask, God Hears

> *This is the assurance we have in approaching God: that if we ask anything according to his will, he hears us. And if we know that he hears us—whatever we ask—we know that we have what we asked of him.*     1 John 5:14, 15 NIV

Have you ever tried to talk with someone who was not interested in listening to what you were saying? Difficult, wasn't it? Perhaps he or she was looking over your head for a better audience or someone he would rather talk with. No matter how important our words, they are not being heard when the other person is not listening.

Have you ever wondered if God is listening when you talk with Him? Most of us have. If we don't seem to be getting what we want from God, we feel that He just isn't listening to us.

God is not a vending machine into which we insert our prayer requests. We don't pull God's handle and get a neatly packaged answer.

God's promise is that He will hear our requests if we ask in accordance with His will. In other words, our request needs to fit God's master plan that He has prepared for our lives. If our request is for self-consumption and self-glory, it will not be in accordance with His will for our lives.

God doesn't just hear our verbal requests. He hears how our requests fit His life plan for us. If they fit, they will be granted.

As a parent knows the difference between good and bad things for a child, so God knows what is good and bad for each of us.

God hears you when you ask, and He knows what is best for you!

# *Promise:* God's Spirit Sets Us Free

> ... *wherever the Spirit of the Lord is, men's souls are set free.*
>                                                  2 Corinthians 3:17 PHILLLIPS

Freedom is not understood very well by those who have never lived under oppression. When freedom comes to the oppressed, there is both an inner and outer release of the spirit of the person. Once freed, that spirit would fight any restraint that would again bind it up.

Around the world, millions of people still struggle for their freedom— freedom of choice, freedom to come and go as they please, freedom to think and to say what they think. The freedoms I take for granted, others dream about and fight to obtain.

Physical freedom is vital to life, but it is not the only kind of freedom. Spiritual freedom lies at the very center of our beings.

Today's promise tells us that the Spirit of the Lord at the center of our lives will bring us spiritual freedom. We will no longer be bound by our fleshly nature or by the control of Satan. We will be set free.

Spiritual freedom unlocks our lives and causes us to operate with a God-given confidence in all of life's situations. Our fear of control by other forces dissipates. We have the Spirit of the Lord in our lives, and nothing can bind us.

Do you sense and feel God's spirit of freedom in your heart today? Have you asked Him to set you free from anything that would prohibit you from serving Him? God will give you His freedom today if you just ask for it!

## *Promise:* Guarantees for the Journey

*"Remember, I will be with you and protect you wherever you go. . . . I will not leave you until I have done all that I have promised you."*

Genesis 28:15 TEV

Jacob was on a journey to choose a wife. He made camp at the end of the day and soon fell into a sound sleep. As he slept, God spoke to him in a dream and equipped him with some promises for the rest of his journey and the remainder of his life.

Upon awakening, Jacob exclaimed, "God lives here!" (Genesis 28:16 TLB). God's communication to Jacob was so real and vital that he felt he was literally in God's house.

Jacob started his journey with only the encouraging words of his father, Isaac. God interrupted the journey with words that would change his life forever.

Has God interrupted your life lately to share His promise of guidance with you? He promised Jacob the same thing He promises you and me. He will be with us and He will protect us *wherever* we go.

Jacob wasn't sure where he was going at the time, so God gave him an all-inclusive promise.

The second part of God's promise to Jacob and to us is that He will not leave us until He completes all that He promises to do in our lives. In other words, God doesn't leave us with the job half-done. He stays on the construction site of our lives until we are finished.

If you feel a little alone on your journey today, remember that God is with you, just as He was with Jacob. You are surrounded by His presence and protection!

## *Promise:* **God's Person Lives Forever**

> *The world and its desires pass away, but the man who does the will of God lives forever.*                                                    1 John 2:17 NIV

Life is a passing parade that often hooks us into joining the band. Once we join, we find ourselves marching to the tune of different desires than we would normally choose. Sometimes those desires in the parade of life completely distract us from the ones God has for us.

It is sometimes difficult to believe that the world around us, along with the things we desire in it, will all pass away. Our human tendency is to believe everything is permanent. To see things as only temporary gives us an unsettled feeling. Permanence is security.

John tells us that the world is temporary, but doing the will of God in our lives causes us to live forever. In other words, the house (our world) is a temporary shelter. The resident of the house (God's person) is permanent. John seeks to give us a new value system by which we can evaluate priorities in our lives.

Doing God's will is simply living in fellowship with Him and following His instructions one day at a time. It is learning the things of eternal value as opposed to those of momentary value.

Someone has said, "Things are to use, people are to love." God seemed to have this in mind when He placed us in this world.

Are you working on permanence in your life today? God's person lives forever!

## *Promise:* **The Wisdom and Counsel of God**

> *You will keep on guiding me all my life with your wisdom and counsel; and afterwards receive me into the glories of heaven!*          Psalms 73:24 TLB

Are you more used to giving counsel to people than taking it from them? We all have a lot of quick answers for other people's dilemmas. It is so easy to tell a person what to do when we don't have to do it ourselves.

We all need to be open to the wisdom and counsel of our sisters and brothers in God's family. God often speaks through them to help us with our own needs.

David received very wise counsel, at a critical time in his life, from the Prophet Nathan. God used Nathan to convict David of his sin and point him in the right direction for renewal.

Years later, David could affirm not only Nathan's wisdom but also the fact that God was the source of guidance, wisdom, and counsel. As David discovered this, even so do you and I need to rediscover it for ourselves.

David also speaks of the reward for following God. He tells us that God is planning a great reception for us when we are promoted to His presence.

Do you find yourself in need of some guidance and counsel today? First, seek God for direction. Then, don't be afraid to ask God to speak through some of your friends in His family. It is not always easy to follow directions unless you know that they are directly from God!


## *Promise:* **What's Your Primary Concern?**

*"All mankind scratches for its daily bread, but your heavenly Father knows your needs. He will always give you all you need from day to day if you will make the Kingdom of God your primary concern."*     Luke 12:30, 31 TLB

Have you ever thought of yourself as scratching out a living? Few of us have unlimited funds and resources. We carefully guard our incomes and expenditures. Most of the time we are just barely getting by.

Luke's analysis of how we live is pretty accurate. He doesn't say that we *have* to live by just getting by, however. He tells us that God knows exactly what we need to make it each day. God's list of our needs and our list of our wants would be vastly different.

God's way of supplying our needs is not to dump the storehouse of heaven upon us but to simply give us enough to get through each day. He wants us to focus our desires on making His Kingdom our basic concern. If we are focused on His Kingdom, we will not consume our energies on our wants from an earthly kingdom.

Too often, we are living in our tomorrows and worrying about tomorrow's needs. This takes away our energies for living and serving God today.

Is living for God your primary concern today? Are you trusting God to supply that long list of needs you are carrying around in your head? Give Him your list and enjoy living in today!

## *Promise:* **On Speaking in Public**

*". . . Do not be anxious how you are to speak or what you are to say; for what you are to say will be given to you in that hour; for it is not you who speak, but the Spirit of your Father speaking through you."*   Matthew 10:19, 20 RSV

How would you feel if your pastor asked you to preach the Sunday sermon in your church next week—a little frightened or scared out of your mind?

Sometimes people ask me if I ever get nervous when I am about to speak to an audience. I think I always feel a little nervous until I get started and feel a rapport with the audience.

The biggest fear that most of us have in standing before an audience is that we will forget what we want to say or make ourselves look foolish. There is nothing worse than being embarrassed in public.

Matthew tells us not to worry when we have to speak. God will put the right words in our mouths, even if we don't know ahead of time what they are to be. On numerous occasions in the Scripture, God's servants and leaders were told what to say at the right time. God spoke through His servants to give us the very Scriptures we read and study.

God never runs out of what to say. He will speak His words through us if we trust Him.

Are you looking for the right words in some situations in your life today? Ask God to speak through you with His words!

## *Promise:* **How to Treat One Another**

*Be kind to each other, tenderhearted, forgiving one another, just as God has forgiven you because you belong to Christ.*   Ephesians 4:32 TLB

Paul always spoke about the practical things in the Christian life. He did not live in the clouds of biblical doctrine all the time, as some would have us believe. Much of his writing to the Early Church was highly relational. He wanted the members of God's family to learn how to live with each other in peace and harmony.

The Early Christians were just like today's models. They had to be reminded and encouraged repeatedly. Paul did this by constantly reminding them what Christ had done for them. They were "forgiven" and they "belonged." It was that spirit that they were to show to one another.

God's relational glue is comprised of kindness, tenderheartedness (a warm spirit), and forgiveness. God's love gives us these ingredients in great quantities. We are to transmit them to our brothers and sisters in God's family.

When was the last time you shared a kindness with someone? How recently has your warmth of spirit shown through to someone else? How long has it been since you washed some hurts in the detergent of forgiveness?

God has forgiven you and you belong to Christ. Let someone in your life know that today by sharing what you have!

## Promise: Alive in the Beginning

*Christ was alive when the world began. . . . He is God's message of Life.*
1 John 1:1 TLB

How many beginnings have you been a part of in your life—hundreds, perhaps thousands? There is always a special joy in being involved in something from its inception. Feelings of ownership, pride, and creativity come from being part of a birth experience.

What a sense of exhilaration Christ must feel in knowing that He was around when this whole world started. His sense of viewing us and knowing us stretches from eternity to eternity. He is not bound by any horizon. His view is limitless.

John tells us that Christ was more than just a spectator of creation. He became a participant in creation by coming to earth with God's message of life more than two thousand years ago. He did not simply *bring* a message of life—He *is* the message of life.

Has your life been touched by the new life that Christ can bring? He first touches our lives by bringing us the gift of salvation. We become a part of His family by receiving this gift. He continues to touch our lives daily through the process of renewal and growth.

Christ wants you to be alive. Don't settle for less than the fully alive experience that He can give you!

## Promise: Nothing Is Too Hard for God

*"O Lord God! You have made the heavens and earth by your great power; nothing is too hard for you!"*                    Jeremiah 32:17 TLB

Whom do you give your problems to if you think they are too difficult for God to handle?

Most of us don't look for a higher person to hand them to, since we know that God is the highest power. If we think our problems are too big for God, we usually just take them upon ourselves to try to resolve. Self-resolution of problems usually becomes self-frustration with problems. The harder we try to find our own answers, the more confused we become.

We know that we can take our needs to God, but many of us simply don't want to bother God with them, or we are not sure that He will give us the answers we want.

Jeremiah wrote today's words while he was in prison. He was looking beyond the problems Israel faced to its future. He saw disarray and impending defeat all around him. Yet he called forth the reality that the God who made everything by His power still had enough of that power available to meet daily situations. He affirmed that God could handle His own problems as well as those of Israel.

Do you have two lists of problems in your life? One contains the things *you* will handle, and the other the things you want *God* to handle. I suggest that you make one list today and simply give it to God. Then believe that you can't come up with anything that He is not able to take care of.

## *Promise:* Living in Love

*"As the Father has loved me, so have I loved you. Now remain in my love."*
John 15:9 NIV

The surest way to survive the blows and attacks that the world directs toward us is to live within a circle of love. Jesus knew this when He gathered His disciples around Him on the Mount of Olives. The survival plan He presented to them was vastly different from what they were expecting. He presented no military or miracle strategies. He simply explained how love worked and what it would do. He knew that people could explain away anything that happened except love. Real love defies explanation.

Jesus presented three circles of love to His followers. The first was the circle of love that God surrounded Him with. The second was the circle of love that He surrounded His disciples with. After three years of following Him, they knew they were loved, if little else. The third circle of love was the growing love that they were to have for one another.

Jesus redefined love on a mountain that day. He moved from that mountain to a hill called Calvary to live out that love. He set a price on the fulfilling of love. The bonding effect of love only began to be understood in the lives of the disciples after the Crucifixion and Resurrection.

Are you living today within the circle of love? God's love and the love that our brothers and sisters share with us help us meet the challenges of living. Throw a circle of love around someone today!

## *Promise:* Bouncing Back

*The Lord guides a man in the way he should go and protects those who please him. If they fall, they will not stay down, because the Lord will help them up.*
                                                          Psalms 37:23, 24 TEV

Have you ever felt that if you could get high enough on the spiritual ladder, you would never fall off? We listen to the spiritual success stories that people tell and wish we were more spiritual so that we would stumble less and celebrate more.

David seemed to understand spiritual growth better than many of us do. In today's verse, he tells us that God promises two things to those who follow Him: guidance and protection. David does not say, however, that these two things will enable us to keep from stumbling or falling on our spiritual journeys. He intimates that we all will fall down, but the good news is that we will not stay down. Because God is in the restoration-and-recovery business, He will keep picking us up.

The secret to growing is to learn what makes us fall and to gain the strength to avoid that obstacle the next time it appears. A part of guidance is the recognition of our weaknesses.

If you have fallen flat in your spiritual life lately, remember that God is reaching out with His hand to lift you up. Reach out and place your hand in His, and your journey will be renewed!

## *Promise:* If I Could Just Have ...

*So you have everything when you have Christ, and you are filled with God through your union with Christ. He is the highest Ruler, with authority over every other power.*                                    Colossians 2:10 TLB

Have you ever gone to a bookstore looking for the perfect book? Perhaps you have been struggling with certain issues and feel that someone has all the answers for you neatly tucked away between the pages of a book. Most of us have realized that our answer book has yet to be published.

When Paul wrote to the Colossian Christians, he warned them about looking for answers in the wrong places. He knew that the Early Christians were susceptible to people pressures and would fall prey to listening to secular ideas and philosophies. Some of what they heard would sound sensible, appealing, and inviting. There would be a temptation to hear those voices rather than the voice of Christ.

Paul's word is simply put. When we have Christ, we have everything we need. We will not need to tack on a little of this or that to add spice to what God has given us. In our society there are many subtle cults and doctrines that want to add on to what we have in Christ. What they offer sometimes looks good on the surface. But the truth is that they cannot give us what we already have.

As a Christian today, you have it all!

## *Promise:* No Room for Doubt

*Now we can look forward to the salvation God has promised us. There is no longer any room for doubt, and we can tell others that salvation is ours, for there is no question that he will do what he says.* Hebrews 10:23 TLB

Salvation through Christ rather than the keeping of rules, rituals, and sacrifices was a brand-new thought for the Early Christians. Obtaining salvation through performance was the accepted way of life. It was into this arena that Paul walked with his message of new life in Christ by a simple act of faith.

Perhaps there were those who felt that they should still keep some of the rituals just in case Paul was wrong. Years of culture and historical practice are difficult to change overnight.

There are four things in this promise that stand out. First, we are told that we can look forward to the salvation that is ours. It is a present thing with eternal implications. We have only experienced a part of the joy it can bring.

Second, we are told that we can put all our doubts aside now. There is no longer a reason to have them because of what Christ has done for us. Third, we can share this Good News with others. It is not to be self-consumed but passed along. Finally, Paul tells us that God will always do what He says. He will not waver, change His mind, or back out on what He has promised.

God's guarantees are certainly more valid than those we hear about in today's world. Salvation is God's gift to us. We can trust Him to do exactly what He says!

## *Promise:* The Perfecting of Love

*... if we love one another, God lives in union with us, and his love is made perfect in us.*                                      1 John 4:12 TEV

Perhaps a good way to approach today's promise would be to ask the question, "What happens if we choose not to love one another?" Some would say that many have made that choice and as a result, the world is degenerating day by day. Family relationships are crumbling, world communities are in disarray. Violence and anger dominate human relationships. It would appear that many people are choosing not to love.

Love is never an option for the person who chooses to follow God. Our union and growth with God always begin with the way we choose to love one another.

Love is demonstrative. It has to be expressed in order to be fulfilled. It takes a giver and a receiver.

To be loved by someone is to allow God to have a new access to your soul. One of the ways God chooses to love us is through other people.

To feel and know the closeness of God's love in us means we have to be open to being loved by others and giving love to others.

How's your love life today? Do you feel loved by God and those around you? Love isn't love until you give it away!

## *Promise:* The Light of Service

*If you pour yourself out for the hungry and satisfy the desire of the afflicted, then shall your light rise in the darkness and your gloom be as the noonday.*
                                                    Isaiah 58:10 RSV

The blessings we expect from God in our lives stand in direct proportion to the blessings that we give out to those around us. We cannot experience the blessing of God without experiencing service to those in need. The Christian is to be an aqueduct of blessing rather than a reservoir of wealth.

Many of us do little to help others because the mountain of need looms so large. Since we cannot remove the mountain, we choose to ignore it altogether.

Helping those with human needs is a one-to-one task. If we help just one person today, we not only brighten their darkness but we illuminate our own pathway as well.

Jesus's style of ministry while He was on earth was to reach out and help all He could. Some of the time He responded to physical needs while at other times He healed emotional needs. On a hot hillside He fed a multitude and met the need of human hunger. He demonstrated that little is much when God is in it.

Who are the people with needs who will cross your path today? Will you have time for them? Will you have time for just one of them? God promises to lighten our pathways when we help lighten their loads!

## Promise: God Has a Big Shadow

*We live within the shadow of the Almighty, sheltered by the God who is above all gods. He will shield you with his wings! They will shelter you. His faithful promises are your armor. Now you don't need to be afraid of the dark any more, nor fear the dangers of the day; nor dread the plagues of darkness, nor disasters in the morning.* Psalms 91:1, 4–6 TLB

We all have a secret list of the things we fear most. Some of our fears are conditioned by past experiences. Others are the result of overindulgence in our imaginations. All fears can pile up in our lives and cause one gigantic roadblock to our growth.

David went through some fearful passageways in his life. In the Psalms he drew some very graphic images of his fears. Yet, in the midst of his collected fears, David seemed to understand that God's shadow hovered over him and moved to eradicate his fears. He depicted God almost as a giant bird that swoops down upon us as our perils mount, and enfolds us in the shelter of His protective wings.

When we are surrounded by His protection, we no longer need be afraid of anything that the darkness or the dawn holds. The power and protection of God is an eradicator of our fears.

As you walk into today, do you sense and feel His protective shield of promises about you? Let your fears go and let God's big shadow fall across your pathway today!

## Promise: The Condition of Forgiveness

*"Our Father in heaven. . . . Forgive us the wrongs we have done, as we forgive the wrongs that others have done to us."* Matthew 6:9, 12 TEV

When was the last time you forgave a person who had wronged you? How difficult was it for you to enter into that forgiveness and then move beyond it to new growth in that relationship? It probably was not easy.

Forgiveness is never a one-way street. It is always a two-way street, most often separated by the hedge of our humanity.

When the disciples asked Jesus to teach them to pray, He carefully tucked a forgiveness promise right in the middle. Jesus knew that there would be no real forgiveness in our lives on the God-man level if we did not practice forgiveness on the man-to-man level. Our relationship with God is always hinged on our relationship to our brothers and sisters.

Many people find it easy to ask God to forgive them for something they have done, but find it nearly impossible to ask and receive forgiveness from a brother.

Forgiveness is a constant in our lives. It enables us to live and serve in relationships with those around us. To withhold forgiveness is to cut a person off from life. The result is that we die along with that person.

Is your life a free-flowing channel of forgiveness to those who bend you the wrong way? As God forgives you, let your forgiveness be your gift to them.

## *Promise:* **You Won't Be Alone**

*"I am not going to leave you alone in the world—I am coming to you."*
John 14:18 PHILLIPS

One of the greatest fears that most of us experienced as small children was being separated from our parents and being lost in a crowd. The greater the crowd, the tighter we clung to their hands. It was not so much the crowd we feared as the possibility that we might be left alone and never be found.

This same fear seemed to dominate the minds of the disciples in the last days of Jesus' ministry on earth. It seemed as though everything they had built and worked toward was unraveling. The one who had been their center was moving away from them. It appeared that they were going to be abandoned.

At the very moment of their heightened fears, Jesus gave them His promise. They would not be left alone. He would come again to them in resurrected power. When He finally ascended to heaven, He would send the Holy Spirit to minister through them.

We all have those lonely moments. Friends and family leave us. We stand alone in the crowd and look for a hand to grab. In that moment God reaches down His hand to us with the promise that we are not alone. He is present and He is coming again. That's God's promise to you and me today!

## *Promise:* **The Cure for Worry**

> *Don't worry about anything, but in all your prayers ask God for what you need, always asking him with a thankful heart. And God's peace, which is far beyond human understanding, will keep your hearts and minds safe in union with Christ Jesus.*　　　　　　　　　　　　　　　Philippians 4:6, 7 TEV

What's your biggest worry right now? How many hours do you have invested in your current worry project? Will your worry time change the outcome?

No matter how you answered those three questions, you know that worry is essentially a waste of mental energy. For the Christian, it is simply the wrong way to live. When Paul told the Early Christians not to worry, he gave them an alternative to worrying. He said to stop talking to yourself about your worries and start talking to God about them—big worries, small worries, all worries. They don't belong in the churning mill of your mind. They belong to God.

When we turn our collection of worries over to God, His promise is that He will give us a peace that defies human understanding. Wouldn't you love to amaze your friends with your peace in stressful and worrisome situations? You can, if you let God manage your worries. When they are His problem to resolve, they are not yours.

Worry will rob us of our Christian joy. It will keep us from a right relationship with God.

Give the ownership of your worries to God today and know the joy of a peaceful heart!

## *Promise:* **Giving Is Receiving**

> *Honor the Lord by giving him the first part of all your income, and he will fill your barns with wheat and barley and overflow your wine vats with the finest wines.*　　　　　　　　　　　　　　　　　Proverbs 3:9, 10 TLB

Our society is in the business of getting. The world of advertising is geared to make us pursue the race for acquisitions. Little is said about giving. Everything is directed toward getting.

Solomon tells us that receiving always starts by giving. When we give the first part of our income to the work of the Lord, God multiplies our gift and returns it to us with great abundance. In other words, you cannot outgive God.

Many of us are very reserved givers when it comes to putting our finances to work for God. In fact, we are misers. We seem to feel that God will take all we give and give nothing in return.

Giving always involves trust. We trust that our gift will be used, blessed, and bring returns to the work of God. We are never to give with only the thought of getting something back. At one time or another, many of us have received a gift with a string attached. We knew we were being bought and paid for with the gift. Instead of joyful, we felt angry and used.

When was the last time you gave to the work of God with a happy heart? When was the last time you gave with only the thought of getting more? Our promise today indicates that we only receive from God when we give to God.

Try living by giving today!

## *Promise:* **The Dream of New Things**

*And the one sitting on the throne said, "See, I am making all things new!" And then he said to me, "Write this down, for what I tell you is trustworthy and true."* Revelation 21:5 TLB

Revelation is the book of endings and beginnings. It is a book that tells God's ultimate plan for each of us. That plan includes new experiences, which can be both exciting and frightening.

There is no guarantee in new experiences unless God is the master planner of them. As the words of God came to John on the island of Patmos, it became clear that God had a new plan in mind for those who belonged to Him. Things would someday not be as they once were. Revelation 21:1–5 explains the changes.

First, God will live with man. There will be fellowship and communion with God in person. No more long-distance connections!

Second, there will be no tears in the new kingdom. We will still have our tear ducts, but the reasons for our tears will be gone.

Third, there will be no more sorrow, pain, or death. The *big three* of the human predicament will no longer exist.

It is difficult for us to catch that kind of dream. It is the dream of new things never before experienced. It will happen, for God authored the dream.

God is trustworthy and true to what He has said. The promise has yet to be fulfilled, but it is there for us. We live today with the knowledge that God has some exciting changes in store for us in the future. Enjoy the dream! It comes from God.

## *Promise:* Getting God's Good Health

*This prayer made in faith will heal the sick person; the Lord will restore him to health, and the sins he has committed will be forgiven.* James 5:15 TEV

The last time you thought of this verse was probably when you had the flu or some more serious illness. Perhaps someone stopped by and quoted it to you as he left. Being well is only appreciated when you are sick. Any way of leaving the illness behind is thought of as relief.

James offers a remedy for sickness that is more effective than anything your local druggist can prescribe. He simply tells us that our prayer, made in the faith of what God promises, will heal us of our sickness. In the previous verses, we are told that God also uses others to speed our healing along. In this case, James suggests that the elders of the church be involved.

Healing is often more effective when shared in a community. It lets others share in the process and experience the joy of the results.

Many people confuse healing with instant results. Healing is a process that begins with prayer and is continued by God. Some people experience instant healing while others go through a restoration process.

James adds that forgiveness is a part of the healing process. Sometimes our sins lead us into our illnesses. With our healing, God is able to take care of our sins. Restoration includes both the physical and the mental aspects.

Place your healing needs before the Lord today. He gives us good health!

## *Promise:* No Fear in the Valley

*Even though I walk through the valley of the shadow of death, I fear no evil; for Thou art with me; Thy rod and Thy staff, they comfort me.*

Psalms 23:4 NAS

When was the last time you heard the Twenty-third Psalm read? In all probability, it was at a memorial or funeral service, or perhaps in the hospital room of a dying person. Contrary to popular usage, this entire psalm is a psalm of life, not death.

Life is a valley surrounded by shadows of our imminent physical death. Each day that we live, we move one step closer to our departure from this life. Our thoughts are not to be directed solely toward the end of our journey but to the way in which we take our journey.

The Psalmist's strong word to us is that we will not fear any evil that joins itself to our journey. We are accompanied by the very presence of God in this life. We are not alone.

David speaks of support when he writes about the rod and staff. Both were the tools of the shepherd. Without them, a shepherd could not function to his fullest capacity.

In our journey through today, God is with us, and He promises to give us support. His support is a comforting awareness that we can complete our journey one day at a time.

Are you living today with a collection of fears around your life? God is with you. He will support you and comfort you. Don't allow the shadows to rob you of God's sunlight!

## *Promise:* Help With Saying and Doing

*May our Lord Jesus Christ himself and God our Father, who has loved us and given us everlasting comfort and hope which we don't deserve, comfort your hearts with all comfort, and help you in every good thing you say and do.*
                                        2 Thessalonians 2:16, 17 TLB

Most of us would get into little trouble in life if we said nothing and did nothing. All of us have had the experience of wondering why we did a certain thing or why we said something. It probably happened to you yesterday and will undoubtedly happen again today.

The Early Christians had the same problems we have. Their struggles were not lessened because they lived in biblical times. Their humanity was present in their experiences.

Paul had a good word for them and for us today. Today's verse is a promise-prayer statement. Two things came from Paul's heart to the hearts of his friends: he desired that they experience comfort and help in all they said and did.

*Comfort,* according to the dictionary, means to cheer or encourage. I can face life if I know I have friends who cheer for me and encourage me. It is difficult to live without affirmers.

Help in saying and doing means to say the right things at the right time and do the right things when they need to be done. God alone can give us the wisdom we need each day to be people whose words are backed by our actions.

Our lives are a collection of what we say and do. What would God like to say and do through you today?

## *Promise:* **God Is Delighted With Me**

*The Lord your God is with you; his power gives you victory. The Lord will take delight in you, and in his love he will give you new life. . . .*
Zephaniah 3:17 TEV

How do you think God feels about you? Does your mind race to all the things you know you have done to displease God? You tally up the long list and respond by saying, "Not too good." It is fortunate for us that our Christian lives are based upon acceptance and not performance.

The Old Testament Prophet Zephaniah tells us that God promises us four things. First, God is with us. He doesn't want us to think we are lone rangers. He walks through life with us. Second, our victories come through the power that He gives us. We are powerless on our own. We are powerful when we tap into Him. Third, the Lord delights in us. He is ecstatically happy and exuberant about you and me. He enjoys us! Fourth, we are given a new life because of His great love. We can't earn it or perform for it. It is a love gift from God.

This Old Testament promise contains our vitamins from God for our daily walk in life. These gifts of God energize us to meet the everyday struggles that we all are challenged by.

God is delighted with all you are today. He is excited about what you are becoming. If God is delighted with you, you can wipe the grim frown of despair from your brow and get excited about God's working through your life. Enjoy His delight in you!

## *Promise:* **Turn Your Thoughts to God**

*He will keep in perfect peace all those who trust in him, whose thoughts turn often to the Lord! Trust in the Lord God always, for in the Lord Jehovah is your everlasting strength.*
Isaiah 26:3, 4 TLB

Have you ever caught your mind wandering as you tried to talk to someone? Perhaps he or she was doing all the talking and you found it difficult to tune in and listen. Your mind took off on its own thought journey.

Life has a way of attracting our attention to its sounds. When God tries to reach us through the noise, we are easily distracted and our minds wander away. God certainly has some powerful competition for our attention these days.

Isaiah tells us that we had better learn to fine tune our thoughts to the

Lord. If we don't, turmoil will replace the peace that God intends for us to have.

Peace comes from trusting God and knowing that He is in charge of all situations. Panic comes from trusting ourselves or sources outside of God.

Many of the people in your world will question your quiet peace and assurance in the midst of a turbulent society. They will find it hard to accept the source of your peace. They may even try to distract your thoughts from the Lord.

God's formula is to think about Him, to trust Him, and receive the perfect peace He brings in all situations. He is the ultimate in strength!

## *Promise:* **Who's First**

*In everything you do, put God first, and he will direct you and crown your efforts with success.*                                    Proverbs 3:6 TLB

Being first is important. People never remember who finishes in second or third place. Winners finish first and are always remembered.

The problem with most of us is that we want to be first. That's where the power and the glory are. There is one place in life, however, where this is not true.

The Christian life is the reverse of the secular life when it comes to being first. God's instructions are that we put Him first in our lives and put ourselves in second place. And His directive is not just in a few things but in everything.

We often have a tendency to put God first only in the things that are of no consequence to us. In the important things, we place ourselves in that spot.

Perhaps this is why we often fail. Today's promise specifically tells us that there are great rewards for putting God in first place in all things. First, He promises that He will direct us and second, He promises His blessing on our efforts. That's a gold-plated promise.

Why are we so hesitant to follow God's plan? We sometimes tend to feel that we can do it better than God. The Bible is full of people who tried to go that route and failed. It was only when they put God first that their lives were successful.

Who's first in your career? In your time schedule? In your relationship building? Try putting God first today!

## *Promise:* **God Is a Road Builder**

*For I'm going to do a brand new thing. See, I have already begun! Don't you see it? I will make a road through the wilderness of the world for my people to go home, and create rivers for them in the desert!* Isaiah 43:19 TLB

There are two kinds of roads. One leads somewhere while the other usually ends nowhere. There is a road like the second one not far from where I live. You can travel on it for several miles until it very abruptly ends. It is not a dead end—it just stops going anywhere. Most of us prefer the oft-traveled road when we have a destination in mind.

One of the promises that God made to the Israelites was that He would build a road for them that would take them home. It was a promise that many doubted. It seemed to be a long time coming. But the promise was made and fulfilled by God.

Many of us have run out of road in our lives. We meet dead ends. We face expanses of wilderness. We wonder what direction to take. God's promise to us stands as tall as it did to the Israelites. When there seems to be no roadway and no direction, God tells us He will lead us home by building the road for us to walk on.

Don't you see the road God is building for you? It is there. Some of us are more inclined to see the wilderness than the walkway. That wilderness can become a formidable object that all but obscures our direction. God is doing a new thing in your life today. He is building a road especially for you!

## *Promise:* **Here's a Happy Man**

*The man who knows right from wrong and has good judgment and common sense is happier than the man who is immensely rich! For such wisdom is far more valuable than precious jewels. Nothing else compares with it.*
Proverbs 3:13–15 TLB

What makes you happy? Psychologists say there are three basic things that people need to be happy. They are 1) someone to love; 2) something to do; and 3) something to look forward to. As you think about personal happiness, you are probably shaking your head in agreement. These three things certainly contribute to a person's happiness. But there is more.

The wisest man who ever lived listed three important qualifications for personal happiness.

1. A knowledge of right from wrong is the first qualification. In today's world, the lines between right and wrong seem to be colored dull gray. The ethics of the moment seem to prevail in many right-wrong situations. We have trouble deciding whether we are right or wrong.
2. The second quality is good judgment. Most of us think that referees, umpires, and judges have that quality all locked up. Not so. God gives us the ability to judge wisely in situations that demand discernment.
3. The third qualification is common sense. It is a quality greatly lacking in our culture. Our society relies on the fact that most people can be conned. Common sense is the ability to look into and beyond a situation and see what is really there.

Would you rather be rich than possess Solomon's attributes? Nothing compares with being a happy person!

## *Promise:* Getting to Know God

*As you know him better, he will give you, through his great power, everything you need for living a truly good life: he even shares his own glory and his own goodness with us!*                                      2 Peter 1:3 TLB

Have you ever met a person for the first time and had the feeling that you really wanted to know that person better? Perhaps you felt that he would not be interested in knowing you, or that he was too important or too busy.

Getting to know someone is a decision that requires the investment of time. It seldom happens overnight, even when there is a kinetic spark in the relationship.

How do you get to know God better, and what happens when you do?

As in a human relationship, you have to spend time with God. Prayer, meditation, and scriptural study are the three most common ways. As you get to know Him better through this process, He becomes a friend, and the several things Peter talks about in today's promise begin to happen.

First, He will supply everything you need to live a good life. Second, He will share His own glory with you. Third, He will share His own goodness with you. In other words, God will not hold anything back from you as you get to know Him better.

Are you receiving the best God has to give in your life right now? Are you getting to know Him better as your relationship with Him grows? It is not a relationship that simply falls out of the air. It is one that you have to work at and invest your energies in. The rewards are worth the investment!

# *Promise:* **A Friend Who Doesn't Change**

*Jesus Christ is the same yesterday and today and for ever.*

Hebrews 13:8 RSV

Have you ever met an old friend whom you had not seen in years? Perhaps an old college acquaintance. You wondered what the person would look like, act like, think like, and talk like. You built a certain degree of speculation in your mind, based on past experience with the person. Then you met, and your expectations were blown apart. He or she was nothing like he once was. You felt that you hardly knew him. You walked away, saying, "Boy, has he changed!"

People change. It's a fact of life.

In today's world, it seems as though everyone and everything is changing. You go back to your roots in your old neighborhood for a visit, and discover that a high-rise building sits where you once played sandlot baseball. Perhaps even your old home has been replaced by a new highway. You go away saddened, with only your memories intact.

In a world that seems to thrive on change, we find ourselves looking for stability. Paul, writing to the Hebrew Christians, gave them a promise of the permanence of Christ. Their world was changing, much as ours is today. New religions were sweeping in then as now. Paul told the Christians, as he tells us today, that Jesus Christ does not change. He is the same as He was yesterday, is today, and will be tomorrow. He is constant!

Christ is your anchor of stability. Don't be afraid to tie your life to Him.

# *Promise:* **God Is a Thirst Quencher**

*"Everyone who drinks this water will be thirsty again, but whoever drinks the water I give him will never thirst. Indeed, the water I give him will become in him a spring of water welling up to eternal life."* John 4:13, 14 NIV

Jesus had stopped by the well for a drink. In a few moments, He was deeply engaged in a conversation with a Samaritan woman regarding water supply. In this conversation He pointed out the fact that human thirst will never be satisfied, but spiritual thirst *can* be satisfied. In fact, Jesus told the woman that He could supply the water of real life in such abundance that it would be no mere trickle but a spring of water that never dries up.

All of us become thirsty. The easiest kind of thirst to quench is physical. The toughest kind is spiritual. Jesus wanted to point out to us that there is only one source that can relieve our spiritual thirst. That source is Himself.

Have you felt dried up and parched lately in your spiritual walk with God? Perhaps you have tried to ease that thirst through other sources in life, only to find out you are still thirsty. When Christ invades our lives, He turns the water of life on in us and keeps it running.

Trust Him today to refresh you from His spring of living water!

## *Promise:* God's Humble Server

*... all of you serve each other with humble spirits, for God gives special blessings to those who are humble, but sets himself against those who are proud. If you will humble yourselves under the mighty hand of God, in his good time he will lift you up.*                                      1 Peter 5:5, 6 TLB

Is it easier for you to give or to receive? I have asked many people that question and found out that most people feel more comfortable giving than receiving. Giving seems to put a person in control of a situation. Receiving, for some strange reason, makes many people defensive, or causes them to feel that they must now reciprocate.

Giving and serving are quite different. In giving, we give what we want. In serving, we give what is needed.

Peter encourages some young men, who will someday be elders in the church, to learn what serving is all about. He tells them they are to serve each other with a humble spirit. Their attitude in service cannot be to think they are better than others but to know that they are equal with others.

Peters tells them that if their service is done correctly, God will bless them in special ways. Peter also shares the consequences of a lack of humility in service by saying that God will set Himself against a proud spirit.

We are encouraged to humble ourselves before God as we humble ourselves in serving one another. If we do, God promises to lift us up.

Are you ready to serve others with humility today?

# Instructions

Almost everything we buy today comes with instructions. If we follow them, the results are good. If we choose to ignore them, the results can be disastrous.

The Christian life comes with instructions. They are found scattered throughout Scripture. They cover a multitude of situations. They are there for our growth and guidance. There may be times when you wonder what to do in certain situations. One of these instructions could be sent from God directly to you.

Instructions are not to be read and filed. They are to be read and followed.

If you are failing at something, try following God's instructions for your day!

## *Instruction:* **Have Fun**

*So I conclude that, first, there is nothing better for a man than to be happy
and to enjoy himself as long as he can.*　　　　Ecclesiastes 3:12 TLB

What kind of facial expression do you see on most Christians—happy,
somber, or sad? Many Christians I meet seem to fit into the somber category. After all, the world is a tough place to live in, and trying to win
others to Christ is somber work. Perhaps the race to join God's family
would speed up if some of the members of the family looked a little
happier.

God is the author of happiness. His creative work expresses His happiness in every dimension. You and I are a part of that creative work. I believe God expects us to be happy. Solomon seemed to think it was all
right when he stated that there is nothing better for us than happiness and
enjoyment. He also expressed that we should enjoy both as long as we
live.

The world is full of sad people with heavy problems. The challenge of
the Christian is to share the happiness that Christ has brought into his
life. That can be done only by expression and example. We either kindle
the fires of happiness or extinguish them.

How can you share your happiness today? The first thing you need to
explore is your facial expression. Do you spend more time frowning than
smiling? Is your smile an invitation to happiness? Are you involved in opportunities and situations that promote the happiness of those around
you as well as your own?

Light up your face today with a happy expression! It will be a magnet
to those you come in contact with!


## *Instruction:* **Hang On to the Truth**

*With all these things in mind, dear brothers, stand firm and keep a strong grip
on the truth that we taught you in our letters and during the time we were with
you.*　　　　2 Thessalonians 2:15 TLB

Paul has just issued a warning to the Early Christians who lived
at Thessalonica. The same warning can be updated nineteen hundred
years and be right on target. Paul's caution for yesterday and today

is to watch out for false teachers and those who would pose as the Christ.

Paul's instructions to us in dealing with detractors are to stand firm and hang on to the truth. Standing implies planting your feet firmly in one place so that nothing can push you around. Some of us run from place to place trying to catch different glimpses of truth. A wandering Christian can be a setup for wrong teaching. If we don't stand firm on something, we are liable to fall for anything.

We are also told to keep a strong grip on the truth. Any who play sports know that the secret to accomplishment is usually found in how to hold the bat, glove, racket, club, and so on. If truth does not come from solid teaching, our grasp of it will be anything but firm.

Are you able to stand firm each day in what you believe? Do you have a solid grasp on the truth of God?

Paul's many letters to the Early Christians contained teaching and encouragement. When he was physically present with them, he taught and affirmed. We need to know God's truth for our lives. We need to be around a community of those who share it. God's truth helps us stand securely. God's people support us in that stand.

## *Instruction:* A Good Mixture

*"But take courage, O Zerubbabel and Joshua and all the people; take courage and work, for 'I am with you,' says the Lord of Hosts."*

Haggai 2:4 TLB

The Book of Haggai occupies only a page and a half in my Bible. It is only two chapters and thirty-eight verses long—certainly not a book to spend much time on. Perhaps that's why they call Haggai a minor prophet. But his message is a major one. It is there to remind us of how God works and what He promises.

The words of this prophet are words to live by today. He tells us that courage and work are a potent mixture to bring into our lives. Courage seems to be a lessening trait in our society. Periodically we read stories of courage in our newspapers. Someone rescues a person from a mugger's attack or puts out a fire before it ravages a building. We give him or her an award and put his picture in the paper. He is somehow an oddity when he should be the norm. We are hung up with minding our own business rather than performing acts of courage.

Work also seems to be vanishing from our society. The prevalent attitude is to do as little work as possible to get by. Our work ethic has been replaced by leisure living. Haggai's call to Israel is simply a reminder that God honors courage and work. They go together.

We are again reminded that God will be with us as we mix courage and work in our lives. These two elements cannot stand alone without the surrounding strength God gives us.

Take a little courage into your work and world today. It is a lofty ideal, but God is the enabler!

## *Instruction:* **Everyone Is a Minister**

*In fact, in everything we do we try to show that we are true ministers of God.*
2 Corinthians 6:4 TLB

Two garbage collectors were recently arrested in New York for not paying their income taxes. They claimed that they were exempt from taxes because they had purchased ministerial credentials. Indeed, they claimed to be ministers. They simply were not true ministers!

Most of us know that buying a credential of any sort does not mean we are qualified to perform a task. You do not become a minister of God by a mail-order certificate. Even attending the best seminary in the country does not make a minister.

The Scriptures teach that every believer is called to be a minister. Some believers are set aside for full-time ministry work. Often they are called reverend, the clergy, and so on. They are true ministers, but they are not the only ministers.

True ministers of God are all those who have received Christ as Savior into their lives and who try to live out the principles set down in Scripture for the Christian journey. In verse 3, Paul tells some simple ways that we will be known as true ministers. He says we will live in such a way that no one will be offended or kept away from God because of our actions. That's a tough command to follow! He also adds that we should live so no one can find fault with us and blame it on the Lord. We have all heard the famous saying, "Well, if that's a Christian, then I don't want to be one." Sometimes it is a judgment. Other times it is an escape clause. Sometimes it is the truth.

You are a minister! Are you ministering through your life today?

## *Instruction:* **The Power of Praise**

*Let everything alive give praises to the Lord!* You *praise him!*
Psalms 150:6 TLB

If you were to read all 150 of David's psalms at one sitting, you would feel that he had taken you on an emotional roller-coaster ride. In the first psalm, he draws the line between the godly man and the wicked man. In the next 148 psalms, David identifies with both sides in his struggle to grow. In his attempt to be godly, he expresses his despair and frustration with his own wickedness. Psalms could well be called the struggle to grow up!

The important part of all David has to say is found in the closing words of the last verse of the last psalm. In spite of all he has gone through, David can conclude with the upbeat exclamation of praise.

How do you give praise to the Lord? What is an adequate way to express praise?

The dictionary tells us that *praise* means, "Commending or lauding in words or song." It also says, "An act of worship." Most of us would express a hesitancy to verbally express praise to God. We seem to believe that God likes silence better than noise. As little children we were told to be quiet in church. That quietness dominates our behavior today.

David says that you qualify to praise God if you are alive. That includes most of us. How can you find some ways to lift a note of praise to God today? Don't expect someone else to do it for you. David says, "*You* do it!"

## *Instruction:* **Putting My Desires on Hold**

*Next, learn to put aside your own desires so that you will become patient and godly, gladly letting God have his way with you.* 2 Peter 1:6 TLB

Letting go of what we possess and what possesses us is a lifelong struggle. We start building our desire list early in life. Our parents reinforce this by telling us what they want us to attain. We add their list to our list and move along. As we grow older, our list grows longer. Then we reach the golden years, and we start unloading what our desires have caused us to collect. It's like cleaning out the garage or attic. We wonder where it all came from.

When Peter wrote his letter to some scattered Jewish Christians, he understood and spoke about the wrong use of desire. He knew and witnessed the power of wrong desire in Christians' lives. He watched them being blown off course when they put their own desires first.

Our society, like that in Peter's time, has picked up the banner of "Do your own thing." Follow your own desire and you will satisfy your longings.

The Christian soon discovers that consistent growth comes from discerning and following God's desires rather than his own. We are instructed to do this in order to bring about two commodities that are much needed for our journey: patience and godliness.

How does your personal list of desires compare to what God desires in your life? Is God in all the things you are pursuing?

Letting God have His way is a slow but worthwhile process. The process can be more fun than the pursuit!

## *Instruction:* Keep Your Ears Open

*Come to me with your ears wide open. Listen, for the life of your soul is at stake. I am ready to make an everlasting convenant with you, to give you all the unfailing mercies and love that I had for King David.*   Isaiah 55:3 TLB

A friend of mine told recently how his young son gets people to listen to him. He simply goes over to them and pulls their faces close to his before he starts talking. When you are that close, you can't help but listen.

Do you envision God getting your attention in that way? We usually listen in two ways: with the ears of our heads and with the ears of our hearts. Some of us don't listen at all. We hear sounds but not words.

Isaiah pleads for his people to come to God with their ears open. He injects an awesome challenge as to why they should listen to God. He says their very lives are at stake.

What sounds in our society get your ear? The sirens on emergency vehicles; the train whistle at a crossing; the scream of another person; a child's crying. These sounds crash into your brain and get your attention.

God seldom yells at us in order to get our attention. Yet His "still small voice" is often louder than any earthly sound. Are you listening when God is talking? If not, you might miss the directions He is giving out for this day.

Getting the ear of God is usually easier than giving Him our ears. Perhaps we are afraid of what He might say to us.

Keep your ears open to God today!

## *Instruction:* Who Owns Your Body?

> *That is why I say to run from sex sin. No other sin affects the body as this one does. When you sin this sin it is against your own body. Haven't you yet learned that your body is the home of the Holy Spirit God gave you, and that he lives within you?... For God has bought you with a great price. So use every part of your body to give glory back to God, because he owns it.*
>
> 1 Corinthians 6:18–20 TLB

Every time I go to my health club, I am conscious of my body. Most of the time I don't think about the extra inch on my waistline, or my under-developed biceps. Then I walk into the exercise-and-weight room and view the varied assortment of bodies with everything in the right place. I automatically pull in my stomach, stand straighter, and wish I could work out inside my own private tent. The message my club sends me is that we live in a body-beautiful, body-conscious age. And I'd better get mine in control.

The age in which Paul lived was as body conscious as today. There was use and abuse of the body everywhere. The apostle's plea to his fellow Christians was to use and care for the body properly because it was God's home. Proper usage of every part gives glory to God.

Today misuse of the body is everywhere. Excess use of pills and chemicals, junk foods, polluted air, and sexual promiscuity are all destroying the temple in which God desires a residence.

Society says that you are in charge of your body and you can use it any way you choose. God says He has paid a great price for you. He lives within you and desires you bring glory to Him through care of your body.

Does God feel at home in you?

## *Instruction:* Share the Ups and Downs

> *When others are happy, be happy with them. If they are sad, share their sorrow.*
>
> Romans 12:15 TLB

The toughest thing about living alone is not having someone special to celebrate your triumphs or share your downers with. Both happiness and sorrow need to be shared commodities in life. We grow from both experiences. Everyone grows in a shared experience, no matter how good or bad.

In the twelfth chapter of Romans, Paul gives instructions about how to live with and love one another. He spells out the undying principles of Christian community. Right in the middle of these guidelines, he injects the principle of human expression. He affirms both celebration and sorrow as a part of the human experience. Which is easier for you to share in with another brother or sister in God's family?

In sharing another's sorrow, it sometimes seems that we cannot find the right words to share adequately in the grief. Most of us fumble through other people's sorrow.

In seeking to share in someone's happiness, we often find ourselves jealous that the experience is happening to them rather than to us. Their success seems to highlight our lack of accomplishment. It is difficult to celebrate another's triumphs when we wish they were ours.

Being with someone in both happiness and sadness means we care. We sometimes have our feelings of inadequacy or jealousy. That just affirms our humanity. Being there for another person is important to his growth and to ours. Someday the situation may be reversed!

## *Instruction:* **Out of the Spotlight**

*"Take care! Don't do your good deeds publicly, to be admired, for then you will lose the reward from your Father in heaven."*          Matthew 6:1 TLB

Most of us like to be in the spotlight once in a while. We enjoy that moment of glory and the accolades that go with it. We work hard to reach a goal and receive the accompanying prize. We feel a real sense of accomplishment and human worth. Without these experiences, our lives would lack meaning.

Today's instruction from Matthew has to do with our motivation and reason for what we do more than the reward for doing it. In every group of people there are those who seek the glory and spotlight to merely lift themselves beyond the reach of others. Whatever they do is done in full view of everyone so that they might achieve public admiration. We could call this kind of motivation a service to self rather than a service to others.

Self-serving deeds always have a hollow ring to them. The person who has to let everyone know what he or she has done will receive only a self-injected glory.

The Pharisees of Jesus' time seemed to fit the self-serving, self-seeking category. They publicly displayed their religious acts so that they might be noticed. Jesus had harsh words for them. He called them phonies.

Do you do good things for the right reasons? Can you be unconcerned with the glory and credit and more concerned about the end result? What is your motivation for what you will be doing today?

## *Instruction:* We All Need a Little Respect

*Show respect for everyone. Love Christians everywhere. Fear God and honor
the government.*                                                    1 Peter 2:17 TLB

A well-known comedian has built his career around the problem that
he doesn't get any respect. Every time he appears on television, we wait
for his famous line to be spoken. He plays the part of the loser in life in all
situations. No one takes him seriously, no matter what he says or does.
He never gets any respect.

How about you? Do the people in your life take you seriously? Do they
respect you?

As Peter writes to the Early Christians, he gives a simple pattern for
getting respect from other people. You have to give it in order to get it
back! That's both profound and simple—and very hard to do. Most of us
want things without having to give anything for them. Sometimes we fall
into the trap of treating people in a special way only because we want
them to treat us the same way. We are not showing respect—we are ex-
changing favors.

Respect is showing consideration for the feelings and personhood of
another. It comes with no qualifications. It knows no barriers of age, race,
education, or position. Peter seemed to know that love and respect are
intertwined. You can't have one without the other.

Are you showing respect to both your Christian and non-Christian
friends? They are all God's unique, unrepeatable miracles. God respects
them. You should, too!

## *Instruction:* A Long Fishing Trip

*Jesus called out, "Come along with me and I will show you how to fish for the
souls of men!" And they left their nets at once and went with him.*
                                                    Matthew 4:19, 20 TLB

What caused those early fishermen to leave their nets and follow Jesus
on a lifelong fishing trip? Were they bored with fishing? Did they know
who He really was? Were they captured by His awesome appearance and
authoritative command? We really don't know what magnetized them
into leaving their nets to follow Jesus. Perhaps it was the challenge and its
magnitude, or the simple invitation to join Jesus and learn what He was
all about.

Has anyone ever invited you to go fishing? If you are not a fishing en-
thusiast, you will probably not get too excited. In place of fishing gear,

you will take lots of food to eat and a few good books to read. You know that between the catching of fish there are long periods of patience and boredom.

Life was never boring with the great fisherman, Jesus. Every day new challenges were faced and miracles of healing took place. I am sure the disciples wondered many times just what they had gotten themselves into.

Every Christian is called to a fishing trip with the Master. Once you begin, it lasts your entire earthly life. Sometimes there are flat, dry, boring, uneventful times when it seems as though the fish aren't biting. At other times, when we are leading people to Christ, it is very exciting.

How is your fishing trip going? Jesus has promised to show us each day how to fish for Him. Don't be afraid to ask for help!

## *Instruction:* How to Respond to Another's Sins

*Dear Brothers, if a Christian is overcome by some sin, you who are godly should gently and humbly help him back onto the right path, remembering that next time it might be one of you who is in the wrong.*

Galatians 6:1 TLB

A prominent Christian leader is accused of tax evasion or exposed on morals charges. What is the general response of the Christian community? We know all too well that most of us want to line up on the judgment side rather than on the restoration side. Sometimes we almost applaud the fall of another Christian. It seems to make us look better and put that person in his or her place.

Many of the New Testament instructions for living are directed at how we live with one another in the body of believers. The writers seemed to know, perhaps because of their own experience, that living and loving one another in Christian community would not be easy. They knew that we would all fall into sin every so often. Their concern was centered more on restoration than condemnation and criticism.

Paul urged the Christians at Galatia to rally around the one who commits sin. He implored them to gently and humbly lift the sinner back onto the right pathway. With tongue in cheek, and perhaps a sly smile on his face, he told them that they could be next. They were asked to give the kind of treatment to others that they themselves would like to receive if the sin were theirs.

Do you surround those who sin with your gentle love? Can you lift them and affirm them back to God? Perhaps God will bring someone to you today for restoration!

# *Instruction:* **A Word to the Gripers**

*In everything you do, stay away from complaining and arguing, so that no one can speak a word of blame against you.*                     Philippians 2:14, 15 TLB

Have you ever tried to avoid someone because you knew that all he or she did was complain? Even listening to him for a few minutes had a negative effect on your own life. Gripers are seldom looking for ways to solve problems. They merely want to highlight them and blame them on someone else. As their lists grow, few things are affirmed as being right. Everything becomes wrong. Gripers are pessimists in action.

Griping and complaining usually lead to arguing. When others don't agree with your complaints, an argument ensues. Most arguments are left to dangle and, as a result, relationships are broken.

If you were to write a list of complaints today, how long would it be? Where would you start and where would you end? Would your complaints be based on others' lack of performance or on your own failures?

In his prison letter, Paul tells his friends to avoid complaining and arguing in *everything!* That's a tall order for most of us. Paul tells us that there is no room at all in our lives for this because even a little bit has a way of growing and polluting us. It is a little like gossip. There is no small portion. It grows in an overpowering way if we allow it into our lives.

We can shut down the griper by refusing to enter into and enforce the complaints. When we quit griping and start taking action, we will have a positive effect on others.

Get your gripe eraser out today!

# *Instruction:* **Here Comes the Singing Heart**

*Oh, come, let us sing to the Lord! Give a joyous shout in honor of the Rock of our salvation! Come before him with thankful hearts. Let us sing him psalms of praise.*                                             Psalms 95:1, 2 TLB

David knew the value and joy that music could bring in a believer's life. Many of his writings encourage us to sing to the Lord. Making music was David's way of celebrating God's goodness. He did not hold praise for his own expression to God but encouraged everyone to participate.

We have all had the joyful experience of having a song of Christian praise drop into our lives at just the right moment. Sometimes it brings tears of joy to our eyes. At other times, we just say a silent *Yes, Lord!* to the music.

I believe every Christian's car should be equipped with a cassette tape player. The glove compartment should be stuffed to overflowing with praise music. As we grind our way through the traffic of life and live through the many moods of our day, we will need a musical uplift. Music ministers to and lifts our spirits. It puts our minds at ease and draws a cloak of calm around our frenzy.

Try singing along with the music. God is not that concerned with our melodic gifts. He tells us to make a joyful noise. You can turn your car into a bubble of song and praise.

All of creation's sounds are a part of God's great orchestra. Make your own kind of music as you lift your voice in praise to Him today!

## *Instruction:* Being Different Is Okay

*Give a warm welcome to any brother who wants to join you, even though his faith is weak. Don't criticize him for having different ideas from yours about what is right and wrong.*                                    Romans 14:1 TLB

Accepting people who differ from us is never easy. That's why our friends usually are similar to us in thoughts, actions, feelings, likes, and dislikes. It is easier to be with "your own kind" than to walk along with those who march to a different drummer.

The sign on the front of a church usually says a lot more to the reader than just a name. It often defines what the members of that church believe theologically and socially. It can tell what hymnal is used and what translation of the Bible is read. It may even tell how affluent its attenders are. It is comfortable to be with people who are just like us. It can also be a dreadful bore!

A good test of Christian acceptance is how we receive those who don't see eye-to-eye with us in our community of Christian fellowship. Do we want to straighten them out quickly so that they can conform also? Are we afraid they might change us to their way of thinking and believing about something? Sometimes new Christians threaten old saints. They don't have it all together and they ask a lot of questions. We want to give them a dose of instant answers and make them veteran travelers overnight.

Is there a place in your Christian group for the weak, the uninformed, the different? Is it easier for you to criticize than to accept a brother or sister who differs from you?

Try giving Paul's warm welcome to that "different" person today!

## *Instruction:* It's God's Battle

*"Listen to me, all you people of Judah and Jerusalem, and you, O king Jeho-shaphat!" he exclaimed. "The Lord says, 'Don't be afraid! Don't be para-lyzed by this mighty army! For the battle is not yours, but God's!'"*

2 Chronicles 20:15 TLB

Who in the world was Jahaziel? Well, let me introduce you to him. He just happens to be the author of the above instructions. He probably never said or did anything else of significance in his life, but to the Israel-ites under threat of invasion, he was God's spokesman.

Israel was about to be invaded by three armies. The odds were over-whelming. King Jehoshaphat had called his people to prayer and fasting. As they waited, watched, and probably trembled, God gave them a word through a nobody, Jahaziel. God's word for His people was a battle strat-egy that did not make sense. *Don't be afraid and don't be numbed by the odds. This battle problem is the Lord's, not yours!*

How many times have you wanted to make your battles your own rather than God's? How often have you been full of fear and numbness as you looked at the problem rather than the opportunity? How often has God sent you a message via an unlabeled messenger?

God operates in very unusual ways. He is never comfortable with man's strategies and plans. He has His own methods—and they work. You can read on in this chapter and see how very unorthodox God can be when He goes into battle for you.

Are you frustrated in fighting your own battles? Let your call to arms be answered by the Lord!

## *Instruction:* God's Payback

*See that no one pays back evil for evil, but always try to do good to each other and to everyone else. Always be joyful. Always keep on praying. No matter what happens, always be thankful, for this is God's will for you who belong to Christ Jesus.* 1 Thessalonians 5:15–18 TLB

Have you ever wanted to get back at someone for something that he or she did to you? At one time or another, most of us have climbed aboard that ship. The feeling of revenge is really a cry from the heart that says, *You can't do that to me! If you think you can, I will show you that you can't. I will get even.*

Trying to get even only makes you lopsided. The writer of the above instruction knew that, and he wanted Christians in his time to know it also.

As we journey through life, we will bang heads and hearts with all kinds of people. Some of them will really try to do us in. Their philosophy will be to get you before you can get them. Paul tells us we are to be thankful when that happens, so we can demonstrate the love of Christ to them. They will be expecting our vengeance, but we will give them our love.

Christians in Paul's time were being oppressed by the government. Many were slain for their faith. Some wanted to retaliate. They were told that this was not God's way. Retaliation was to be replaced by a forgiving spirit, a joyful attitude, a prayerful heart, and a thankful life.

Are you wasting excess energy in your life planning to get even with those who have wronged you? Start forgiving and begin living!

## *Instruction:* **Four for Prayer**

*Don't be weary in prayer; keep at it; watch for God's answers and remember to be thankful when they come.*                    Colossians 4:2 TLB

Prayer, a process that God intended to be simple, natural, and spontaneous, is one of great complication for most Christians. Bookshelves spill over with countless volumes on prayer. They range from the "how to" to the "how not to." Prayer is basically a conversation with God.

There are four things in today's instruction for living that define our attitude toward prayer. First, we are told to not be weary in prayer. That could mean that we are not to pray when we are too tired to think, or it could mean that we are not to give up in our praying. In another passage of Scripture, we are told to pray without ceasing. In other words, hang in there. Don't quit because the answers don't appear to be forthcoming.

Second, we are told to persevere in prayer. We learn things by doing them, not by abandoning them. The disciples asked Jesus to teach them to pray. They were given a prayer model, but the learning process continued for the rest of their lives. They struggled with prayer, but they prayed!

Third, we are told to watch for the answers. Why are we shocked when our prayers are answered? Didn't we expect God to answer? A right prayer attitude is one of expecting God to respond, and seeing how God works things out.

Finally, we are told to give thanks for answered prayer. "Thank you" is a simple statement but an important one. God receives our thanks.

These four for prayer will work in your life today if you will work at them!

## *Instruction:* **Running From the Devil**

*So give yourselves humbly to God. Resist the devil and he will flee from you.*
James 4:7 TLB

How does a person get away from the temptations that Satan brings into his life? Many Christians want to flirt with the things that Satan offers. They try to convince themselves that they can handle the presence of sin and not get involved in it. Their philosophy seems to be, "Go away closer."

Resisting Satan is never an easy proposition. He comes to wreck our lives in all kinds of disguises. Contrary to popular opinion, he does not come dressed in a red suit with accompanying horns and pitchfork. If anything, he comes as an angel of light, but bearing a world of darkness.

Joseph had one good idea in dealing with Satan's temptation. When Potiphar's wife tried to seduce him, he literally ran away from her, leaving his cloak in her grasp. We can choose to run as fast and as far as we can from Satan. It is a good way to deal with temptation.

James's advice is to be so strong and so dedicated to God that Satan will not be able to stay around you. He will do the running. You can sit tight.

It is easy for the Christian to think that Satan is on vacation when in reality, he is just around the next corner. Satan seldom drops a hydrogen bomb in our pathway. He subtly and quietly goes about his business of blasting us apart, bit by bit. His attack on our lives is very deceptive.

How is your resistance level today? The more you give of yourself to God, the less there will be for Satan to tempt and attack!

## *Instruction:* **Growing Some Patience**

*Dear brothers, is your life full of difficulties and temptations? Then be happy, for when the way is rough, your patience has a chance to grow. So let it grow, and don't try to squirm out of your problems. For when your patience is finally in full bloom, then you will be ready for anything, strong in character, full and complete.* James 1:2–4 TLB

Problems are the builders of patience. Few of us want to encourage problems so that we can expand our patience. Our immediate response to problems is to find a way to get rid of them. They are the pebbles in the shoes of life that make us walk funny, feel funny, and generally make us very uncomfortable.

James seems to share today's instruction with tongue in cheek. I am sure that the people who read this for the first time responded much as you and I do. They probably thought James was joking when he affirmed the positive nature of problems.

James, in fact, says that we are to be happy when struggles come, and not to try and squirm out of them. The end result of facing them will be a great increase in our own strength and confidence.

Can you look at your problems as God's opportunities? Can you be patient enough and excited enough to watch how God will work His plan through them? Will you give God the time to do that, or will you rush in and try to solve them yourself?

Being happy with your problems is having a quiet confidence and a smile in your soul. You would prefer not to have problems, but you know that God has them there for a purpose. You will ultimately be the beneficiary of your problems.

Your patience will come to full bloom through your problems!

## *Instruction:* **Pass It On**

*For you must teach others those things you and many others have heard me speak about. Teach these great truths to trustworthy men who will, in turn, pass them on to others.*                                  2 Timothy 2:2 TLB

Every Christian is a teacher. We communicate to others what Christ is to us by word, deed, and action. One of the great mistakes in the contemporary Christian world is to assume that there are only a few teachers but many students. It is easy to relegate the role of teacher to the pastor of your church or the leader of your Bible study. When we place that responsibility solely on another, we relinquish what God would have each of us be.

Timothy was a young student of Paul. Paul spent time with him as his mentor and friend. Timothy's responsibility was to carry the things that Paul taught him into the lives of others. In teaching others, Timothy was to encourage them to pass it on to others who could be trusted.

Who are the Timothys in your life? We all should have a few whom we are teaching, sharing with, and helping grow. We start by sharing the simple things of Christ with new converts, or the converts we lead to Christ. As they grow, they also share. This is called discipleship. And that is the example Jesus set up for the evangelization of the world.

It is easy to leave the teaching up to those who are wiser than we are. That becomes a cop-out. We are all teachers, passing on the truth of God. To whom will you pass it on today?

## *Instruction:* **Honor and Love**

*"Honor your father and mother, and love your neighbor as yourself!"*
Matthew 19:19 TLB

A man had pressed through the crowd to Jesus and asked Him how he could have eternal life. Jesus replied by telling him to keep the commandments, and then listed them for him. As he did, He mentioned today's instruction as a part of the commandments.

Honoring and loving are emotional commitments to other human beings. It is far easier to keep laws that are tangible than ones that are intangible. We see results from the tangible as we carry them out. The emotional and intangible come from inside of us and are centered in our hearts.

Honoring your parents means lifting them to the highest level of respect. They stand above all others. Our respect is the result of our years of loving and being loved by them. It is more than the two days a year that we single out for mothers and fathers. Honor is a forever thing. Have you shown that honor in a tangible way to your parents recently? You may *feel* the love, but it is good to *show* it.

Loving your neighbor is harder than loving your parents. Your neighbor might do some things that could dissolve any love you had for him. In a modern world, we usually define our neighbor as the person who lives in the house next door or on our street. In reality, everyone we come in contact with is our neighbor. Jesus is really just getting specific with the same love principle He shared with His disciples when He told them to love one another. It is easier to love generally than specifically. You and I are called to love specifically.

How are you doing today with honor and love?

## *Instruction:* **Tearing Down or Building Up?**

*In this way aim for harmony in the church and try to build each other up.*
Romans 14:19 TLB

Have you ever been part of a church fellowship that specialized in living with each other in harmony? To most of us, that would be a wonderful idea yet to be realized. Usually the reverse is true. We often find ourselves trooping from church to church and fellowship to fellowship looking for a loving, harmonious group to grow with. Harmony is not something you go looking for. It is something you bring with you. It is transmitted from you to others.

Paul constantly urged the Early Christians to live in harmony with each other. He knew too well what their human excesses were. He knew that the Spirit of the Lord in a person's life was the source of harmony. But even with God's Spirit in evidence, the human spirit has to be contended with.

When there is disharmony, there is a tearing down of relationships and community. People are set at odds with each other. The ultimate disharmony is war.

Paul urges God's people to be builders and not wreckers. When you spend your time building someone up, it increases the harmony in relationships and supportive communities.

Are you a builder of other people? Are you always lifting them, affirming them, and seeing the Christ who dwells within them?

Harmony comes from you as you become a builder of others. Think about a building project you can work on today!

## *Instruction:* Watch Out

*Be careful—watch out for attacks from Satan, your great enemy. He prowls around like a hungry, roaring lion, looking for some victim to tear apart. Stand firm when he attacks. Trust the Lord; and remember that other Christians all around the world are going through these sufferings too.*

1 Peter 5:8, 9 TLB

If anything, today's verses should scare the wits out of you. They mean that someone is after you and his desire is to tear you apart. That sounds like the story of a lunatic from a horror movie. It's not. It's a reality for the Christian—one we often forget about.

Many of the Christian sounds we hear are soothing and somewhat numbing. They seem to be lullabies rather than fight songs. Peter gives us a short fight song and sounds an alarm in the process.

It is easy to forget that Satan is very much in business today. He is on the prowl, looking for victims whom he can devour or possess. Peter's instructions are to have your feet on solid ground when the inevitable attacks occur. We are also told to trust as we stand firm.

Our trust is found in the hundreds of promises contained in Scripture. God has promised us protection, but He did not promise us we would not be attacked. Sometimes we forget that until satanic attacks occur.

The final note that Peter sounds involves the fellowship of sufferers. There is always a river of strength that flows from those who suffer in similar situations. We know we are not alone. We know we all stand together. Watch, stand, trust, and share. Good words for today's walk!

## *Instruction:* **Peace Inside and Outside**

> *Let the peace of heart which comes from Christ be always present in your hearts and lives, for this is your responsibility and privilege as members of his body. And always be thankful.* Colossians 3:15 TLB

How long has it been since you felt a true spirit of peacefulness in your life? With the busy, frenzied lives that most of us live, peace seems to be reserved for the front of Christmas cards. We even race through our times of rest.

Peace comes from God and is found on both the inside and the outside of our lives. Inner peace is the quiet confidence of knowing God is in charge in all situations. Outer peace is expressing a visible calm when exterior events want to drown you in their turbulence. It is next to impossible to express outer peace if one does not have inner peace. Peace, like happiness, comes from within. The inner impression that peace makes on our hearts helps us to make an outer impression on situations and people.

Paul notes that peace is not a happenstance. It is both a responsibility and a privilege. We, as the people of God, are responsible to be conveyers of peace to a troubled world. We are honored to be the bearers of peace. It is a privilege conferred only on those who belong to God.

There is a great deal of crazy-making in our world. We find it at home, in the office, on the streets, in our churches. You and I are called to help make some sense of this madness we live with. The only way we can do this is by letting the peace of Christ flow through us to those desperately in need of it.

Are you willing to be a channel of His peace today?

## *Instruction:* **Who Prays for You?**

> *Dear brothers, pray for us.* 1 Thessalonians 5:25 TLB

When was the last time someone said he or she would pray for you? Perhaps you shared a concern or a problem with him. As you walked away, almost as an afterthought, he told you he would pray for you. "I will pray for you!" Those five words have too easily become a parting benediction for many Christians. We literally toss them over our shoulders as a way of dismissing the struggles of others.

Praying for someone is never to be taken lightly, or forgotten. Missionaries become the most frequent recipients of our promises to pray. Then they go back to their places of service, and once every six months their names appear in the church bulletin. We say a quick "God bless them."

Paul, Silas, and Timothy needed the prayers of God's people. They were not afraid to ask for them. They did not want an "over the shoulder prayer." They wanted a daily remembrance before God in their behalf. Perhaps the Thessalonian Christians told Paul they would pray for him when he left them. Here, in his letter back to them, he asks for their prayers.

There is power in having others pray for you. There is also the spirit of a shared struggle. Praying for someone is being there for him.

Prayer is two-sided. We promise to pray for others and we ask them to pray for us. Don't treat either lightly. If you say it, do it. If you ask it, expect it.

Whom are you praying for today? Who is praying for you today?

## *Instruction:* Sharing the Load

*Share each other's troubles and problems, and so obey our Lord's command.*
Galatians 6:2 TLB

There are no lone rangers when it comes to problems and troubles. I have met only a few fellow travelers in life who want to hug their own struggles to themselves and not have them shared by others. Most of us feel better when we can share our hassles with other members of the body of Christ.

We are sure to meet a few people who don't just want to share their load but who want to transfer it to someone else. Watch out! That gets dangerous. If you have a messiah complex, you will feel like gathering up everyone's problems and taking them upon yourself. That's dangerous.

Problems, if we understand Scripture, are to help us grow and to produce patience in our lives. When you take someone's problems away from him, you deprive him of a growth opportunity.

God calls us to walk alongside of those who have struggles so we can encourage and affirm them. It is easier to carry a problem if you know that you are not alone.

There is a danger in seeing other people as your answer rather than your assistance. Some of us are problem dispensers. Others are problem collectors. God calls us to be problem assisters.

How are you doing with your load of problems? Are you looking for relief in the form of another person? Look for someone who will walk with you through them. You will be better for the struggle!

## *Instruction:* **The Collector Syndrome**

*"Don't store up treasures here on earth where they can erode away or may be stolen. Store them in heaven where they will never lose their value, and are safe from thieves."* Matthew 6:19, 20 TLB

Have you ever met a collector? I once walked through a house that was up for sale and discovered that the owner was a clock collector. I lost track of the number of different clocks in the house. Every square inch of wall was covered. Every piece of furniture was covered. The closets were full. Even the garage was full of every sort of timepiece. The owner's comment as I looked through the house was, "As you can see, I collect clocks." Really!

His house was also wired with numerous burglar systems to protect his collection. What a collection! What a responsibility to keep it!

Many of us are collectors. We collect material things and fill our lives to overflowing with them. We place value on them and try to protect them. We can consume all our energies in acquiring and securing. If the possessions were ever stolen or burned up in a fire, we would feel as though we could not go on without our collections.

Jesus warns us about spending too much time stacking our treasures up in this life. What we collect we must protect. His advice is to only collect heavenly treasures and send them on ahead of us. Heavenly treasures are our investments in the lives of others. It is being God's person to another. It is making disciples. People should matter more than things. They should be our investments.

What are you collecting? Are your collections giving you so much excess baggage that you have no time to spare for people loving?

Maybe it's time to clean house or have a garage sale!

## *Instruction:* **Some Parting Thoughts**

*I close my letter with these last words: Be happy. Grow in Christ. Pay attention to what I have said. Live in harmony and peace.*
2 Corinthians 13:11 TLB

The Corinthian Christians were one of the most troubling groups for Paul to deal with. It seemed as if they would never get their church fellowship living in harmony. Their controversies over Paul's teaching and the teaching of others seemed endless. They even challenged the authority of Paul. Certainly Paul had every right to close his last letter to them with the words, "Good-bye and good riddance." But he didn't. His closing words to them, after many storms, were words of encouragement and love.

How many times have we been glad to say a good-bye and toss a "good riddance" in for good measure. We tend to be hasty in writing people off. Paul wasn't. He had a patience with people that came from his many problems with them.

It is difficult to deal with affirming endings. It is easier to rush on and forget. Paul's last words to the Corinthians were almost a form of benediction. He wished them happiness brought about by being happy. He urged them to keep growing. He reminded them of all he had shared with them. He knew his teaching was still valid for them, whether they felt it or not. And finally, he urged them to live in harmony and peace. That would have been a real turnaround from the way they had been living.

Paul was not discouraged.

What kind of parting words have you used lately?

## *Instruction:* **Caring About Others**

*Don't just think about your own affairs, but be interested in others, too, and in what they are doing.*                                    Philippians 2:4 TLB

Self-obsession will be known as the sin of the seventies. The philosophy of "doing your own thing" at the expense of others crept into our thinking as the age of demonstration ended. People spent a great deal of time being consumed with their own interests. History will probably record the seventies as the age of *me-ism.*

Life in Christian community is the exact opposite of what society has taught us. We are not to be consumed with ourselves. We are to be involved with everyone else. There is no such thing as a community of one. There is no such thing as an orchestra of one. It is a combined effort.

It is easy to spend all our time thinking about our own problems and needs. We can become trapped in a "mess of self" if we are not careful. The Young Church at Philippi was warned by Paul about the sin of self-excess. Paul's word was to get interested in others and take some of the focus off yourself.

How interested in other people are you? Do they bore you, excite you, stimulate you? Are they burdens to run from or blessings to be enjoyed?

It takes time and effort to be interested in others. Involvement grows by inches. Paul seemed to know that this kind of relationship would draw people close together. With closeness and concern would come caring. From caring would come loving.

Jesus was interested in people. Just look at some of His conversation in the Gospels. Pick one person to be interested in today and watch your life and his change!

## *Instruction:* **God Is Your Architect**

*Be glad for all God is planning for you. Be patient in trouble, and prayerful always.*                                                                    Romans 12:12 TLB

How would you like to have God tell you everything He is planning for you for the next twelve months? How about six months? Sounds exciting, doesn't it. Or does it?

The good things that we would enjoy from God would be terrific to look foward to. What about some of the struggling and testing times that God has in store for you over the next year? If we knew that those were a part of the plan, we would start worrying now and looking for ways to take the year off.

It is a good thing that God reveals the plan on a daily basis. That way, we can attain the growth that will enable us to meet the struggles.

God's instruction is simply to be happy for *all* God is planning for us. He is the architect of our lives and knows what He is doing. His caution to us as He reveals that daily plan is to be patient when the tough times come, and to always be prayerful. Patience and prayer—the dynamic duo of the Christian walk. Both of them reside near the top of the "tough to do" list in our Christian life.

We do not know how God's plans are going to work out for us today. We do know that we can be glad, because God knows exactly what He is doing. We wait patiently and we pray continually. God reveals the process.

The Architect is at work in your life today. Trust Him!

## *Instruction:* **Keep Your Eyes Open**

*Keep your eyes open for spiritual danger; stand true to the Lord; act like men; be strong; and whatever you do, do it with kindness and love.*
                                                                    1 Corinthians 16:13, 14 TLB

Have you ever felt yourself falling asleep while driving home in your car late at night? Your eyes blink, your head nods, and your tires hit those little bumps in the pavement that signify the lane changes. Your head snaps up and you shake off the drowsiness and go on. There is real danger ahead for those who fall asleep at the wheel. Even though you might feel you can have two nods without a collision, there is no guarantee.

Some Christians fall asleep as they travel through life on their spiritual pilgrimage. Others have a problem keeping their eyes on the journey. Spiritual dangers are usually not advertised by giant road signs. It takes a keen perception to spot them. It takes a person's being wide-awake to avoid them or steer carefully through them.

How are you doing lately in your driving? Are you wide-awake and spotting the spiritual potholes as they come along?

We are urged to do several things to stay awake: stand true to the Lord, act like men, and be strong in everything we do. That sounds like a job for someone who is awake. We are also told to do everything we do with kindness and love. No job for the catnappers!

There are strong demands on the Christian if he is to remain true to God. Satan is hiding behind some of the road signs along the highway of life, just waiting for us to go to sleep. Nod twice and you are under attack.

Keep your eyes open today. Be awake and prepared to live!

## *Instruction:* Foolish Testing Is a Waste of Time

*Jesus replied, "The Scriptures also say, 'Do not put the Lord your God to a foolish test.'"*                                    Luke 4:12 TLB

Did you ever take a test in school that was a waste of time? I did. I have taken some tests in life since then that I felt were also a waste of time. Testing is designed to check the retention of our knowledge. If it does less than that, it fails.

Sometimes tests are designed to embarrass us with our lack of knowledge. At other times, they are designed to intimidate us or even manipulate us. Perhaps that's why few of us really enjoy testing.

Some of us have even gotten the idea of testing God. Satan was the first to try it. He set up what appeared to be fabulous rewards for Jesus if He passed Satan's testing. He invited Jesus to jump off the temple to see if the promises surrounding Jesus would prove true. His test had no validity and no purpose, because Jesus' life was the proof of the promises. He had already passed the test! He had no need to prove anything to Satan or anyone else.

Jesus set an example in His wilderness experience with Satan. He has told us that we don't have to yield to any of Satan's testing games. We are able to live by the authority of the Word and the promises contained in it. When Satan tries to play his testing games with us, we can simply say, "Don't put the servant of the Lord to a foolish test!"

Don't take foolish tests and don't invent them for others. Examine your life today and see how you are doing with the tests that come your way.

## *Instruction:* **What to Do When You Go Home**

*"Go home to your friends," he told him, "and tell them what wonderful things God has done for you; and how merciful he has been."*     Mark 5:19 TLB

Most of the people I know look forward to going home to see their parents, relatives, and friends. Home seems to be wherever the greatest collection of these people are. Going there always has a special appeal. There is an excitement about old places that have a share in our memories. There are people who still remember us as we were, rather than as we are. Going home is special.

Jesus had just healed a man possessed of many demons. Crowds had witnessed this powerful act of healing. They had trouble believing it. The man who had been healed wanted to remain with Jesus, but Jesus told him to go home to his friends and share his story with them. He did, and everyone who heard him was amazed at this new man who had emerged through Jesus' healing power.

Going home for this man was probably both difficult and easy. The easy part was that he could not wait for people who knew him previously to see the change in his life. The hard part was probably wondering if they would believe it was permanent and real. Telling everyone that God had done this miracle would certainly arouse some skepticism.

Do you tell your friends and family what God is doing in your life when you go home? Do you spend all your time talking about old things, or are you eager to tell about the new things God is doing through you? Going home can be good news in many ways. Don't be afraid to share your growth and God's work with those who knew you when you were something else!

## *Instruction:* **Tough Love**

*"There is a saying, 'Love your* friends *and hate your enemies.' But I say: Love your* enemies! *Pray for those who* persecute *you!"*     Matthew 5:43, 44 TLB

Jesus was always in trouble with the society around Him. He kept doing things just the reverse of the way they had always been done. The authority system was always after Him for making changes in the rules and accepted patterns.

The same thing is true today. The worldly system operates on one level. The Christian system operates on another. The world has a problem with Christians because what they do often does not seem to make any sense, according to its system. The world says to love your friends and hate your enemies. That seems to be good sense. No one can fault the directive to love your friends. Hating enemies also seems like good advice. There is always an enemy around somewhere to hate. Enemies are people who are out to get us in some way, shape, or form. They can be next door, down the street, or across the world. It seems to be "us or them"!

Jesus knew that even enemies respond to love. They become confused and perhaps more open when they receive love instead of more hatred, which in turn fuels their hatred for us. Jesus exemplified this kind of love by asking forgiveness for His executioners. They were dumbfounded by this, and wondered how He could do it.

Loving those who are going in the opposite direction is hard—perhaps almost impossible. But it works.

Try some tough love on your persecutors today!

## *Instruction:* Watch Out for the Chains

*So Christ has made us free. Now make sure that you stay free and don't get all tied up again in the chains of slavery to Jewish laws and ceremonies.*
                                                        Galatians 5:1 TLB

Have you ever had someone say to you, "I can't talk to you right now. I'm all tied up"? What do they mean? They are simply saying that they are involved in other things and you cannot be important to them until those things are taken care of.

Have you ever felt that life has you all tied up? You can hardly move because of the knots of problems that have you tied up tight.

Christian freedom is leaving the knots behind you and operating in the open space God has given you. Some of us allow others to tie us up. A few of us tie ourselves up. Either way, we are not free.

Paul urged the new Christians at Galatia to preserve their new freedom and not fall back into old ways. They were urged to enjoy God's grace rather than man's laws.

There is always a great degree of responsibility that comes along with freedom. We must use freedom wisely or it, too, will tie us up.

Many people in today's world dream of freedom and will travel any path to obtain it. They live in countries where freedom is a forgotten word. They are being strangled by the knots of oppression. Many of them run toward the freedom you and I take for granted.

Ultimate freedom is found in Christ. When He sets you free, you are really free. You will never look back.

How free are you today? How many chains are you still dragging around? The Christian is not a chain collector!

## *Instruction:* Looking for an Idea

*The intelligent man is always open to new ideas. In fact, he looks for them.*
Proverbs 18:15 TLB

When was the last time you thought you had a great idea and when you shared it, someone threw cold water all over it? How did you feel? Probably about the same way Jesus felt when He told people they could have eternal life and they yawned three times and walked away.

The Christian is God's idea person. God has given us good, sound minds to use. He expects our juices to be flowing creatively. We look for new ways to grow and serve God. We dream dreams that are bigger than we are.

Ideas flow in two ways: they come from us to others and elicit a response, or they come from others to us and penetrate or die.

How open are you to new ideas? Is it easier for you to say, "Well, we never did it that way before!" Many great ideas have been snuffed out by negative thinkers.

God's Word is full of ideas. How open are you to them? Do you approach Scripture with an "it won't work" attitude? Solomon knew that intelligence is centered in receptivity to new ideas. He tells us that the intelligent man goes looking for ideas. He doesn't sit and wait until they find him.

Do you need some new ideas in your life today? Keep your eyes and your heart open. If you are aware, some that have been flying by will stop where you live.

## *Instruction:* Enjoy! Enjoy!

*This will make possible the next step, which is for you to enjoy other people and to like them, and finally you will grow to love them deeply.*
2 Peter 1:7 TLB

What are the steps to falling in love with someone? You date him or her, you like him a little, then you like him a lot. Somewhere along the line, you wake up in love with the person. You may not be sure how you arrived there, but you know you are there.

Peter offers a process that results in loving people. This kind of love is not romantic love but brother-sister love that builds relationships in the body of Christ.

The process begins with enjoying people. Enjoying someone means accepting him where he is and not wanting something from him or trying to use him. Many friendships are founded upon use rather than enjoyment.

Enjoying people means having fun with them. It means sharing strengths and weaknesses and being able to laugh about both. It means opening the door of your life to them and inviting them in.

If you enjoy people, you will find yourself liking them as persons. They will move from the collective to the individual in your life.

Growing to love a brother or sister takes time. There are no instant friendships with lasting qualities. Only mushrooms grow overnight.

Peter was setting forth a process for building solid Christian community and love toward all members of the body of Christ.

Is the door of your life open to this process today? If it is, God will put people in the doorway!

## *Instruction:* **New Words to the Musical of Life**

*"And so I am giving a new commandment to you now—love each other just as much as I love you."*                                    John 13:34 TLB

Jesus' time on earth was running out. In the message to His disciples on the Mount of Olives, He tried to equip them for living and growing after His death and Resurrection. Gently, He spelled out His marching orders to them. Perhaps they waited with bated breath, expecting some great, earthshaking directive that would lead them to new heights of leadership. It never came.

All of what Jesus wanted the disciples to do after He left was summed up in John's Gospel. They were simply to love each other with the same energy and love that Jesus had directed toward them when they ministered with Him.

What do you think their response was? "No problem! We can do that easily!" Or, "Is that all?"

What would your response have been? What happens when you expect one thing and receive another—happiness or disappointment?

The disciples were just like you and me. They felt some disappointment, some happiness, some misunderstanding, some questioning. They certainly didn't fall in love with each other in that moment. It took years of maturity and living for Jesus' words to become a reality in their lives.

Persecution and struggle enhanced their love for one another as the Early Church grew. They had their highs and lows and in-betweens; their love for each other grew.

Jesus' words are still up front in your life and mine today. We are called to love each other. Jesus certainly put some new words to the music in our lives!

## *Instruction:* **How to Handle Anger**

*If you are angry, don't sin by nursing your grudge. Don't let the sun go down with you still angry—get over it quickly; for when you are angry you give a mighty foothold to the devil.* Ephesians 4:26, 27 TLB

Do Christians ever get angry? Do you get angry? I can almost hear a thundering *yes* coming back at me. We all get angry. Our problem is not in getting it, it is in getting rid of it.

The first thing Paul tells us is not to carry our anger around with us day after day. It has a way of growing and festering. It also has a debilitating effect on our lives. It takes energy to stay angry. We need our energy for more creative things than anger.

Paul talks about the need to resolve anger before we go to sleep at night. Have you ever taken your anger to bed and tried to sleep with a free mind? It doesn't work too well, does it? You have trouble sleeping, and your anger often looms larger in the early-morning hours as you roll and toss in bed.

Unresolved anger is not only a robber of our rest but it also exposes us to the attacks of Satan. Satan uses anger to cloud the real issue and prohibit any resolution. Anger feeds on anger until we can easily reach the point of rage and commit some act that will permanently damage us. Many murders are committed out of anger and a person's inability to resolve that anger.

Anger is something that comes with the human package. It is not wrong to have it. It is wrong to harbor it and not resolve it.

Is anger damaging your life today? Ask God to help you resolve it!

## *Instruction:* **Smothering the Spirit**

*Do not smother the Holy Spirit.* 1 Thessalonians 5:19 TLB

The Holy Spirit is probably the most misunderstood part of the Trinity. We have no problem with the Father (God) and the Son (Jesus). The

Holy Spirit remains a shrouded mystery to most believers. Great controversy abounds in the church as to how the Holy Spirit operates and equips the believer for ministry. The gifts of the Spirit and their operation have caused denominations to split, churches to have open warfare between their members, and a general fear to occupy the hearts of believers. We will not try to solve all of those recurring problems in one short devotion.

Controversy on the operation of the Holy Spirit was prevalent in the Early Church. Paul wrestled with the problem constantly. His words for today, as in his day, can form a rainbow of understanding above all the conflict and mystery. Simply, Paul tells us not to smother the Holy Spirit by our lack of understanding, our doubts, or our fears. Don't put the Holy Spirit in a box.

The Holy Spirit does not operate within the structures and confines of life as we understand it. The Holy Spirit does not do things as we would do them. The Holy Spirit does not fit a stereotype and is not a conformist.

We rational souls have to try and understand everything and, even worse, explain it. That's where we run into trouble with the operation of the Holy Spirit. It is the secret weapon of the Trinity.

Give the Holy Spirit free reign in your life today! You will be amazed at the results.


## *Instruction:* **Praying in Secret**

*"But when you pray, go away by yourself, all alone, and shut the door behind you and pray to your Father secretly, and your Father, who knows your secrets, will reward you."*                                   Matthew 6:6 TLB

Few people whom I know enjoy being alone. Even fewer enjoy praying alone. There seems to be something within each of us that calls us to community experiences.

Jesus recognized that prayer was important work that takes place between a person and God. He knew the need for removing all wordly distractions when conversing with God was to take place. In His own life, He withdrew from the crowds and even the disciples, on occasion, to pray alone.

In a world that gets noisier and more congested by the moment, we need to be able to close a door on it all when we talk to God. It may mean going into a special room in our house or a cabin in the mountains. Regardless of the place, we need to leave the world outside.

Matthew tells us that God knows our secrets, and one of my feelings is that prayer is the open admission of some of our secrets to God. Perhaps this is why it is good to not always have others around when we are praying. We all have secret needs, thoughts, wishes, desires, and concerns. The prayer time alone is a place to share these with God.

Matthew tells us that God will reward us when we follow this prescription for prayer. He does not say what the reward will be. Perhaps a clear conscience and a feeling of release from things we have given to God is one reward.

Will you find time today to close the door to the world and talk with God?

## *Instruction:* The Gifts of Help and Hospitality

*When God's children are in need, you be the one to help them out. And get into the habit of inviting guests home for dinner or, if they need lodging, for the night.*                                    Romans 12:13 TLB

Christians are a combination of the city rescue mission and the Holiday Inn. We are to stand ready to meet the human needs people have, as well as feed and house them. Most of us run from instructions like these because they are time-consuming and probably will not lead to recognition and glory. It is easier to refer the needy to the mission and the homeless to the Holiday Inn. They are the professionals and we are the novices.

In the Early Church, believers came many miles to share in a house-church fellowship or to hear Paul preach. At the end of the meeting, they could not jump in their cars and drive down the highway a few miles to their own homes. They had to find lodging and nourishment. Paul believed that it was the responsibility of the Christians to share what they had because it was a gift from God.

I visited a church where all visitors were recognized in the worship service and invited to the homes of the members for dinner and fellowship. I could detect a "special something" in this church family. They were warm and loving and caring.

How long has it been since someone offered the above gifts to you? How long has it been since you offered the gifts to another? We are both givers and receivers. Some of the best ministry I know takes place when we follow Paul's words. Try it! You might be surprised at the results.

## Instruction: Do You Always Want Your Rights?

*Your attitude should be the kind that was shown us by Jesus Christ, who,
though he was God, did not demand and cling to His rights as God, but laid
aside his mighty power and glory, taking the disguise of a slave and becoming
like men.*
                                                    Philippians 2:5–7 TLB

Freedom and rights seem to go hand in hand. The more freedom we
have, the more we demand our rights within that freedom. We will go so
far as to enter into litigation in order to pursue our rights. Rights have almost become demands.

Christians often fall into the same trap as non-Christians. We want our
rights protected as we live within our Christian communities. We make
demands on one another because of our rights. Some rise to the status of
elitism in the leadership of our Christian communities. Many of our leaders and Christian spokesmen make demands because of their positions.
We have fallen prey to the philosophy of "God's best for His greatest."

Jesus seldom pulled rank. He never said, "Do you know who I am?"
The disciples wished He would call down fire and hail to show people
who He was. He never did. He never dragged His family tree out in order
to obtain His rights. He quietly went about the work of God in a servant
capacity.

Are you the servant or the served? It is much more fun to be waited on
than to be the waiter. Too many of us have followed the former in our
Christian circles.

Take a look at Jesus' attitude regarding rights and freedoms. Then,
contrast His to yours!

## Instruction: A Word to the Loafers

*Now here is a command, dear brothers, given in the name of our Lord Jesus
Christ by his authority: Stay away from any Christian who spends his days in
laziness and does not follow the ideal of hard work we set up for you.*
                                                    2 Thessalonians 3:6 TLB

We live in a welfare society. The more you give to people, the more
they expect. People reach out to the government with open hands to meet
their needs. The government fills those hands, but they never seem to be
full enough. There is no work given in exchange for the handout. In part,
we have affirmed the principles of freeloading in our society.

Paul set a tough standard regarding work and its rewards. He literally
commanded Christians to stay away from other Christians who sit

around with their hands out expecting others to meet their needs. He said what we are often afraid to say of the freeloaders in our world. They are lazy!

Laziness can be contagious. It is easy to say, "Why should I work when those who don't work receive the same reward?" It is even worse when your work pays for their reward for *not* working!

Christians can be as lazy as anyone else. Paul urged the believers to follow his and others' example of the law of hard work. Paul was way ahead of what we call the Puritan work ethic. He was simply following a biblical principle of how to raise one's self-esteem. Productivity makes a person feel good about himself. Accomplishment is self-affirmation.

We can be lazy in many different ways. Use God's yardstick to measure your own life today!

## *Instruction:* **The Specially Able**

*Let love be your greatest aim; nevertheless, ask also for the special abilities the Holy Spirit gives, and especially the gift of prophecy, being able to preach the messages of God.* 1 Corinthians 14:1 TLB

Someone has wisely said, "Shoot at nothing and that is exactly what you will hit!" We could also say that if you don't aim when you are shooting at something, you will still not hit it. Aiming and shooting can be a big problem for the Christian.

What is your greatest aim as a Christian—to be more godly, to read your Bible more, to pray and witness more? These are all important to Christian growth, but the Scriptures tell us to aim at love.

Christian living is perfecting our loving. Everything we say, think, and do is to be cloaked with love. It is God's perpetually blinking neon sign over our lives. If love is our greatest aim, the many other things we need will follow in its wake.

Paul tells us to be free to ask also for the special abilities the Holy Spirit gives to us. There are numerous gifts we can ask for, but one is highlighted. It is the gift of speaking or preaching the message of God to the heart of man.

Notice that we are not called to ask for the gift of being ordained clergymen. There was no such thing yet. This gift and its calling were to be asked for by anyone and everyone. Not all would receive it, but all were to be open to it.

How open are you to God's call to preach? Some of us do it daily in small ways. Others are called by way of profession. Just be open today and every day to God's gifts in your life!

## *Instruction:* **What Does God Want You to Do?**

*Don't act thoughtlessly, but try to find out and do whatever the Lord wants
you to.*                                                    Ephesians 5:17 TLB

Have you ever said, "I don't know why I did that"? We usually say that
when we have done something thoughtless or just plain dumb. It is a
statement that we really don't want anyone to answer. We just hang it in
the air and hope no one will venture a response.

We all do and say some pretty silly things. Most are done without
much forethought. Usually, when we think about things for a while, we
are much wiser in our actions and reactions.

God wants us to be adventurers in finding out what He wants us to do
in all things in our lives. It might be changing jobs, changing friends, or
just making everyday decisions. God does not want us to spend all our
time acting thoughtlessly. He wants to be in our thoughts and directing
them.

Some of us have struggled with finding God's will for our lives. I don't
believe God has one big will and one big answer and that when we find it,
we will no longer have to search. God's will is revealed from day to day.
You just need to know it and follow it today. And it is no mystery. We
simply ask, submit to God, and we will receive the directions.

Knowing what God wants us to do and doing it are two different
things. I know many people who have God's orders in their hands but are
hesitant to follow them.

God gives the plan and the power to follow the plan a day at a time.
Are you looking for the whole road map, or can you be content with just
today's small corner?

## *Instruction:* **The Gift of Money**

*If you are a preacher, see to it that your sermons are strong and helpful. If
God has given you money, be generous in helping others with it.*
                                                        Romans 12:8 TLB

Don't you wish you had the gift of making money—lots and lots of it?
How would you handle that gift if the Lord gave it to you? Someone has
said, "God always knows whom He can trust with money." Perhaps that's
why I don't have that gift.

Most people collect money. Very few are in the distribution business
other than to pay daily bills. The problem with collectors of anything is
that they are never quite sure they have enough. The more they acquire,
the greater the fear of losing it.

Giving in the right areas is a responsible investment of what God has blessed us with. We are not to hold back in our giving because we don't approve of the way it is received and used. When God directs us to give in a certain area, we are to follow His instructions.

Many people who have money give only so that they can get more. This is contingent giving and will always be devoid of the real joy of giving.

The Christian who has anything to give should be a "no strings" giver. That is where the real joy of giving lies.

Most of us don't have the gift of making a lot of money. But we are not excused from giving what we can. Perhaps one day God will give us great wealth and the great responsibility of distributing that wealth.

Does what you give help others?

## *Instruction:* The Secret to Door Opening

*"Ask, and you will be given what you ask for. Seek, and you will find. Knock, and the door will be opened."* Matthew 7:7 TLB

Life is a series of open and closed doors. We are usually afraid to walk through the open ones and curious to know what is behind the closed ones. Occasionally we shut the ones that are open and kick down the ones that are closed. Why does it seem so hard to go through open doors?

Jesus gave the secret to dealing with doors when He spoke with His disciples. To them, there were more closed doors than open ones. The door to their understanding was closed. They were not always sure what Jesus was up to, and they wanted to know.

Asking is always the first step to opening any door. If there is someone on the inside, he opens the door when you ask. Jesus said to ask if you expect to receive.

Seeking follows asking. Once you go through the door, you don't remain in the doorway. You move beyond to exploration. A seeker is an adventurer who will make discoveries.

Knocking is announcing your readiness to enter what is beyond the door. We don't knock unless we are prepared to enter.

God does not take us down a corridor in life where all the doors are kept sealed. He is a door opener for us when we are prepared for entry.

Are you ready to take the steps of moving through closed doors into new rooms of growth in your life? Ask, seek, and knock!

## *Instruction:* When Criticism Counts

*Don't refuse to accept criticism; get all the help you can.*
                                                    Proverbs 23:12 TLB

When was the last time you thanked someone for the criticism he or she directed at you? Probably a long time go—or never! Most of us have a difficult time with any form of criticism. We usually interpret it as a personal attack upon our integrity and behavior. When it is launched in our direction, we immediately throw up a wall of self-defense and start arguing, or retreat into the safety of silence.

Solomon tells us that there is help in criticism. We are to accept it. In another of his proverbs, we are even told to welcome it.

There are two kinds of criticism: constructive and destructive. Constructive criticism is applied gently and with a sense of affirmation. It is designed to help a person improve in whatever area the criticism is directed. It does not attack the person. It is directed toward the problem. It gives the person a chance to respond and make corrections. It is in the best interest of everyone involved.

Destructive criticism is directed toward the person rather than the problem. It dehumanizes and gives the person no place to stand. This form of criticism is often a judgment without mercy.

We are all recipients as well as givers. Are you able to give and receive the right kind of criticism?

Listen with an open heart and mind the next time a criticism comes your way. It may be God's way of helping you improve your life!

## *Instruction:* How to Treat Those From Other Lands

*"Do not take advantage of foreigners in your land; do not wrong them. They must be treated like any other citizen; love them as yourself, for remember that you too were foreigners in the land of Egypt. I am Jehovah your God."*
                                                    Leviticus 19:33, 34 TLB

My wife and I had just arrived in England and were taking our first cab ride. As we arrived at our destination, we asked the cabby how much the fare was. He gave us a mumbled figure in English currency. I held out my hand with English notes and coins in it and told him to select the right amount, since we had not mastered the currency yet. Several hours later, we told an English friend what the cabby had selected and asked if that were correct. We were horrified to find that the cabby had taken four times the amount of the true fare. In our first outing, we had been taken advantage of. We learned the currency fast!

Increasingly, our country is opening its doors to immigrants from other countries. For most of us Americans, they are a source of congestion. They barely read our language. They don't drive properly on our roads. They are often confused by our customs and practices. It is easy to run out of patience with them, and we sometimes even use them to our advantage.

In the Book of the Law, Moses has an instruction for everything for the Israelites. He even tells them how to treat foreigners, because they were often the foreigners themselves. His words are to not take advantage of them, not wrong them in any way, and to treat them as one would treat his own people. Finally, they are told to love foreigners.

Love knows no race, color, religious affiliation, or social status. Let us love *all* our neighbors today!

## *Instruction:* The Boundaries of Blessing

*Stay always within the boundaries where God's love can reach and bless you. Wait patiently for the eternal life that our Lord Jesus Christ in his mercy is going to give you.* Jude 1:21 TLB

Are you living inside or outside the boundaries of God's blessings? I did not ask if you were being blessed. Some people feel that if blessings are not raining down upon them, they must be far from God. I believe that we can live in certain places which we can expect God to bless more than others. By this, I don't mean geographical locations. If there were one geographical blessing spot in our land, we would all head for it immediately.

Living within the boundaries of blessing means several things. First, it is living your life with an expectant attitude that God really has a plan for you. He has a personal investment in you and is daily revealing His plan for you.

Second, it is living your life with a strong supportive community of Christian friends around you. They form a protective and supportive shield for you so that you can grow in the right environment.

Third, it is allowing the Word of God to penetrate your daily life. Reading the Word, studying it, and memorizing it are ways to integrate it into your life.

Finally, living within the boundaries of blessing means that you are free to share the blessings God does give to you with others. A blessing needs to be passed along.

God's love reaches out and blesses when you live within His boundaries of blessing. Where are you choosing to live this day?

## *Instruction:* The Power Within

*Last of all I want to remind you that your strength must come from the Lord's
mighty power within you.* Ephesians 6:10 TLB

I remember reading those wonderful Charles Atlas ads in comic books
when I was a child. I wanted to look like old Charles and be able to mash
the bullies on the beach. We were told you could do it all through
dynamic tension. The problem was that it took months and months of
hard work. You couldn't just paint it on and have it. You had to build
it in through the rigors of hard training and rivers of sweat. If you did
persevere, you could become a walking tower of strength. People could
know your strength by just looking at you. That's one kind of strength. It
is an outward strength.

Inner strength is applying the dynamic tension of God to the muscles
of your soul, spirit, and mind. It is a rather silent and unnoticed growth
that is best built through the trying of your faith.

Inner strength is a resource that we draw upon when the real issues of
life come banging on our doors. The more issues and battles we face, the
greater will be our strength. It is like faith. You only build it by having it
tested. If your reservoir is full when the testing comes, you will come
through the test.

Strength for the Christian comes from the Lord. We draw on that
strength and power each day as we face the offerings of life.

How is your inner strength today? Do you feel a strong reserve from
God that will enable you to meet today's challenges?

## *Instruction:* A Place of Refuge

*How precious is your constant love, O God! All humanity takes refuge in the
shadow of your wings.* Psalms 36:7 TLB

Have you ever felt that you would like to hide behind the wings of
God? When the hassles and tensions of life crowd in on you, when you
run out of mental and emotional gas, have you ever looked for a place to
hide?

There is an increasing need in all of our lives to have a place of refuge.
The dictionary defines *refuge* as, "a place of retreat or sanctuary away
from dangers and troubles." In effect, it is a safe hiding place.

There were many places we used to run and hide in when we were
children. We would escape our parents' wrath and our friends' reprisals
by sneaking into an old barn or a dark corner of our houses.

When you grow up, hiding places become scarce. In the words of the old spiritual, "I went to the rock to hide my face and the rock cried out, 'no hiding place!'" Life can get to be one giant overexposure process. We need to get out of the light and into a quiet corner once in a while.

David realized that God was his ultimate place of refuge. There was no other place that afforded him the warmth of constant love.

Where do you go for refuge? Do you have a special place where God can meet you and surround you with His love?

## *Instruction:* Stop Talking and Start Doing

*Little children, let us stop just saying we love people; let us really love them, and show it by our actions.* 1 John 3:18 TLB

I once heard someone say that the Salvation Army was simply love in overalls. In other words, they worked out the love they talked about in very practical ways.

A theme of constancy in Scripture is putting love into action. The disciples were told to love one another. This meant that they weren't just to say it but they also had to *show* it. One of the ways of showing love, I am sure, was simply putting up with one another each day. They were all very different personalities and needed love to make them into a working unit.

When asked if he loved Jesus, Peter replied by saying, "You know I do." Jesus' response was to make Peter's love into an action word. He told Peter to feed His sheep.

John tells his readers to stop talking about love all the time and start showing love by their actions. Love is fun to talk about. It is romantic to sing about. It is an overworked theme heard many times a day. But there is a world of difference between talking and doing.

How can you make love an action word in your life today? By loving the world? That's too broad. Narrow it down to loving one other person in a constructive way. Don't just tell him—show him. Look for ways to make God's love flow through you into action with another person.

Love isn't love until you give it away!

## *Instruction:* **Let's Do It All Together**

*May God who gives patience, steadiness, and encouragement help you to live in complete harmony with each other—each with the attitude of Christ toward the other. And then all of us can praise the Lord together with one voice, giving glory to God, the Father of our Lord Jesus Christ. So, warmly welcome the other into the church, just as Christ has warmly welcomed you; then God will be glorified.*                                Romans 15:5–7 TLB

The thought of spending eternity with our friends in heaven is fantastic. The thought of spending each day with them here on earth is often something far less. It is an honest struggle to live in Christian community in the body of Christ. The maintenance needed to keep harmony with our brothers and sisters is wearying.

Paul's prayer of equipping the Roman Christians to live with one another contains the elements of patience, steadiness, and encouragement. When these three things are present, we will have the wisdom to know how to work and live together. Over these three ingredients, Paul tells us to have Christ's attitude. That means asking the question, "How would Jesus respond to this situation?"

When we live in harmony, we can rightly praise the Lord together. Perhaps the reason for poor singing and poor praise in many churches is the lack of the bond of love between the members.

Paul ends his instructions by telling us to extend a hand to those who are trying to enter our fellowship. We are to make them feel warm and welcome.

I have been in many groups where the welcome left a lot to be desired. I also noted that I was not anxious to return to that group.

Together in community is God's good idea for growth today!

## *Instruction:* **Enjoying the Good Years**

*Don't let the excitement of being young cause you to forget about your Creator. Honor him in your youth before the evil years come—when you'll no longer enjoy living.*                                      Ecclesiastes 12:1 TLB

Isn't it a shame that youth is wasted on the young! Someone always seems to be saying that as we get older. If we could only have young bodies with old minds, we would do so much better.

Being young is exciting. Just ask your children. They live for today and compress all the living they can into that day. They never want to go to bed. There is too much to do and they can sleep a lot when they reach their parents' age.

Solomon spoke a great deal about time, youth, the seasons, and aging in Ecclesiastes. He planted the idea of how important it is not to forget about God while you are enjoying youth. For many of us, almost everyone this side of retirement is young. I hear many people tell me that they will give God a second look when they retire and have more time. Today they want to pursue their careers and enjoy life. Tomorrow, when they are looking at the short side of life, God will get a few moments.

Have you put God on hold while you race along the road of life? Are you planning to check in later when you have more time and less energy?

God is a front-burner force in your life. He doesn't want to slowly simmer on the back burner until you have time for Him.

Is God a part of your excitement for today?

## *Instruction:* Setting Up Your Face

*Because the Lord God helps me, I will not be dismayed; therefore, I have set my face like flint to do his will, and I know that I will triumph.*
Isaiah 50:7 TLB

Have you ever tried reading people's minds by the expressions on their faces? Spend an afternoon in your local shopping mall and try it. You will soon discover that only two feelings show right through. Happiness and sadness.

Sometimes we go through tremendous pain in different situations. We decide to either let it show or hide it. There is always a well-meaning friend around who, if we are hiding it, will tell us how amazed he is at our strength and outward calm. You can't always tell the interior by looking at the exterior.

We all put different expressions on our faces to augment the different moods we are going through. Isaiah tells us that he is setting his face like flint on doing the will of God. Flint is a tough, unyielding substance known for its hardness. Isaiah says he is going to be tough about doing God's will. He is not concerned about the faces around him. He sets his own face with a purposeful expression.

Our expressions should radiate our confidence in His strength as it flows through us. What message does your face express to the world?

Isaiah knew he would triumph as he set the right face to God. So will you!

## *Instruction:* **A Distribution of Gifts**

*Now God gives us many kinds of special abilities, but it is the same Holy Spirit
who is the source of them all. . . . There are many ways in which God works in
our lives, but it is the same God who does the work in and through all of us
who are his.*                                              1 Corinthians 12:4, 6 TLB

I have always wanted to stride up to a microphone, pick it up, nod at
the pianist, and break into song. The problem is that in this desire I have,
I don't want to sound like me. I want to sound like Bev Shea or Andy
Williams. Perhaps you have wished that you had someone else's gift, as I
have.

As my own gifts increase and are utilized, I find that I have less desire
to want someone else's. I become more content and committed to developing the gifts God has given me.

Your gifts and mine are from the Lord. The Holy Spirit empowers us
to use those gifts for the building up of the body of Christ. We can be
thankful for the gifts and abilities we see in others. We don't need to envy
them or desire them. The source of all our gifts is the Lord.

Paul also tells us that God works in different ways in different people.
He has no carbons. We need not be jealous when we see God doing something through another person. Just be thankful for it and affirm it.

What special abilities and gifts has God given you? Are you using them
to His glory?

## *Instruction:* **Why? Why? Why?**

*Since the Lord is directing our steps, why try to understand everything that
happens along the way?*                                      Proverbs 20:24 TLB

Have you ever caught yourself thinking, *Why did God allow this to
happen?* Or even, *Why* didn't *God allow it to happen?* It is a good thing
that we will have eternity to spend with God. For me it will take that long
to have all my "whys" and "why nots" answered.

It is easy to feel that we are pawns on a chessboard some days. It seems
as though God is moving us around in all directions and we can't make
any sense out of where we are going. The important thing is not to always
know where you are but to know who is going with you and preparing the
way before you.

Confidence in living is knowing that God is directing our steps. The
Scripture tells us that the steps of a good man are ordered by the Lord.
One order of good steps, please, Lord!

How much time have you wasted recently trying to analyze your footprints? It should be enough to know that God is directing your feet.

I often look back over my life and wonder how I got where I am today. If I do retrace my steps in my thoughts, I conclude that they all led me up to where I am. I still have a lot of unanswered questions from the journey, though. They will remain unanswered for a long time to come.

Give only a fleeting glance to the "whys" in your life. They are God's property!

## Instruction: **Directions for Being a Follower**

*Then Jesus said to the disciples, "If anyone wants to be a follower of mine, let him deny himself and take up his cross and follow me. For anyone who keeps his life for himself shall lose it; and anyone who loses his life for me shall find it again."* Matthew 16:24, 25 TLB

How do you get people to follow you? If you have ever been in a leadership role, you know how difficult a question that can be. It seems that people are always looking for ways to do things differently than you want them to. Leadership certainly isn't easy. But then, neither is being a follower!

The disciples were slowly being pulled in closer to Jesus. They were beginning to sense that this journey they were called to involved a deeper commitment than they had planned on. What may have started out as a fun trip was getting serious.

Jesus' call to be a follower, as recorded by Luke, had more teeth in it than the initial call to be fishers of men. It was almost part two of the original call.

Jesus hit upon three requirements for a deeper commitment from the disciples. The first one was self-denial—in other words, putting oneself in second place. The second was cross bearing. This involved work. It was to be no fun-filled trip with a few miracles tossed in. The final requirement involved following the One who was leading, in any direction He chose to go. Jesus knew that this would ultimately lead to Calvary for Him, and later, certain death for the disciples as they sought to expand the Kingdom.

Making a decision to follow Christ is an important step. Taking action on that decision and walking it out daily is even more important.

How are you doing today at following?

## *Instruction:* **Paying What Is Due**

*Don't withhold repayment of your debts. Don't say "some other time," if you
can pay now.*                                      Proverbs 3:27, 28 TLB

The one thing I like most about the Book of Proverbs is its practicality
in dealing with the everyday issues of life. The overarching theme of Solomon's writing is that we will be wise and do well if we follow the practical principles that, for the most part, are good common sense. If we
choose not to follow them, we will bring a great deal of sorrow into our
lives.

One of the most practical things we all deal with is paying our bills.
That problem has never changed. Only the currency varies.

If you are like most people, sitting down with your stack of bills and
checkbook the first of every month is a traumatic experience, especially in
these times of economic recession and climbing inflation. Our prayer is
that we can reduce the stack of bills in proportion to the money available
to pay them.

Solomon's word of wisdom in this area is one that brings relief and release to the bill payer. He says that we are to pay all our bills now if we
can. We are not to withhold payment because we want to use the money
for other things or because we feel our creditors can wait until next
month. We are to pay what is due now.

I know I always feel a sense of relief when I toss all those envelopes in
the mail after writing my checks. My credit remains good, and I fulfill
one of the practical responsibilities I have as a Christian.

How are you doing in this area? Christian responsibility invades the
practical areas as well as the spiritual areas of our lives!

## *Instruction:* **What to Do When You Would
Rather Worry**

*Don't worry about anything; instead, pray about everything; tell God your
needs and don't forget to thank him for his answers.*     Philippians 4:6 TLB

How much time will you spend worrying today—a few minutes, an
hour, a few hours, all day? Worry, once it gets your attention, will take
over your thoughts. What starts out as a small worry, or even a minimal
concern, can escalate into an anxiety attack. Worries often loom larger
after dark, or when we wake up in the middle of the night and can't sleep.

For the Christian, worry is basically distrusting God. It is probably the
number-one sin in the lives of most Christians. The more time we devote

to worry, the more insoluble the worries become. You simply can't win the worry game.

Much of the last chapter of Philippians is devoted to combating the sin of worry. Paul doesn't just say, "Don't worry." He tells what to do in place of worry and how to build a peace-of-mind attitude in all situations.

His first advice is to turn your worries into prayer requests. Give the ownership of the worry over to God and trust Him for the right results. No matter how small or how large, give it to God. Many of us want to take care of the small things and give God the big ones. Give them *all* to God.

We are also told to thank God for the answers, whether or not they have arrived. Thanking Him is trusting Him.

What will you do with today's mound of worries? Do you want to own them or would you rather let God own them? Let them go and get some peace into your life today!

## *Instruction:* Build Up Your Life

> *But you, dear friends, must build up your lives ever more strongly upon the foundation of our holy faith, learning to pray in the power and strength of the Holy Spirit.*
> Jude 1:20 TLB

What is the strongest vitamin a Christian can take? It is not Geritol, Centrum, or the multivitamins you buy at the health-food store. The strongest vitamin for building strength in the Christian is prayer—one in the morning, one in the evening, and liberal doses throughout the day.

Jude encourages us to build our Christian strength through the power of prayer. If we fail to do this, we will be weak and ineffective as God's people. Jude adds another dimension to prayer. He says we need to learn to pray in the power and strength of the Holy Spirit.

When Jesus went alone to the garden to pray just prior to His arrest, we are told He sweat great drops of blood. That is praying in the power and strength of the Spirit. Human power here would have been useless.

Prayer is like building muscles. It takes time, practice, and consistency. Understanding the work of the Holy Spirit in prayer takes time. To pray in the Spirit means to be empowered in our prayers by that same Spirit. It means to pray with an intensity. Sometimes this kind of praying is exhausting.

Praying in the Spirit means to be in complete and immediate communion with God. It is getting directly through to the Source.

The Holy Spirit will give you power and strength to build up your life. Ask for it today!

## *Instruction:* Are You Running to Win?

*In a race, everyone runs but only one person gets first prize. So run your race
to win.*                                              1 Corinthians 9:24 TLB

This year several thousand people started out in the Boston Marathon.
They were all runners and had trained long and hard for the event. They
looked like runners as they went through their prerace warm-ups. They
packed together into one great sea of human congestion as the starter's
gun went off. One person finished first and one person finished in position
987. Who will be remembered in the history of the race? The winner! The
spectators will remember it, the other runners will remember it, and the
winner will remember it. The only one who remembers who finished in
spot 987 is the one who finished there.

The Christian life is a race. Everyone who knows Christ is in the race.
Paul tells us that we are to run to win. Our attitude in running the race
should be the attitude of a winner. We have trained, we are strong and
confident, and we know who is calling us toward the finish line. At times
we will feel like quitting. But we are called to keep going. The prize is up
ahead, not behind.

How are you doing today as you get set to run this section of the race?
Are you tired before you start? God gives strength. Don't look back at
where you have been. Keep your eye ahead. Run for the prize!

## *Instruction:* How to Get Red Cheeks

*"If someone slaps you on one cheek, let him slap the other too! If someone
demands your coat, give him your shirt besides."*          Luke 6:29 TLB

Jesus was spending some time instructing the disciples in how to get
along with people. He wasn't teaching them the techniques of Dale Car-
negie. He wasn't concerned that they learn how to win friends and influence people. He wanted them to know what it was like to be a person for
others—a servant. What He told them flew in the face of common sense
and human practices of that time, as well as those of today.

If someone were to slap us, we might respond by either slapping him
back, asking him why he slapped us, or running away so that we would
not be slapped again. Jesus introduces a fourth response: turn the other
cheek. It sounds like an easy way to get red cheeks!

I am sure that Jesus was not intimating that the disciples should simply
go through life getting beaten up. He was trying to introduce a nonvio-
lent, nonreprisal way of living. He wanted them to be peacemakers, not
warmongers. He wanted them to display love, not violence.

Turning your other cheek does not mean that you are to be a doormat in life. It is developing an attitude that leaves the possibilities of wrong self-reaction up to God. It is also a way to leave a witness with someone. The world says, "You hit me, and I will hit you back." Jesus says if we do that, we will spend all our time hitting others.

You and I will be hit a few times today. How we respond will be indicative of how we are growing and maturing in Christ.

## *Instruction:* **Twice Born**

*Jesus replied, "With all the earnestness I possess I tell you this: Unless you are born again, you can never get into the Kingdom of God."* John 3:3 TLB

Nicodemus probably experienced the shock of his life when Jesus shared these words with him. He was accustomed to obeying rules and regulations as a part of working toward a spiritual reward. He may have wanted to find a few new ones from Jesus that would help him do the job better and faster.

Jesus introduced a whole new way of meeting God and living forever. Goodness, rules, rituals, ceremonies, and status had nothing to do with it. He brought to life the "born again" principle.

What does it mean to be born again? It means being invaded by the living Christ in every area of your life. It means letting go of the old ways of living and letting Christ bring in the new ways. It is giving all that you know of yourself to all that you know of God. It is making a decision that will last a lifetime.

In the words of an old song, "I have decided to follow Jesus, no turning back!"

Jesus came to give life and to give it more abundantly than we could ever know. It is His gift to us. Your sins and mine have been paid for by His death on Calvary. We can be born into a new life with Him. He invites us. We choose to accept or reject that invitation.

Are you walking into today knowing that you have been born anew? If you are, celebrate it by telling someone else about it. If you aren't, do it right now!

## *Instruction:* **Look Out for Imposters**

> *Watch out for the false leaders—and there are many of them around—who don't believe that Jesus Christ came to earth as a human being with a body like ours. Such people are against the truth and against Christ.*
>
> 2 John 1:7 TLB

False religious leaders don't travel around with a sign depicting their lack of credibility. Most of them sound and act responsible. Some of them even come from sound roots. All of them have one thing in common: they are not true representatives of Jesus Christ.

We are living in the age of cultists and false voices. Many people, young and old, are following false teachers. Some are so impressive that their very acts seem to be a stamp upon their call and authority.

Jesus' disciples were on a healing mission one day. When they returned to Jesus, they were upset. They had healed people in Jesus' name, and yet some stranger came along after them and did the same acts apart from Jesus' power. Jesus said that this was part of what the disciples would face—a power close to His, but false. They were told to test the spirits to determine if they were from God.

A new religious guru seems to be born every day. P. T. Barnum told us that a sucker was born every minute. If that is true, there will always be a following for the false teacher.

It is getting tougher to spot them. God has to give each of us a discerning spirit and an abundance of wisdom. Run from false teachers. The sounds they make can be enticing and convincing, but they are false.

Listen carefully to the sounds that come to you today in your journey!

## *Instruction:* **The Danger of Self-Praise**

> *Don't praise yourself; let others do it!*                    Proverbs 27:2 TLB

Praise, like perfume, is to be sniffed but never showered in.

There are two distinct kinds of praise: the kind that comes from others to us and the kind that we inflict upon ourselves. The first is affirmation, and we all need that to survive. The second is a form of annihilation that comes from taking ourselves too seriously and believing our own press releases.

The self-praisers are the people who ask you how you are doing and before you can answer, start listing all their own accomplishments of the past half century. They may not tell you in so many words how great they are. They let all they have done speak for itself.

Self-praisers demand attention. They always want to be at the center of everything. They demand special treatment and often make huge demands on other people. Their presence announces their importance.

Solomon believed praise that is due you will come your way. You don't have to initiate it or solicit it. Your acts will speak for themselves. They will be recognized and rewarded by others.

We live in an age of hype and promotion. It is easy to get caught up in it with our self-promotion and self-praise.

A good rule in avoiding the self-praise trap is to give God the glory for all that He is doing through you. Without His working through you, very little would be happening anyway.

Be a praise distributor today rather than a praise collector!

## *Instruction:* **How Do I Look?**

*"So my counsel is: Don't worry about* things—*food, drink, and clothes. For you already have life and a body—and they are far more important than what to eat and wear."* Matthew 6:25 TLB

We live in a sensory world. Advertising and marketing is directed to our senses. The two most prominent areas aimed at us deal with appearance and appetite. When you are well dressed and your stomach is full, the media barrage doesn't affect you much. When you are hungry and have nothing to wear, it always hits the target.

The disciples whom Jesus was training were susceptible to both man's inner needs and the outer covering. Perhaps they even awakened in the morning wondering what they should wear that day. *What part of my wardrobe would look best for a day full of miracles? What should I wear when I know the rulers will be watching our every move? Should I stand out in the crowd or merely blend in? What will we have for lunch today? Where will our next meal come from?*

Perhaps Jesus overheard their conversations. His response was to help them get their priorities straight. He did not recommend a dress for success manual. He told them not to worry about dress and food. He stressed that life and body were where their emphasis should be.

There is nothing wrong with looking good and eating right. It is only when these things become an obsession that we get in trouble. God still looks through what we wear to our hearts. He promises to fill us with good things other than food. He promises to meet all our needs.

Are you obsessed with the wrong priorities today? If so, work a little on setting them straight!

## *Instruction:* **How to Stay Close**

*So keep on believing what you have been taught from the beginning. If you do, you will always be in close fellowship with both God the Father and his Son.*                                                    1 John 2:24 TLB

Have you ever wanted to get close to someone? I don't mean just standing next to him or her, but to be close to him both physically and emotionally. Perhaps you have just met someone new and you have a desire to get to know him better and have him as a friend. How do you do this?

First, you have to be with him and invest time in him. It is not important that you always have some agenda to discuss. You simply have to be open to sharing your spirit with his spirit.

Second, you have to be patient with a growing friendship. It does not grow overnight. It takes time and a form of processing. It has to be exposed to many different situations.

Third, it has to contain an element of giving and receiving. No relationship is one-sided.

Our growing relationship with God is much like the ones we seek to build with other people. A spiritual relationship, much like a human relationship, has to have a foundation. On the spiritual side, we have to take all the things we believe and have learned about God into the relationship. We have to believe what we have been taught.

Most of us desire human closeness as well as a closeness to God. As the slogan says, "If you don't feel close to God, guess who moved?"

Are you close today? If not, maybe you should move in a bit!

## *Instruction:* **A Key to Health and Vitality**

*Don't be conceited, sure of your own wisdom. Instead, trust and reverence the Lord, and turn your back on evil; when you do that, then you will be given renewed health and vitality.*                                   Proverbs 3:7, 8 TLB

I love to wander through hardware stores and health-food stores. In the hardware stores, I wonder what everything is. In the health shops, I wonder what everything they sell will do if I take it. I have to admit to trying a few different pills, potions, and vitamins that guaranteed that I would have more stamina and alertness. (No, I have not found the secret weapon.)

Most of us would pay a few dollars for a vitality formula that works. Solomon offers a prescription with guaranteed results. He starts with our humanness by telling us to bury our nature to be conceited. We have to let go of the feeling that we know all the answers and can rely on our own wisdom.

In place of conceit and self-wisdom, we are to trust the wisdom of the Lord and have a sense of reverence for Him. We have to believe that He knows what He is doing.

As a final word, Solomon tells us to turn our backs to evil. Why? Well, evil has a corrupted and disturbing nature. It is something akin to eating junk food when we really need protein in our diet. Evil is enticing. So is a chocolate cake. But the ultimate value to our being is questionable. The Christian cannot attempt to live for God and play with the things of Satan on the side.

If you don't believe Solomon was right, go and visit your local friendly psychologist or psychiatrist. He or she will tell you that these simple ways really work. Get the garbage out of your life and the good things into it.

Are you full of God's vitality today?

## *Instruction:* **Getting Good Returns**

*"Try to show as much compassion as your Father does. Never criticize or condemn—or it will all come back on you. Go easy on others; then they will do the same for you."*  Luke 6:36, 37 TLB

A day will seldom go by when you will not find yourself dealing with criticism, condemnation, or compassion. Our world seems to be filled to the brim with the first and second, rather than the last. Cheap shots come more easily than caring shots. We can toss them out and run away from the debris. Caring is cleaning up the debris that is often left by someone else.

Jesus was a model of compassion. He saw human need and was moved to do something about it. In many instances, He responded to sickness by healing people. He was never afraid to come close to a hurting person. He even wept over the crowds and their needs.

Criticism always has a boomerang effect on the person giving it. Much of it is in the form of gossip. Gossip is one of the most deadly diseases of the human race. There is no defense against it and no way to nail it down as truth or untruth.

Whenever a group of people get together, there is the risk of conversation turning from the constructive to the critical. Others find it easier to jump on the criticism bandwagon and add their own.

The instruction from Luke's Gosepl is to go easy on others, and they will go easy on you. Temper your words of criticism and condemnation with love. The Scripture says we are to speak the truth in love. The key is to make sure that what we are saying is the truth.

Try to replace the bad *C*s in your life with the good *C*!

## *Instruction:* **The Key to Forgiveness**

*"And forgive us our sins, just as we have forgiven those who have sinned against us."*                              Matthew 6:12 TLB

Have you ever had a difficult time being forgiven for something? At least once in our lifetime, we really lay a huge egg. In the very next minute we know we have goofed and we try to seek forgiveness from someone for the mistake. What happens when you ask for it and it is not granted? What happens when you fear asking for it and never do? What happens when you feel it is not your problem to deal with?

These are tough questions, and sooner or later you will tangle with them.

Jesus seemed to know we would all eventually do wrong things. Some of those wrong things are called sins. When we commit them, we have to deal with them.

Forgiveness is not carte blanche for sinning. It is not our justifiable excuse. Forgiveness is our way of healing and restoration with both God and man.

Jesus told us that God's forgiveness and the forgiveness of others comes via the pathway of our taking the initiative. If we have a forgiving spirit toward those who sin against us, we will experience a joy in forgiveness.

Forgiveness is the glue of God that holds us all together in community. It puts together broken things with a permanent bond.

How is your forgiveness factor today?

## *Instruction:* **Avoiding Garbage**

*Let there be no sex sin, impurity or greed among you. Let no one be able to accuse you of any such things. Dirty stories, foul talk and coarse jokes—these are not for you. Instead, remind each other of God's goodness and be thankful.*                          Ephesians 5:3, 4 TLB

Have you ever taken a trip to the local dump? You race in, dump your trash, hold your nose, and race out. But you will always notice a few people climbing over the piles of refuse and picking things out to take away.

You wonder how they can stand the smell and the filth. They put up with it or get so used to it that it doesn't affect them anymore.

Sometimes our world seems to be one big dump. Everywhere we look there are piles of refuse with burning odors rising from them. Hardly a day goes by that we don't hear profanity, dirty jokes, or foul language. Sexual license has so inundated our world that we barely notice any longer. Greed appears to be the final motivation for business and government alike.

How do you negotiate your pathway through the piles of garbage in your day? With great difficulty, to be sure. Paul tells us that we are to be careful that these things don't contaminate us. They have a way of creeping into our lives because they are so prevalent.

Paul says an antidote for garbage contamination is to remind each other of God's goodness, and be thankful for it. In other words, get your eyes off the garbage and onto the Lord. We see either the garbage or the good.

It is getting tougher to find your way as God's person. Don't get trapped into being a garbage collector!

## *Instruction:* Watch Out for the Dividers

*And now there is one more thing to say before I end this letter. Stay away from those who cause divisions and are upsetting people's faith, teaching things about Christ that are contrary to what you have been taught.*
Romans 16:17 TLB

There will always be imitators. Any good idea draws forth a copy. I recently read that thousands of pairs of designer jeans were confiscated in a warehouse. They carried a famous logo, but they were imitations. Potential buyers would have been deceived, thinking they had purchased the real thing. I doubt that it would have affected their walking, but it might have affected their minds, knowing they were wearing imitations.

There were many imitators in the Early Church. They wanted to grab a share of the glory and excitement of a new movement without paying the price of real discipleship. They became abusers rather than users of the faith. They took what they liked and added their own variations. New believers constantly ran afoul of these false teachers. They caused divisions and greatly upset the basic Christian faith that was being taught. It seemed that every time Paul turned around, some new and confusing idea was being launched. This became a problem. It is still a problem today.

Do you know what you really believe? Do you know it well enough that you can spot the error of a false doctrine? I meet many roaming Christians in my travels who seem to always be searching for a better angle to the faith. These people become prime candidates for erroneous teaching.

Know what you believe and why. Watch out for the imitators. They are getting harder to recognize. Keep the eyes and ears of your heart open and discerning!

## *Instruction:* **What Do You Do for Others?**

*"Do for others what you want them to do for you. This is the teaching of the laws of Moses in a nutshell."*                          Matthew 7:12 TLB

How would you like to have the people in your life treat you? If I were answering that question, I would say things like honestly, with tenderness and caring, with respect, with love, and with gentleness. I could fill this page with other hopes, as you could. We all spend a lot of time trying to get people to treat us right. We manipulate, motivate, intimidate, and frustrate in order to get the flow of fair and good treatment heading in our direction. If we could just get everyone going in our direction, we would be living in Camelot. The truth is, it will never happen with that kind of thinking.

Many have called Jesus' words of instruction for today the "golden rule." Some in our world have reversed the words and tell us to "do others in before they do us in." This is a moldy rule and it doesn't work.

Jesus always set a positive initiative for living. He was always taking the lead. He said, "If you want to be served, then be a servant. If you want to be great, be humble." To the people listening, these statements sounded like contradictions. They certainly had never lived His way before.

The golden rule is elasticized! When you stretch out in doing things for others with no thought of reward, they in turn will do things for you. And even if they don't, you will have the joy of serving that they don't have.

Pull your golden rule out today and let it measure your gift to others!

## *Instruction:* **Some Good Thoughts**

*And now, brothers, as I close this letter let me say this one more thing: Fix your thoughts on what is true and good and right. Think about things that are pure and lovely, and dwell on the fine, good things in others. Think about all you can praise God for and be glad about.*          Philippians 4:8 TLB

What do you think about most when you allow your mind to wander—vacations in Tahiti, owning a castle in Bavaria, your problems and how to solve them? The list could go on for days. We all catch ourselves daydreaming from time to time.

The mind is much like a computer. What we punch in largely determines what comes out.

Paul closes his letter of joy to the Philippians with what appears to be a side thought. He sort of says, "Oh, yes, one more thing!" But that parting thought really helps determine whether one will have God's mind and thoughts, or will let His thoughts be crowded out and replaced by worldly ones. Paul tells us to think about things that are true, good, right, pure, lovely, and fine. "Well," you say, "that won't take long. *Then* what do I think about?"

You could start making a list of the things in your life that fit that description. You may find many more than you anticipated. Paul also tells us to praise God for all we can be glad about. Ah, your list is getting longer, isn't it?

Our minds and thoughts often get filled with wrong things. When we let God's good things in, our minds will be renewed.

Start on your list today!

## Instruction: Loving Our Leaders

*Dear brothers, honor the officers of your church who work hard among you and warn you against all that is wrong. Think highly of them and give them your wholehearted love because they are straining to help you. And remember, no quarreling among yourselves.*                1 Thessalonians 5:12, 13 TLB

Very few Christian workers in our churches are spoiled by love. The attitude of many congregations toward pastors and staff members is summed up by the words, "You keep them humble, Lord, and we will keep them poor!"

What a tragedy that we too often take those who serve the Lord and teach us truth for granted. I have watched many pastors leave the ministry in despair because of poor treatment.

Paul knew the dangers and the joys of Christian service. He had the same experiences that we who work in full-time service today have. First, he tells us to honor those who lead us. Honor is showing respect and love. He asks that we think highly of our leaders. Don't criticize them and talk about them behind their backs. Finally, he asks that we give them our wholehearted love. Much of the love directed toward Christian leaders is a halfhearted variety. Pastors and Christian workers need love and affirmation, too. Just because they are in a "spiritual business" does not mean they do not have human needs.

Paul adds a footnote in telling church members not to fight among themselves. Many a pastor has resigned because of open warfare among the members.

Have you expressed your love and appreciation lately for those who shepherd and care for you? You need to give it, and they need to receive it!

## *Instruction:* **What Pleases the Lord?**

*Learn as you go along what pleases the Lord.*        Ephesians 5:10 TLB

In many of Paul's letters, his opening paragraphs contain doctrinal concerns for the believers. His closing comments contain practical instructions on living the Christian life. Many of his instructions are so practical, we wonder why he even takes the time to offer them. Our common sense seemingly would bring them to our minds.

Today's instruction for Christian living is so practical that it must be processed to be of any value. Paul intimates that we learn many things about Christian living as we live. There is no other way to learn them. Experience is always the best teacher. Paul knew that the Christian adventure had to be experienced on a daily basis. He knew that the early believers would learn as they traveled God's pathway.

Many people memorize Bible verses. They have a verse for every occasion. They know where everything is found. One soon discovers that this does not mean these people are mature and growing Christians. In order to be that, they have to practice the verses in living that they are committing to memory.

We learn by trial and error as we grow. We learn what pleases God by living.

A good measure of your growth is to think about what would please God in every situation that you encounter each day. If you put that thought at the front of your mind, you will be spared many mistakes and injurious actions toward others.

Learn as you go and as you *grow!*

## *Instruction:* Serving and Teaching Is a Gift

*If your gift is that of serving others, serve them well. If you are a teacher, do a
good job of teaching.* Romans 12:7 TLB

The Scripture lists more than twenty spiritual gifts that are given to believers to equip them for serving God and living the Christian life. Believers do not have all the gifts, nor do they have the same gifts as those
around them. God has a way of gift distribution that fits His plan for
every group of Christians.

We don't select our gift from God's stockpile. If we did, perhaps too
many of us would want the same gift and there would be a big lack of
certain gifts in some groups. God gives us the gifts that He wants us to
have and use.

Some of us have the gift of serving and teaching. Although they are
two different gifts, they are seldom apart in those who have them. Serving
is helping others with no reward in mind. It is learning to be a waiter—
not a very glamorous job, to be sure. Servants are usually not the people
who are on center stage in life. They hover around the edges fulfilling the
needs of others.

Teaching is communicating knowledge to others. It is a responsible
job. Paul emphasized its importance numerous times to those who
worked with him and in the Early Church.

Teaching demands a servant attitude. Teachers wait while students
learn. They serve the needs of the student, not themselves. Often, they are
not around to receive the credit for what they have taught when their
students succeed.

We all do a little serving and a little teaching. It is a part of everyday
life. If we do it well, we will grow and others will benefit!

## *Instruction:* God Will Turn On the Light

*So be careful not to jump to conclusions before the Lord returns as to whether
someone is a good servant or not. When the Lord comes, he will turn on the
light so that everyone can see exactly what each one of us is really like, deep
down in our hearts. Then everyone will know why we have been doing the
Lord's work. At that time God will give to each one whatever praise is coming
to Him.* 1 Corinthians 4:5 TLB

Leadership always causes controversy. Leaders often want to make
sure that everyone knows they are in charge. They want the prestige and

authority perhaps even more than the responsibility. Those who have to follow certain leadership often try to shoot it down by criticism or by deciding not to follow it at all. Undermining seems to be the close companion to leadership. Leadership always draws fire from the crowd.

In the Corinthian church, there was some confusion over the leadership of Paul and Apollos. Some were for Paul and liked his style. Others gravitated toward Apollos and wanted his leadership. There may have been others without name who also attracted their own following. Perhaps the potential for the first denominational split was in the Corinthian church. One thing is certain: the problems of Paul have not disappeared over the years.

Paul's word to the Early Church and to us today is simply that God will take care of the job evaluation of His leaders when He sends Jesus back. In other words, avoid the judgments and the battle over popularity and let God make the definitions. God gives the rewards, not man.

We all have a tendency to replay the Paul-Apollos controversy. Don't get caught there. It is a dead-end street.

## *Instruction:* **Submission Is Expensive**

*Honor Christ by submitting to each other.*                    Ephesians 5:21 TLB

Submitting to leadership and authority is an everyday experience for most of us. Directions from the boss are handed down to us and we follow them. We can do it with joy or great complaining. The truth is, we do it if we want to work where we do. Taking orders is a part of the working world.

How do you feel about taking orders from someone who is not your boss? Simple! You just tell that person to mind his own business.

In the Christian community, there is always a very fine line between what is our own business, what is God's business, and what is the business of every other member of the body of Christ.

Scripture teaches that we have to be responsible for and responsive to one another. Christian community is like a family. What one does often affects others. We cannot tell everyone to mind his own business. If that is our wish, we should move to a cave and live alone.

Submission is not letting everyone else direct your life. That is not what God intends. His concern is that we are open to the input of others both in instruction and in correction. It is a mature Christian who can take both of these from his brother. Only an immature Christian refuses to submit to his brother or sister in Christ.

Submission is not living under a club. It is floating on a cloud because we will always be lifted by it. None of us has all the answers. We need all the help we can get.

Do you honor Christ by receiving instruction and correction from your Christian friends? It certainly isn't easy. But you need it!

## *Instruction:* **Going Deeper**

*May the Lord bring you into an ever deeper understanding of the love of God and of the patience that comes from Christ.* 2 Thessalonians 3:5 TLB

What level of your Christian growth are you living on? Many people I meet seem to be living on the surface of their faith. Even though they have been Christians for many years, they never seem to go any deeper in their faith and growth. They practice a "maintenance faith" that keeps a routine going in their lives. They never explore and become creative Christians.

A prayer that Paul echoed for the Christians at Thessalonica was that they would not remain as surface saints but that they would have two things happen that would mature their faith.

The first was that their love would deepen to the level of understanding God's love. The more they knew and understood God's love, the more their own love would grow and affect their lives.

Understanding God's love is knowing the ingredients that are in it and inviting them into our lives. We could list a whole page of those ingredients. Forgiveness is just one big one.

The second part of Paul's prayer was for a patience that comes from Christ. It is learning that God is never in a hurry. We don't need to be, either. He is patient with us and expects us to be patient with one another and with ourselves.

We need to get in over our heads once in a while with God. Playing it close to the surface may be safe, but it is also boring.

Christ won't toss you into deep water. He will walk with you as you take the steps!

## *Instruction:* **Caring for Your Own Family**

*But anyone who won't care for his own relatives when they need help, espe-*
*cially those living in his own family, has no right to say he is a Christian. Such*
*a person is worse than the heathen.*                              1 Timothy 5:8 TLB

Who will help take care of you when you are aged and infirm? Most of
us seldom give that a thought because we know that we will be healthy
and vivacious forever. We pass by retirement homes and convalescent
homes with never a thought that we might one day be occupants. Then
that moment comes for our own parents when their health fails and we
have to decide how to help them. There is never an easy answer to this
problem, and I am not trying to rain guilt on you by mentioning it.

There are scriptural ways of doing things and there are our own ways.
If we follow God, we need to look first to His Word for our instructions.

Paul instructs Timothy in family responsibility. A witness to the love of
Christ is shown by how we respond to the needs of our own relatives.
Love is always two-sided. Our parents loved us and cared for us when we
were small and could not care for ourselves. Fifty, sixty, seventy years
later, the procedure is often reversed, and we find ourselves returning the
care and love. Love is a responsibility to be assumed. It starts with family.

Old age is not a fun time in our society. It is often lonely and full of fear
for the aged and infirm. Many have been abandoned by their families.
Others have no families.

A family is a trust from God to be loved and cared for. How are you
doing with your family?

## *Instruction:* **Looking Up or Looking Down?**

*You have no right to criticize your brother or look down on him. Remember,*
*each of us will stand personally before the Judgment Seat of God.*
                                                    Romans 14:10 TLB

How many people in your life do you look up to? You could probably
fill a few pages with their names and the reasons you look up to them.
How many people in your life do you look down on? Another page or two
full of names, and perhaps plenty of good reasons to go along with the
names?

We have relationships with many different people. We rate most of
them on a scale in our minds. Some relationships we are glad to continue,
others we are glad to end.

Living is viewing and reviewing people. It is deciding how we will deal with them. Will we look up to them with respect, or look down on them in disrespect?

If you have a long list of people on the "down" side, you probably will not feel too comfortable with today's instruction for living. The Scripture tells us not to criticize those who are our brothers and sisters, and not to look down on them for *any* reason. Usually, if we don't criticize them, we will have no reason to look down on them. The only way some people elevate themselves is to put everyone else down. They are not growing. They are just keeping others from growing.

This Scripture gives us a warning that few people seem to heed or be aware of. God's judgment line puts everyone on the same level. We will all stand equally before the Lord. That's good news for some, and really bad news for others.

How's your elevation today? Are you looking down on and putting down those around you? Start lifting people. You will be amazed at how tall some of them are!

## *Instruction:* **Go to Church**

> *Let us not neglect our church meetings, as some people do, but encourage and warn each other, especially now that the day of his coming back again is drawing near.* Hebrews 10:25 TLB

Is going to church an exciting experience in growth and fellowship for you? Or is it a boring, dull routine that you would just as soon get out of? What do you think life was like in the Early Church? If you read the opening chapters of the Book of Acts, you probably feel that you could get excited about attending one of the Early Church meetings. Things really happened there!

In writing to the Hebrew Christians, Paul makes a point of telling them how important it is to attend their church meetings. He tells them to do something when they are there. They are to encourage one another and warn one another. In some churches today, there is not a lot of encouragement exchanged when the members gather. Many go home feeling the same struggles they came with. Few are warned about the snags and snares of life. In many churches, even the fire in the pulpit has burned out.

Church ought to be a time when gifts are exchanged. It should be a lifting and exciting time. Being with each other should be a happy experience. Worshiping God in community should highlight the event.

What can you bring to your church next Sunday? What can you take away? It is important to be with the people of God regularly!

## *Instruction:* **Doing or Undoing?**

*Remember, too, that knowing what is right to do and then not doing it is sin.*
James 4:17 TLB

How often have you known what was right in a certain situation, but failed to do it? If you are as human as I am, your answer is probably, "Often!" Sometimes we call this frustrating experience the sin of omission. We don't talk much about it because we are more often engaged in the sin of commission.

There are some excuses for the sin of omission. An often-heard one is that we are never really sure what is right. Sometimes we need to have a crowd vote on it, and if there isn't a crowd around, we do nothing. Another reason for this sin is that we are afraid of what others might think of us. If we jump into a situation that is right but not too popular, others will think less of us. Another reason is simply that we don't want to get involved in things outside of ourselves.

In my area, a man recently jumped into a fight and literally saved a girl's life. He imperiled his own, but did not think about that. Many people simply stood by and did nothing. It wasn't their problem. Or was it?

Most of us know what is right and what is wrong. We know when we should jump into something or remain outside of it. It takes a risky Christian to be on the edge of personal involvement. The Bible is full of risky Christians.

The next time you get a chance to do what is right, take the plunge. You might experience some serendipity blessings from it!

## *Instruction:* **Directions From the Spirit**

*I advise you to obey only the Holy Spirit's instructions. He will tell you where to go and what to do, and then you won't always be doing the wrong things your evil nature wants you to.*
Galatians 5:16 TLB

As a Christian, you will constantly fight the desires of your flesh to go in the opposite direction from God. Some of the things of the world that are not for the Christian will look very enticing. Your human nature will beckon you many times.

God's word for today tells us to obey the Holy Spirit's instructions. If we do, we will know where to go and what to do in all situations. Knowing the "where" and "what" is important in our lives. It is easy to get confused and sidetracked. Satan's biggest weapon seems to be confusion. I have listened to many people tell me that they did not know what to do about certain things or where to go with their lives.

The Holy Spirit takes no delight in seeing us confused. The Scripture tells us that God is not the author of confusion—the devil is. God's intention is that we might have direction through the leading and power of the Holy Spirit.

How do you get it? You ask for it in everything. The Spirit works through the teaching of Scripture, through other Christians, and through His own mystical way that often defies description. Sometimes we get confused because we can't explain the Spirit's leading. We just know, and that is enough.

Are you struggling with the Holy Spirit's leading in your life today? Ask for directions. You will receive them!

## *Instruction:* Watch Out for False Messiahs

*So Jesus launched into an extended reply. "Don't let anyone mislead you," he said, "for many will come declaring themselves to be your Messiah, and will lead many astray."* Mark 13:5, 6 TLB

Recently a press conference was called by a man in my city. At the conference he announced that the Messiah had come and was in seclusion until the next week, when he would reveal himself to the entire world via a telepathic message. It made the evening news and the local papers. It all had the ring of sanity and clarity about it. The man who made the announcement was not a deranged derelict or an escapee from a mental institution. He seemed very normal and very, very serious. I wonder how many believed his report. I wonder how many instant disciples were ready and waiting in the wings to follow this imitator once he revealed himself.

Jesus warned His disciples and followers to expect false teachers. He even said some would declare themselves to be the Messiah. That warning has been in effect ever since.

How susceptible to a false teacher are you? It is easy to look for a credible source of "new truth." Many times, even very mature and well-informed Christians fall for false teachers.

Jesus' warning needs to be heeded now more than ever. People want to believe and follow someone. That's human nature. Some of those false teachers look so good and sound so sincere.

Recognize truth from error. Only God's truth makes us free.

## *Instruction:* **Listen and Receive**

*Come to me with your ears wide open. Listen, for the life of your soul is at stake. I am ready to make an everlasting covenant with you, to give you all the unfailing mercies and love that I had for King David.*   Isaiah 55:3 TLB

Do you ever find yourself quietly listening for the voice of God? It is hard to listen to a voice that speaks to your soul rather than your ears. Soul listening demands the utmost in concentration and fine tuning.

Isaiah issues a warning to us. He instructs us to come to God with ears and hearts open to the voice of God. In response to our listening to God, we are told that we will receive unfailing mercies and love.

If there were ever two important ingredients for the believer, it would be mercy and love. Mercy affects how we deal with others in our lives. Mercy is directed outward from us to someone else. God has to plant and germinate the seeds of mercy within us before we can distribute them to others.

When we are promised the kind of love that King David enjoyed, we know we are receiving something special. David tested the love of God in numerous ways. He did not always follow God as he should have. Yet God's love rang through David's life with a sharp, clear tone.

David was perhaps one of the greatest scriptural examples of God's love, so much so that Jesus was born of David's lineage. God had to love David in order to honor him in that way.

Do you have your ears and heart open today to the voice of God? Listen and receive the great gifts God holds out to you!

## *Instruction:* **The Blessing Boomerang**

*If someone mistreats you because you are a Christian, don't curse him; pray that God will bless him.*                           Romans 12:14 TLB

What do you do when someone mistreats you? You can feel sorry for yourself and have a good cry. You can get angry with the person who is mistreating you and look for ways to get revenge. Or, you can pray that God will bless the person.

Paul knew that many believers would be mistreated because they were followers of Christ. They would be thrown into prison, beaten, and killed. Society would not understand the way they lived or the way they died. Few of us have that problem. At least, not yet!

We all deal with various forms of mistreatment. It happens every day. Paul prescribes an attitude to take in dealing with mistreatment. I call it the "blessing boomerang."

We all know if you throw a boomerang properly, it comes back to you. When you are hit with a mistreatment, throw a blessing back. Pauls says to pray that God will bless the person who is not blessing you.

There is always a great tendency to react like everyone else in a situation. Reacting in God's way demands taking the time to think through how God would have you respond. Praying for a blessing for the person who mistreats you shows Christian maturity. Cursing that person only adds to the problem and improves nothing. Think before you act!

The test of Paul's instruction is doing it. Pick a situation in your life and do what the Word tells you. You will be amazed at how your attitude will change, and even the other person will change as he or she becomes the recipient of a blessing sent by you through God.

## *Instruction:* Giving Thanks More Than Once a Year

*Always give thanks for everything to our God and Father in the name of our Lord Jesus Christ.*                                                    Ephesians 5:20 TLB

Are you in the habit of thanking God for really big blessings in your life and just passing by the smaller ones? Do you even take the time to thank God for anything He gives you? Many people nod to God just before they eat a meal. A quick, "Bless this food," three times a day seems to be the extent of our thanksgiving for what God gives to us.

Thanksgiving is an everyday part of the Christian life. Thanking God is counting the blessings and celebrating the joy they bring to us.

When I give a gift to my children, the only thing I want in return is a simple thank-you. By those words, they are expressing how they feel about both the gift and me. Their thanks make me feel loved, appreciated, and affirmed. I think the same feeling ascends to the heart of God when we thank Him.

I have discovered another thing about receiving thanks: it makes you want to keep on giving! I think that is why God keeps on blessing us when we give thanks.

How many gifts does God give you in the course of a day—ten, twenty, hundreds? Try to pick out a few and say a simple, "Thanks, Lord!" You will be amazed how much more you will appreciate God's love when you say thanks.

Oh, and don't forget, the word Paul uses is *everything,* not just some things. That means good things and some not-so-good things. Thanking God for some unwanted gifts can turn into blessings, too!

## *Instruction:* **How to Be Right in His Sight**

*Consequently, it is clear that no one can ever win God's favor by trying to keep the Jewish laws, because God has said that the only way we can be right in his sight is by faith.*                                                  Galatians 3:11 TLB

Have you ever met someone who told you he expects to go to heaven because he is not a bad person and he has tried to obey the golden rule? I meet many people who try to affirm their goodness by keeping the rules.

In the Early Church, there were many believers who tried to mix their new lives with their old lives. They were truly born anew by the Spirit of God, but they couldn't quite give up the idea of keeping rules and laws that had been with them for centuries. There were still others around who had not received Christ as Lord, and lived under the rigidity of Jewish laws in an attempt to please God.

Jesus threw out the rule book when He came to earth. He became the rule. Many people had a hard time with that. They were so steeped in custom and tradition that they had tunnel vision.

There was always a battle between the laws and the grace of God in the Early Church. We still fight that battle today. Many people build their lives on doing good and believing that's good enough. God is not interested in your performance. He is interested in your faith in Him as the Son of God and Savior of the world.

Do you know some people who are trying to do it their way instead of God's way? Are you one of them? God accepts no substitutes!

## *Instruction:* **It's a Full-Time Job**

*So everywhere we go we talk about Christ to all who will listen, warning them and teaching them as well as we know how. We want to be able to present each one to God, perfect because of what Christ has done for each of them.*
                                                  Colossians 1:28 TLB

Do you talk about Christ everywhere you go? Probably not. You are either too busy talking about other things or you are simply fearful of what people will think if you talk about God too much. Who wants to be branded a religious fanatic?

From my experience, most people do not talk about God a whole lot because they are simply not excited about their faith. Not much is happening in their lives, so there is little to talk about.

Can you imagine what must have happened when the Early Church let out from a meeting in the Book of Acts? Those people were so excited that they couldn't keep from talking about the acts of God in their lives. It was a natural process. It wasn't canned or memorized. It wasn't a speech they learned in an evangelism class. They simply told what was happening. And people found God!

There are more people out there who are willing to listen to us than we realize. But they want to see something in us and not just hear our speeches about God and His love. Real faith is an action word.

Finding faith is like finding a bargain. It is simply no fun to keep it to yourself. You want to tell everyone where you got it. That was really the secret of the New Testament Church and a few scattered churches today. They were and are excited people telling others about the Source of their excitement.

How exciting and contagious is your faith?

## *Instruction:* **The Big Four**

*Dear brothers, warn those who are lazy; comfort those who are frightened; take tender care of those who are weak; and be patient with everyone.*
1 Thessalonians 5:14 TLB

Warning, comfort, care, or patience. Pick the one that is easiest for you to give to others. Some people will pick *warning,* since that can be resolved by a few quick words and little involvement. A few might pick the word *patience* because that can be worked on privately, whenever they have time. *Comfort* and *care* demand a personal involvement and an investment of time. Sometimes there is no end to care and comfort giving.

Our Christian responsibility always demands involvement with others. We only survive, thrive, and grow in concert with one another. The demands of a supportive fellowship include all four words that Paul shares.

We will always have a few lazy members in the body of Christ. We are to warn them that they must carry their responsibilities along with everyone else. There will be those around us who are frightened of some things, and those who are frightened of everything. A Christian is a fear remover. Giving comfort helps remove fears. The frightened are never helped simply by being told not to be afraid.

Weakness is a part of our human condition. We will always have a weaker brother or sister around to take care of. We can't will their weakness away, but we can give the gift of tender care.

Being patient with everyone is the impossible dream for most of us. We feel we are climbing the mountain if we can be patient with a handful. Somehow, that doesn't get the job done. If we can become patient people with God's help, we will find it easier to be patient with everyone. Four big words of instruction to take along today!

## *Instruction:* **Words for the Wealthy**

*Tell them to use their money to do good. They should be rich in good works and should give happily to those in need, always being ready to share with others whatever God has given them.*                    1 Timothy 6:18 TLB

What does it mean to be rich? How rich is rich? How rich are you and I? To many of us, rich means Rolls Royce, Beverly Hills, the summer in Europe, and never running short of money. Rich is a relative word and often bears the definition of the user.

In Paul's letter to Timothy, we are told not to put our trust in money. That's a different philosophy from today's business community. Money makes money and is trusted more than people, in many cases.

The Scripture, contrary to popular belief, is not opposed to the making of money. It is often opposed to the ways money is used. The Scripture tells us that money is to be used to do good. It has to be spent in order to achieve that kind of result. It is a tool to help people, not to cause them sorrow or ultimate joy.

I don't think Paul's directive is only issued to those who make over a million dollars a year. I think it is directed to everyone who makes any money whatever. You and I are called to do good things with whatever money God entrusts to us. What we have is meaningless unless we use it to bring meaning to others.

Paul tells us to be rich in good works and give happily to those who have needs. Rich is not what you have. It is what you give away! The Scripture tells us that much shall be required from those who have much. That doesn't mean we are excused if we have little. We all have so much to give and share with others.

Have you experienced the joy of giving lately?

## *Instruction:* **An Openness to God**

*Seek the Lord while you can find him. Call upon him now while he is near.*
                                        Isaiah 55:6 TLB

Where would you go if you went looking for God? To a church at the corner of Fourth and Elm; to a clergyman's office; to another person; to your knees in quiet prayer?

Isaiah intimates that we have to seek the Lord while we can. These words were directed to Israel, but they are relevant to us today. There are some people who tell us that God is everywhere, while others tell us God is nowhere. A few others would tell us that God is somewhere, but they are not sure where.

Followers of God are seekers after Him. It is not so much finding a specific place where we think God might reside. It is discovering His presence that is with us constantly. His promise is to be with us wherever we go. Yet we still seek after Him in our lives.

Isaiah tells us to call upon Him. How do you do that? If it were as easy as dialing our telephones, we would do it more often. The truth is that it is easier than dialing a phone number. We can call upon God anytime and anyplace.

There are special times in all of our lives when we feel that God is very close to us and when we can feel His presence in a certain way. These are truly mountaintop times. But when we don't feel this way does not mean that God has abandoned us. Perhaps God has an active presence and a passive presence in our lives. He is still at work in the slow times—He just works differently.

Seek and call. Both demand an openness to God as you live through today.

## *Instruction:* **Putting Your Go in Gear**

*And then he told them, "You are to go into all the world and preach the Good News to everyone, everywhere."*       Mark 16:15 TLB

This instruction, given in the final verses of Mark's Gospel, has long been known as the Great Commission. It was given as a directive to the disciples and apostles. It became the marching orders for Christian missions right through today. Yet, nineteen hundred years later, we have failed to fulfill its call. Perhaps we should call it the Great Omission.

The problem with these marching orders, many times, is that we have left them in the hands of the professional Christian workers who are trained in special areas and with special knowledge. We have let it become someone else's job. We have even paid others to do it so that we would not have to face the call ourselves.

The Great Commission is a neighborhood project. It was never intended to start in Africa or some far-flung land. It was supposed to start at home, reaching out in concentric circles that would eventually touch everyone. Somehow, we have reversed the process.

Every day, you and I go into our world—the world of our work, business, recreation, community. This is the world that needs the Good News that Jesus is Lord. We are the missionaries to our world.

Share the Good News with one other person today. You will be amazed how easily it can be done!

## *Instruction:* God Tells You What He Wants

*No, he has told you what he wants, and this is all it is:* to be fair and just and merciful, and to walk humbly with your God.          Micah 6:8 TLB

Israel always seemed to have a problem dealing with God. The things they wanted to give to God, He did not want. The things God wanted from Israel, they would not give. An endless line of prophets tried to get Israel back on track. Micah was one of the prophets whom God used to speak to Israel. In today's instruction, Micah tries to tell Israel that God does not want their offerings and sacrifices.

God wanted four simple things from Israel. First of all, He wanted them to be fair and just. Many of them had acquired their wealth by dishonest means. God did not bless that. He asked them for honesty in all their dealings.

God wanted them to be distributors of mercy. Mercy is often the gift of love wrapped in a rainbow of understanding. It dramatically involves our dealings with others.

Finally, God wanted Israel to walk humbly before Him. That was a large problem for them. They were obsessed with pride and arrogance. They thanked God for little and boasted much of their own ability.

Thousands of years later, you and I are still called to these four things. It is sometimes easier to give money and material things to God, but these are not the essentials for what makes real life happen. God wants us to give the things that make our relationship with Him grow, and make our relationships with each other better.

God is telling you what He wants. Are you listening?

# *Instruction:* Away With Pretending

*So get rid of your feelings of hatred. Don't just pretend to be good! Be done with dishonesty and jealousy and talking about others behind their backs.*

1 Peter 2:1 TLB

Have you ever missed getting your garbage cans out on the appointed pickup day? I have, and there is nothing I hate more than garbage that sits around for two weeks. If it's hot, it takes on a strong odor and becomes more of a nuisance than anything I can think of. Many mornings I find myself racing to get my garbage out as the truck comes rolling down the street. Empty garbage cans make me feel better.

Have you ever caught yourself carrying mental garbage around for days at a time? It has a way of polluting you and driving others away from you. I guess we could say it makes a person very smelly.

Hatred, pretense, dishonesty, jealousy, and gossip combine to make a big pile of garbage. When they are evident in our lives, there is little room for the good things of God to move in.

Peter cautioned the Christians of his time to get rid of the excess baggage in their lives. It may be hard for us to believe that Christians struggle with these things, but they do. Love, joy, and peace are often crowded out by the five things Peter warns about.

Sometimes we pretend that these things are not in our lives, when some of them actually are. As you look at your life today, are some of them evident? You will have a better day if you let them go and ask God to fill your life with His things of the Spirit.

# *Instruction:* Just Getting By?

*Never be lazy in your work but serve the Lord enthusiastically.*

Romans 12:11 TLB

There are two kinds of work that you and I are involved in. First, there is the work of the Lord in our lives. A part of this is working on our own Christian growth each day. The other part is the work of God we do in Christian community, worship, service, love, care, and study. The personal and the corporate combine to become the work of God.

The second kind of work in our lives can be defined as the way we make our living. Our vocation is important. We not only derive our living from it but we also receive affirmation and feelings of self-worth. We either love our work and do it well, or we dislike it, and going to our place of employment is akin to serving a sentence each day.

In all of our work, we are urged by Scripture not to be lazy. In the Old

Testament, there is a verse which says that those who will not work cannot eat. If this were true today, we would not need a welfare system.

Laziness is a sin. I have met people who were lazy both physically and mentally. They expect the world around them to meet their needs. Some Christians are caught in the grips of doing nothing. They say they are waiting for God to do it. The problem is that God is waiting for them to get moving.

Enthusiasm is the electricity of God. It generates the potential that is within us, and gives a positive response to life. It is also contagious.

Laziness is negative. Enthusiasm is positive. Which of the two will control your life today? It is a choice you can make!

## *Instruction:* **The Song of Your Heart**

*Talk with each other much about the Lord, quoting psalms and hymns and singing sacred songs, making music in your hearts to the Lord.*
Ephesians 5:19 TLB

What do God's people talk about when they get together—sports, the weather, the economy, their families, their problems? Most of the time, they sound just like everyone else in the world. If you don't believe that, stand outside your church doors next Sunday and listen to the conversations around you. I doubt that they will be much different from those you would hear at the supermarket or the hardware store. Perhaps occasionally, God might get a few lines or a church problem might be discussed. The sermon of the day might even get a minimal word or two.

There is nothing wrong with good conversation and talking about the things we mentioned above. That should be a part of our conversation with others. The problem is the missing part that Paul tries to tell the Ephesians about.

How much do you talk with others about the Lord? What about quoting psalms and hymns and singing sacred songs? Probably the last one is the easiest for most of us. We can sing all day long, and no one thinks much about it. Start talking about the Lord, and people might think you are a religious nut.

Talking about the Lord is talking about what He is doing in your life and what He is saying in your life. It is also listening and recognizing His voice.

Letting the things of God increasingly fill your mind will enable you to make God's kind of music in your heart. Let the sounds of God fill your being today!

# *Instruction:* **Watch Out for the Spoilers**

*Don't let others spoil your faith and joy with their philosophies, their wrong and shallow answers built on men's thoughts and ideas, instead of on what Christ has said.*                                    Colossians 2:8 TLB

Ever since the tower of Babel, man has tried to get to God through his own ideas and processes. Somehow, the simplicity of the Scriptures is not quite enough for some people. New life through receiving Christ as Savior and Lord is too easy for many. So they set about contriving their own philosophies and standards in reaching God.

We could call this ever-growing band of people "the spoilers." They were everywhere in the Early Church, and they are everywhere today. You meet them in airport lobbies, in front of shopping malls, at your front door, and in beautifully decorated churches. Many of them even use Scripture to back up what they say.

There is one tried and true test when you are confronted with glowing new philosophies. Go to the Scriptures and see for yourself what Jesus had to say. Don't fall into the trap of accepting what someone tells you. Check it out for yourself. If that doesn't work, make an appointment with your local pastor, or even a Christian counselor. Don't be afraid to check out the source of what you are told. Even the disciples were encouraged by Jesus to do the same.

Men don't have the answer. God does. Look out for the spoilers in life. They usually catch you in an unguarded moment, when your defenses are down. Keep alert today!

# *Instruction:* **Avoid the Angry**

*Keep away from angry, short-tempered men, lest you learn to be like them and endanger your soul.*                                    Proverbs 22:24, 25 TLB

How can you tell an angry person when you see one? He usually carries a big sign that says, I AM AN ANGRY PERSON! What? You say you haven't seen anyone lately with a sign like that? You just forgot to read the fine print on the face of the person who is angry. He may not be carrying an ANGRY sign but the word is usually carved deeply into his countenance. Even if it is not on his face, it comes from his spirit the minute he opens his mouth.

How much time do you enjoy spending with an angry person? Probably very little. You soon discover two things: you can't still someone else's anger, and there is a danger that it will infect you.

Solomon knew the best way to deal with angry people. He simply told us to stay away from them. If a soft answer will stifle wrath, staying away from an angry person until his or her anger subsides will help us deal with anger more effectively.

Trying to talk with an angry person only seems to kindle his anger. He may even get angry with us, even though we were not the cause of his anger.

Anger must be worked through by the possessor. That takes time and thinking. If anger is built up through many years of living, it will not be diffused in a few minutes of talk. Sometimes that takes the skilled help of a professional counselor.

Watch out for the angry people in your life today. Try to quietly step around them and be on your way!

# *Instruction:* **How to Deal With Your Brother's Sin**

*"If a brother sins against you, go to him privately and confront him with his fault. If he listens and confesses it, you have won back a brother."*

Matthew 18:15 TLB

Isn't this a simple formula for dealing with all the sins that brothers and sisters in God's family have directed at you? It is simple, but extremely hard to do.

First of all, you have to be able to explain what the sin is. If it is gossip that has harmed you, you have to be able to pinpoint it. If you have been slighted in some way, you have to be able to define it. If someone has cheated you, you have to be specific.

After you identify what the sin is, you have to have the courage to go to that brother or sister and tell him or her what the problem is and how you feel about it. It means confronting the other person, and you will need the help and wisdom of God to do that effectively.

After confrontation, there has to be receptivity from the other person. If he is not receptive, little will be accomplished. The next step is to return with several witnesses. Even this may not work. Jesus then tells you to take the problem to the church. If nothing works, then you have done your best. God has to be the final judge.

There will always be disagreements in the body of Christ. Open wounds need healing. Healing is a process that demands vulnerability.

How have you been dealing with the sins directed at you by others? Try God's way! You might be surprised at the end result.

## *Instruction:* **Dealing With Envy**

*"You must not be envious of your neighbor's house, or want to sleep with his wife, or want to own his slaves, oxen, donkeys, or anything else he has."*
Exodus 20:17 TLB:

We have all heard people say, "I'm green with envy." I am never quite sure why they use the color green. Perhaps someone decided it was the color of greed. Being green with envy means that you wish you had what someone else has. It doesn't matter whether it is something great or small. You would like to have it for yourself.

I have always wanted a 1941 Ford Convertible. I saw one the other day. It was perfectly restored and a real classic. I had to confess that I was green, purple, red, and blue with envy. I wished it were parked in front of my house. I wanted to drive it and watch heads turn with envy in my direction. Then I jumped in my Honda and drove away—still green and still envious!

Envy becomes a problem when it turns into a consuming obsession—when we don't just look and dream but we take action to obtain. We try to scheme, cheat, steal, lie, and intimidate in order to get something. That is where envy becomes one giant, consuming domination.

The Ten Commandments attempt to throw a warning to us regarding envy. It has ruined the best of people and the greatest of nations. It is a sin that starts in the back corners of the mind and can soon take over our sanity. There is seldom an end to envy. It grows bigger each day. The more we acquire through envy, the more we desire.

Envy will stare you in the face a few times today. Look right back at it and recognize it for what it is. Stop, but don't stay at the intersection of envy!

## *Instruction:* **What Really Matters?**

*In this new life one's nationality or race or education or social position is unimportant; such things mean nothing. Whether a person has Christ is what matters, and he is equally available to all.*
Colossians 3:11 TLB

Have you ever been seated at the head table at a banquet or dinner? How did it make you feel—important, obvious, afraid? How does it make others feel who are sitting at lesser tables?

As speaker, I have sat at many head tables. There is always a place for me, whether or not I am there on time. And the head table is usually served first. Apparently, it is special to sit at a head table. It must mean you are up there with the heads!

There is a status or pecking order even in Christian groups. Social position is often of very obvious importance to some Christians. Isn't it interesting? Paul says the things that mean so much to us mean nothing at all in the Kingdom of God. God's measuring stick of status is simply whether or not you have Christ. There are those who do and those who don't. Now, that doesn't mean that those who know Christ personally should get all the good seats. It simply means that God welcomes those who are members of His forever family and is equally concerned about those who are not.

The new life is lived on level ground. As someone has said, "The ground at the foot of the cross is level."

Where are you choosing to live today? It doesn't matter what you have. It matters to whom you belong!

## *Instruction:* Have You Entertained an Angel?

*Continue to love each other with true brotherly love. Don't forget to be kind to strangers, for some who have done this have entertained angels without realizing it!*                                    Hebrews 13:1, 2 TLB

When was the last time you invited an angel over for lunch? Or, when was the last time you invited a person to lunch who turned out to be an angel? How do you tell angels from other people?

I am sure that there were many visitors in the Early Church. At some of the meetings the walls may have been bursting with people. Some of the regulars probably started grumbling about the crowds. Perhaps this was why Paul wanted them to know that some of the strangers who crowded into their meetings might be sent from God.

I am not sure that this text means literal angels. I am inclined to believe it might mean that some people who appeared as strangers were really gifts of God to the rest of the body. They probably weren't even called angels, just people with angelic missions or a loving touch.

God sends a never-ending stream of His people through our lives. Some stay awhile. Others are just passing through. Some are on divine missions from God to us. They won't announce it. We have to discover it.

We are to show love to all and treat all who come to us in a brotherly fashion.

Many times emissaries from God come without calling cards. If we are not careful, we will miss the message and the messenger.

Look for the angel unaware that God might be sending to you today. Be open to the person and the message he brings!

# *Instruction:* **A Very Big Change**

> *Now your attitudes and thoughts must all be constantly changing for the better. Yes, you must be a new and different person, holy and good. Clothe yourself with this new nature.*
> Ephesians 4:23, 24 TLB

Conversion is as much a process as it is a decision. We can decide to follow Christ by an act of the will and a repentant spirit. From the moment of decision on, we enter a process that ends only at our physical death.

As we are caught in the process of becoming what God wants us to be, our attitudes and thoughts are undergoing changes. An attitude is how we feel toward something or someone. A thought is how we might carry that attitude into reality.

What is your attitude toward God now that you know you belong to Him? What about your attitude toward yourself? Are you accepting the fact that you are a unique, unrepeatable miracle of God's love? How is your attitude changing toward other people in your life? Do you see them through the eyes of Christ? Do you see the needs they have?

Striving to have the "mind of Christ" is not easy. Sometimes it is asking the question, "How would Jesus feel and respond in this situation?"

A big part of Christian growth is getting rid of our old, selfish nature. That doesn't happen by submerging it in invisible ink. It is a very slow process with most of us.

Paul tells us to wear new clothes as new people. New clothes are not always the most comfortable ones. Sometimes they make us too obvious. As we grow, the new nature we are clothed in becomes more comfortable and more familiar.

What will change in you today? What will you view differently?

# *Instruction:* **Shaping Up Your Kids**

> *Don't fail to correct your children; discipline won't hurt them! They won't die if you use a stick on them! Punishment will keep them out of hell.*
> Proverbs 23:13, 14 TLB

Solomon believed in correction. He would not have been too popular in today's permissive society. His books would not have sold too well. He would have gotten a lot of negative mail concerning the adverse effects discipline could have upon a child's future life.

Perhaps we should listen to Solomon. We are getting drowned in a tide of youthful permissiveness.

Contrary to popular opinion, discipline won't hurt children. If it hurts anyone, it hurts the parent who dispenses it—not physically, but emotionally.

Children of all ages need correctional help. Parents are able to give it because they have lived longer and have a much wider range of vision than children do. They can measure a child by what they know and have learned through living.

Solomon tells us that children won't die or even be warped by physical punishment. I can remember that the most feared thing in my days in elementary school was the principal's leather strap. Now I think when it was thrown out, love went out along with it.

Love and discipline go hand in hand. Discipline stings, but love heals the sting.

Correction, discipline, and punishment are rapidly fading ingredients in our society. In some cases, you can murder someone today and be freed from prison on good behavior after ten years.

Our children, the sacred trust of God to us, need all three of Solomon's reproofs applied to their lives. It may well spare them their own private hell years from now!

## *Instruction:* **Ah, the Good Old Days!**

> *Don't long for "the good old days," for you don't know whether they were any better than these!*
> Ecclesiastes 7:10 TLB

Once in a while, I see someone bang his fist on the side of a new car and exclaim, "They sure don't make them like they used to!" That's right. They sure don't. I haven't found a new car yet with a crank sticking out of the front end in place of an electric starter. I wonder how many arms were broken, sprained, or lost in the good old days of auto engineering.

We all have a tendency to remember only the good and forget the bad of yesterday. Perhaps that's a good idea for our minds, but a bad idea for our growth.

Even the Israelites thought Egypt was better than the wilderness, after they had gotten sweaty and bored with the manna God provided.

We tend to file things into good and bad drawers in our lives. We have good and bad days, depending on the events we experience. If you tallied up your life right now, which column would be the longest—the good or the bad?

Our mistake is comparing one day to another instead of celebrating one day after another. When a bad day comes along, we think only of the good day we had last week, and then fall into a depression.

The Psalmist said, "This is the day the Lord has made. We will rejoice and be glad in it" (Psalms 118:24 TLB). He never told us to compare it with yesterday!

If you want to long for anything, long for the good *new* days yet to come in your life. You can't live backwards. Don't get caught in nostalgic comparisons. Today is all you have, and it is a gift from God to you!

# *Instruction:* A Blessing on Your House

*"Whenever you enter a home, give it your blessing."*                Luke 10:5 TLB

Is your home a place where blessings are received and given out? Probably few of us think of our homes as blessing centers. We just go in and out, try to keep it clean, and sleep and eat there. Homes today are often places where people pass through rather than live. Many homes seldom have a visitor to welcome.

Today's instruction was given to the band of disciples whom Jesus sent out on a short missionary journey. As they ministered and visited different homes, they were to leave their blessing upon the homes and their residents.

I am sure that some of those homes had a collection of problems living in them. They needed to be blessed. Perhaps others had happy families living in them. The disciples' blessing upon them was simply an affirmation of God's love to them.

Some of the disciples were probably glad to find a home that warmly received them to rest and bathe and eat. The blessings in those instances were directed toward the disciples.

Have you ever stood in someone's doorway as you were about to leave and said, "May Christ bless this house and those who live in it!" That's a simple blessing to leave behind you. It has meaning and love attached to it.

Many of the homes on your street are devoid of blessings. God may direct you to carry His blessing to those homes.

The words of the song put the blessing in perspective:

Bless this house, O Lord we pray,
Keep it safe by night and day!

## *Instruction:* **Let's Get Away From It All!**

*Then Jesus suggested, "Let's get away from the crowds for a while and rest."*
*For so many people were coming and going that they scarcely had time to eat.*
Mark 6:31 TLB

The Memorial Day Holiday is approaching. On Friday evening, thousands of cars, campers, boats, and humans will escape from the city to the quiet of the country. When they get to the country, they will find out that all the noise of the city has followed them. It is getting more difficult to find a place to rest away from the noise and crowds.

In a world that increasingly demands more from each of us, getting away to a place of rest is very important.

Crowds followed Jesus everywhere. They demanded that He heal them, talk to them, and listen to their problems. It is little wonder that He kept retreating to places of quiet and refreshment. He knew the need to get away and regain His strength.

Is it time for you to plan a getaway? Have the problems of life been squeezing that last ounce of human juice from you? Is it time for you to get alone and look at life from a distance and regain your peace and calm?

Life was busy in Jesus' day. It is still busy today. I am always amazed at how small my problems look when I view them from a mountaintop or a lakeside cabin. I think God uses these special times to retune our engines and sort out our priorities.

Everything will be right where we left it when we get back, and we may get some answers that we need while we are away.

Try a weekend away, and let God speak to you!


## *Instruction:* **Letting Your Friend Be Known**

*"If anyone publicly acknowledges me as his friend, I will openly acknowledge*
*him as my friend before my father in heaven."*          Matthew 10:32 TLB

All of us have had the privilege of introducing our best friend to someone. We usually have a deep sense of pride as we introduce that person. We want him or her to be known for who he is, and we want him to be known as our friend. The people he is meeting may accept him instantly because he is our friend. We don't have to sell him, explain him, or even defend him. The word that he is our friend is enough.

Perhaps the greatest compliment we can give someone is to say that he is really a true friend to us. Few words have to follow to describe what a friend is.

Jesus wanted to be known as a friend of the disciples and the people He ministered to. He wanted to be their friend and to be introduced to others as their friend. He made a promise to those who claimed Him as friend. He would openly acknowledge them before His Father in heaven as His friends.

Friendship is often described as a circular pathway. There is no apparent beginning or ending to it. The one thing that keeps it going is a love that knows no limits. Real friendship has no hidden agenda. It is not manipulative. It is universal acceptance.

A real friendship is a warm and loving relationship. Jesus desired that when He lived, and He desires it today. He wants our friendship, and He wants to give His friendship to us.

Have you ever introduced your friend Jesus to someone else? Do you want to be His friend?

## *Instruction:* Avoid the Get-Rich-Quick Schemes

*The man who wants to do right will get a rich reward. But the man who wants to get rich quick will quickly fail.*                    Proverbs 28:20 TLB

My daily newspaper is full of ads telling me how others have obtained great riches in sudden fashion. For only a few dollars, they will share their secret with me, and I will be able to experience the same results. I sometimes feel that they are getting richer by getting my money more than really helping me obtain money. Someone must be answering the ads, because they keep on advertising.

All of us would have to admit to a mild interest in getting rich. It is interesting to me that Solomon, in today's instruction, talks of getting rich, but not in a monetary sense. He talks about the desire to do the right thing rather than the desire for riches.

I want to do the right thing each day. So do you. Few people consciously want to do the wrong things. The problem with some is that they want to do the right things for the wrong reasons. It is important to do the right things for the right reasons. I do the right thing simply because it is the right thing. If no reward comes, I have lost nothing. My reward is knowing I have done my best in doing right.

Solomon warns that the people who only want to get rich quickly will fail. If we put this thought under some of those newspaper ads, I wonder if anyone would listen.

Are you spending a lot of energy racing after the wrong things in life? Are you looking for an easy way to wealth? Do you really know what wealth is?

The world has some pretty weird standards for getting rich. Don't get caught up in them. Get rich in your soul doing what is right!

## *Instruction:* The Marvelous Miracles of God

*Come, see the glorious things God has done. What marvelous miracles happen to his people!*                                     Psalms 66:5 TLB

How would you feel if you received an invitation to attend a party where you were guaranteed you would see miracles performed? Would you go expectantly or suspiciously? Would you believe a miracle if you saw one?

I am always amazed when I see Christians trying to explain what they think God is doing. They seem to feel that God is in great need of an interpreter when He does certain things—like miracles! It is too difficult to let God do what He wants and just celebrate the results.

Some think the age of miracles has passed. Perhaps they feel that God ran out or just got too tired of doing the miraculous. It seems easier for them to credit the unexplained to Satan rather than to God.

David tells us that marvelous miracles happen to God's people. Apparently, David's expectancy level was higher than ours is today.

Are you limiting the miraculous by refusing to expect it to happen, or denying it when it does happen? It might well be time for all of us to stop trying to put God in a human and theological box. I think He would like to be what He is for a time—God! God of miracle power that causes us to say, "Wow!" when we see Him at work.

Sometimes we look for the big miracle when God is at work doing small, quiet miracles all around us. We need to acknowledge the small ones in order to be prepared to recognize the bigger ones.

Have you let a miracle in your life slip by without thanking God? Are you living with the confidence that God knows what He is doing? Come, see and celebrate what God is doing!

## *Instruction:* Hang On to Your Flavor

*"Good salt is worthless if it loses its saltiness; it can't season anything. So don't lose your flavor! Live in peace with each other."*        Mark 9:50 TLB

Will the spearmint lose its flavor on the bedpost overnight? So go the words of a famous song of years ago. The answer, in case you have never tried the experiment, is, "Yes!" Old gum is not worth chewing. Old salt is worthless if it loses its saltiness.

Jesus encouraged those around Him to be the salt of the earth. They were to be the seasoning in society. They were to be its preservatives when the forces of sin tried to infiltrate it. They were to give it taste.

Some of us have forgotten what we are supposed to be. Or, we just throw a sprinkle of salt over our shoulders once in a while, and hope that will do the job.

Jesus saw His followers as influencing society, not just being influenced by it. The Early Christians even infiltrated the courts of Rome with their Christian influence. Agrippa was almost persuaded to follow Christ because of Paul's testimony. The only way the world could handle the saltiness of Christians was to kill them.

God calls us to season our world with His loving influence. That will never be an easy job. It is our calling.

Are you a "good salt" Christian? Will you be aware of the influence God has called you to be today in your job?

Don't lose your flavor!

## *Instruction:* **Just Plain Hallelujah!**

*Hallelujah! I want to express publicly before his people my heartfelt thanks to God for His mighty miracles. All who are thankful should ponder them with me. For his miracles demonstrate his honor, majesty, and eternal goodness.*
Psalms 111:1–3 TLB

I heard a song the other day that had a catchy line in it. It said, "Sometimes Hallelujah, sometimes Praise the Lord!" Those were the only lines I caught, but they made me think about my response to the things God does in my life. I began to wonder if I could add either of these exclamations to the things that happen to me each day. Some days, it is easier to say, "Oh, no!" to many of the situations that clutter up the road through life.

The Psalmist did not hide his expression for what God had done in his life. In one place, we are told he danced before the Lord. Many of us would not be caught dancing in the street because of the joy of God in our lives. People would think we had cracked up. David wanted the people to know what God was doing in his life. He did not want to hide the good news. He also wanted the people to think about these things from God. Thinking sometimes cements things in a more permanent way in our hearts. If we have cause to doubt God in the future, we can think back to what He did in the past, and know He can do it again.

How long has it been since you praised God publicly for what He has done in your life? You will not put God on the spot by doing it. God loves celebration. When He does something in our lives, He wants us to share it as well as enjoy it.

Hallelujah and praise the Lord!

## *Instruction:* **Looking for the Day**

*"So be prepared, for you don't know what day your Lord is coming."*
                                        Matthew 24:42 TLB

The Early Christians spent a great deal of time speculating on when Jesus was going to return for them. Nineteen hundred years later, theologians and students alike continue to predict the imminent return of Christ. Second Coming books have enjoyed huge sales in the last ten years. Home Bible studies have drawn people into open discussion and often disagreement about the Lord's return. Times really haven't changed regarding rapture fever.

Jesus' word in the Book of Matthew was to spend our time in preparation rather than in speculation. His simple advice was to get on with our living, since no one really knows when the Lord will return.

So how do you prepare? I once heard someone say that a Christian should be ready to preach, pray, sing, or die at a moment's notice—not bad advice for living or dying. Living in preparation is living with a plan and purpose, and an expectant heart. It is knowing that I must face the practical things in life as I look toward the promise of the future. I cannot run the risk of being so rapture minded that I am of no earthly good.

Life is the training ground for eternity. We can't float away on a heavenly cloud. Of course some days it is easier to turn our heads toward heaven than our minds toward earth.

The promise of the Scripture is that Christ will return. The time is His secret. My job, and yours, is to be prepared. I will commit myself to growing and sharing my life with others until that day comes. Then I will celebrate my homecoming!

# *Instruction:* **It's Hard to Be a Waiter**

*Don't be impatient. Wait for the Lord, and he will come and save you! Be brave, stouthearted and courageous. Yes, wait and he will help you.*

Psalms 27:14 TLB

Have you ever waited by a busy roadside for a tow truck to come and haul away your dead automobile? I can remember when our motor home broke down while we were on a long trip. Waiting to be towed in seemed to take forever. Having a load of impatient kids did not add to my patience. It is difficult to wait for others as well as wait on others.

Waiting for others is easier than waiting for the Lord. We know that others will eventually arrive, but we sometimes wonder if the Lord has forgotten our address. God doesn't operate on the seconds, minutes, hours schedule that we do. He seems more concerned about equipping us for events, and then leading us through and beyond them. He knows the amount of preparation and waiting we need to take us through certain things.

One of the most frequently used admonitions in Scripture is to wait upon the Lord. I will be the first to admit that waiting is not easy. I tend to be a "right now" person. God tends to be a "wait awhile" God. We clash a lot!

David tells us that we are to do something important while we are waiting. We are to be brave, stouthearted, and full of courage. That is good equipment for waiting. We will not fear whatever we are waiting for if our inner person is strong.

The promise is that God will help us if we wait for that help. Are you running ahead of the Lord today? Or are you willing to wait for His timing in the things important to your life?

# *Affirmations*

An affirmation is a good word about you, or something you did, that comes from another person. Most of us like to collect affirmations and remember them when bad days come. They are the plus sign in life that keeps us going.

The Scriptures are filled with God's good words about us and what we can do with His strength in us. Jesus was an affirmer of the many people He ministered to in His lifetime.

As we are affirmed by one another, we need to be affirmed by God.

As you read an affirmation a day, just sit back and realize that this is how much God loves you and cares about you. He is the affirmer; we are the affirmed!

## *Affirmation:* **Filled With Joy**

*"I have told you this so that you will be filled with my joy. Yes, your cup of joy will overflow!"*
John 15:11 TLB

Have you ever had the joy of being the bearer of good news? You can hardly wait to tell it, and you are overflowing with your own excitement. Wouldn't it be neat to have the kind of job that involved bringing good news to people every day? You could be a full-time dispenser of happiness.

Sharing joy is a part of human affirmation. It is saying that the receiver of the joy deserves it. He or she may not have had to do anything to receive it.

Jesus is excited about people being happy. Too few of us view Him in this light. Our vision is often clouded by the Old Testament image of an angry God dealing with Israel.

Jesus shared some exciting thoughts with His disciples on the Mount of Olives. He wanted them to be prepared for the future, but he also wanted them to have a spring of hope within them. He wanted His words and His love to fill them with joy. The Scripture doesn't say they laughed up a storm or even got slightly happy at what Jesus told them. But Jesus did plant the seeds for future joy in their lives.

Jesus was not a miser in dispensing joy. He did not want the disciples to be just a little happy. He wanted them to be full to overflowing with happiness. I think He knew the effcct a "full to the brim" life would have on others. Joy that spills over is contagious.

You and I are to be filled with joy. It's a gift from God. Share the gift today with someone in your life.


## *Affirmation:* **You Belong**

*Now you are no longer strangers to God and foreigners to heaven, but you are members of God's very own family, citizens of God's country, and you belong in God's household with every other Christian.*
Ephesians 2:19 TLB

Belonging is one of the greatest feelings in the world. We all roam through life looking for places where we are special, places where we belong. From Little League uniforms to designer jeans, we all try to send out a message that says, "I belong!" My wallet is full of plastic cards that tell me I belong to certain unique groups. When I show one of those cards, I am instantly recognized as belonging to a certain organization.

Some people spend their entire lives trying to join groups that will give them a sense of belonging. Some people have told me that they feel as if they don't really belong anywhere. People often get married just so they will belong with and to another person.

Being where you belong is a warm feeling. Paul's word of affirmation to us is a strong one. By it, we are taken out of the nonbelonging world of strangers and foreigners and placed in the family of God. We are not merely there by transfer but by citizenship. As a result, we don't just belong to God but we belong to every other member of His family, too. We are one big household!

I listened to the words of a marvelous song the other day: "I'm so glad I'm a part of the family of God." Every time I hear them, I am reminded that *I belong*. Me. Not the world. Me!

Have you found the very best place for you to belong? You will always belong in God's family. Your search is over!

## Affirmation: **We Are God's Own Sons**

*Now we are no longer slaves, but God's own sons. And since we are his sons, everything he has belongs to us, for that is the way God planned.*
                                                    Galatians 4:7 TLB

Have you ever wondered what it would be like to be the son or daughter of a rich man? Even if you had to live on an allowance, you would know that someday all your father's riches would be yours. In the human sense, few of us are that privileged. We might end up with a few pieces of jewelry, a watch, and maybe even a few thousand dollars from our parents' estates.

In his letter to the Galatian Christians, Paul tells them how very wealthy they are because they are sons of God. Now that did not mean they could write a check on God's account and buy a new herd of sheep. It did mean that all the things God had created and placed in the world for their enjoyment now belonged to them, also. We are shareholders in the wealth of a universe. When we joined God's family, we became heirs to His vast resources.

If what God owns belongs to us also, why do we often live with such a poverty-stricken attitude and spirit, like people who have a million dollars in the bank but don't know it?

If you really believe that the wealth of this world is yours, you will also understand that everything you think you own is really owned by God. In other words, God shares His wealth with us, and everything we have we share with Him, also.

God had a great plan. He would share His world with us. His resources would be limitless. Our responsibility is to use wisely what is ours in trust! You are a child of the King. Don't live like a pauper!

## *Affirmation:* Use Your Ability

*God has given each of us the ability to do certain things well....*
                                                    Romans 12:6 TLB

What ability or gift would you like to have that you do not possess? I would like to be able to fix everything myself and never have to call a repairman. I frequently meet people who have the ability to fix anything. It doesn't matter whether or not they have ever fixed that kind of thing before. They simply size it up, pick up their tools, and go to work. The end result is amazing.

Then there is the kind of person who *claims* to be able to fix anything, but only makes it worse. There are quite a few of those in the crowd as well. This kind of person doesn't just *want* someone else's gift, he feels he *has* it.

God is not a miser in gift giving. All of us have gifts and abilities. You soon discover that God doesn't give all gifts and abilities to one person. He spreads them around so that there is a wide diversity in life.

The secret of functioning well as members of the body of Christ is to discover your gifts and then use them to build up others in the body. Instead of developing their own gifts, some members simply covet the gifts of others, or try to imitate them.

A growing Christian is always honing and developing his or her gifts. If all Christians did this, there would be tremendous balance in the body of believers. All the work would get done because all the gifts would be in operation.

Are you using the gift that God has given to you? Are you at home with it? Are you enjoying the developing of it?

# *Affirmation:* **We Are Wonderfully Made**

*Try to realize what this means—the Lord is God! He made us—we are his people, the sheep of his pasture.*                                    Psalms 100:3 TLB

Psalm 100 is often described as a song of praise. It speaks of celebration, identity, praise, and promise. David tells us four things in this third verse that help us establish our identity.

First, the Lord is God. There are no substitutes and no imitations. I am sure David saw many people in his time trying to put their own god in office. In his own life, he knew that the Lord was God. In the lives of his people, he wanted this affirmation out front.

Second, He made us. This was a planned creative act. You and I are no accident. We did not happen from somewhere via an evolutionary process of millions of years. We were actually designed by God. All the parts are in the right places, too. He is our architect.

Third, we are His people. Our identity is tied to Him when we experience the new birth. We become a part of His forever family. We are no longer immigrants looking for a country. We are now residents of His country.

Fourth, we are the sheep of His pasture. You have to know something about sheep to get the full meaning of this. They need a nourishing place to feed and grow. They also need protection and guidance. You and I are pretty much like sheep. We need the same things, and God promises to give us those things.

It's a good feeling to know that our identity is found in being members of the body of Christ. The care that God has for us intensifies with each passing day.

We are wonderfully made and cared for!

# *Affirmation:* **The Things God Is**

*The Lord is my strength, my song, and my salvation. He is my God, and I will praise him. He is my father's God—I will exalt him.*          Exodus 15:2 TLB

The Israelites had just witnessed the greatest miracle they had ever seen. The Red Sea was awash with the bodies of Egyptians. Moses had led Israel away to safety, and a celebration was in order. A song was composed and sung to the Lord. The song told what had actually happened and what the Lord had done. It gave Him the credit for the miracle.

Today's affirmation tells what the Lord is to Moses, to Israel, and to us.

Moses recognized that the strength for any victory is found in the Lord. It is not found in might or power.

Strength, song, and salvation paint a very complete picture of what God is to any believer. There is nothing left out. As you live your life today, will He be those things to you?

Moses also noted that God has a history with His family. He did not just come on the scene but was also there for Moses' father and his father's father. The strength and help that Moses received was founded in the relationship that others before him had with God.

Moses lifted praise to the Lord. Part of that praise was in the singing of this song of victory. Moses followed instructions and the Lord received the accolades.

God can and will be the same things to you today as He was to Moses. You can sing this same song as you go about your day and wend your way through the struggles of life. Believe what God is, and great victories will be yours!

## *Affirmation:* Love is . . .

*Love is very patient and kind, never jealous or envious, never boastful or proud.*                                     1 Corinthians 13:4 TLB

What sounds does love make? Think about this for a few minutes and see what you come up with.

I have a feeling that the sounds of love are not loud and brash. They are rather quiet and plumb the depths of a person's soul when loosed.

We are so used to things that make noise that it might be hard to believe love is a subdued sound. In the midst of a letter to some Early Christians, Paul takes a short sidetrack in thinking to describe what love is all about.

Patience and kindness are words that can only be expressed by an act. Yet the acts that bring out both patience and kindness are not center-stage material. They are often observed around the edges of life.

Jealousy and envy are certainly not a part of love. They are, in effect, those loud, sharp noises that are merely self-seeking. They are two things that you and I fight off daily.

Love is never boastful or proud. These two negative responses to love usually draw attention to the person desperately in need of love. Their acts try to bring them the love they desire.

We all need to love and be loved. It is so easy to try to get love in the wrong way, or even give it in the wrong way.

Will the love you demonstrate to others today be of the patient-and-kind variety? I hope so!

## *Affirmation:* **My Redeemer Lives**

*"But as for me, I know that my Redeemer lives, and that he will stand upon the earth at last."*                                          Job 19:25 TLB

If you had the kind of friends Job had, you would certainly need no enemies. Sometimes we have friends like that. The words they speak tend to be words of discouragement rather than encouragement. Advice is always cheap and usually comes from a pooling of ignorance with other people.

It was enough that Job had to withstand Satan, but he also had to withstand the bad advice of his friends. Today's words from Job to his detractors remind me of the little saying from my grade-school years, "Sticks and stones may break my bones but names will never hurt me."

Job tells his friends that they can say anything they want, but he is still going to come out on top. Perhaps the strongest statement Job makes in his entire life is the proclamation that he knows God is not dead. He tells his friends that his Redeemer lives and that He will still stand upon the earth, long after Job lives through his hassles.

Isn't it interesting that Job doesn't tell his friends he will still be standing after it's all over. Instead, he draws attention to the power and authority and history of God in men's lives. He literally says that after all is said and done, God will still be around.

That is a strong hope for Christians, especially for those of faint heart. When all of our trials are over, our Redeemer lives! And because He lives, we, too, shall live!

## *Affirmation:* **Strength in Joy**

*"It is a time to celebrate with a hearty meal, and to send presents to those in need, for the joy of the Lord is your strength. You must not be dejected and sad!"*                                          Nehemiah 8:10 TLB

What does the word *celebration* mean to you? How do you celebrate the happy things in your life? Does God want you to celebrate?

I believe that celebration is therapy for the heart. Too few of us really know how to celebrate anymore. We live in a world that casts ominous clouds of fear and pessimism across our lives. We find it difficult to look beyond those clouds and see the rays of sunshine that invite celebration.

The walls of Jerusalem were rebuilt. Ezra was reading the Law to the people. All of a sudden, the people began sobbing as they heard the tough commands of the Law. Ezra stopped them and invited them to celebrate rather than commiserate.

Food was always part of a festive occasion. It still is today for most of us. Gift giving was a part of Israel's party. The gifts were given to those in need, not to those who already possessed much. The sharing of joy was to be injected into the very human part of the celebration. Ezra wanted the people to know that the Lord was the source and center of their joy, and that they were surrounded by His strength. God was literally to be the center of their partying. He was the theme. Whatever else happened, He was recognized as being the center of attention and celebration.

You and I are not to be dejected and sad. God invites us to a celebration today. Put your gloom on the shelf and plan a party with your friends. Let the real joy of the Lord be your strength and source of happiness.

## *Affirmation:* A Universe in Trust

*Then God said, "Let us make a man—someone like ourselves, to be the master of all life upon the earth and in the skies and in the seas." So God made man like his Maker. Like God did God make man; Man and maid did he make them. And God blessed them and told them, "Multiply and fill the earth and subdue it; you are masters of the fish and birds and all the animals...."*
*Then God looked over all that he had made, and it was excellent in every way....*                                                    Genesis 1:26–28, 31 TLB

I remember the numerous times my wife and I have gone away for a few days and instructed our children to take care of everything. If you are like me, you write out a long checklist and then go over it about ten times. By the time you leave, your children are worn out from your instructions. You don't expect your children to improve on what you have while you are gone; you simply want them to guard, protect, and care for it. Little do they realize that what they are caring for belongs to them as well.

You and I are entrusted with the care of a universe. When God finished His last creative work, He turned the whole planet over to that creative work for care and growth. What an infinite amount of trust God had in man! He was not told to simply put a fence around things and keep them as they were—he was to use his own ingenuity and wisdom to help it all grow and multiply.

Some days, it doesn't look as though you and I are doing too good a job with the task God has given us. On those days, I am sure God has a hard time seeing us through the pollution we have created.

God's assignment to you and me said, *I trust you!* That's how God feels about you and me today. He loves us and He trusts us!

## *Affirmation:* **An Open Invitation**

*For I am not ashamed of this Good News about Christ. It is God's powerful method of bringing all who believe it to heaven. This message was preached first to the Jews alone, but now everyone is invited to come to God in this same way.*                                                     Romans 1:16 TLB

The ad said, "Now Open to the Public for the First Time!" The lines were long as customers tried to jam into the wholesale-clothing manufacturer's outlet. The doors of this firm were formerly open only to dealers and store owners. Now everyone could share in the same bargain prices once reserved for the elite. What an opportunity!

We have all seen the ads and raced around for the bargains. We have even directed our friends to the same places. A good deal should never be kept secret.

When Paul wrote his letter to the Church at Rome, he let them in on a little secret. The Good News about Christ was once reserved for the Jews only. Now, for the first time, it was open and available to everyone.

Apparently there were no long lines of people waiting to receive this Good News. Slowly, the Gentiles began to receive Christ into their lives and before long, the message of the Gospel became a universal rather than exclusive one.

Do you feel that the Good News is just for you? Well, it is, but it is also for the people who live on your street and work in your office. When you don't share what Christ is to you, you keep others out of the Kingdom. I meet some people who want to hug the Gospel to themselves. They have found a bargain they don't want to share. That certainly wasn't God's intention!

God's open invitation to others is often through the front door of your life. Keep the door open today!

## *Affirmation:* The Affirmation of the Spirit

*But when the Holy Spirit controls our lives he will produce this kind of fruit in us: love, joy, peace, patience, kindness, goodness, faithfulness, gentleness and self-control; and here there is no conflict with Jewish laws.*

Galatians 5:22, 23 TLB

How do you know who really is in control of your life? You, God, someone else? Probably some days we wonder who is in control, as crazy things seem to be happening to us. The Early Christians struggled with this problem. Their conflict prompted Paul to write them today's words of affirmation.

The measure of our growth is found in what our life is producing. If control of our lives is centered in the Holy Spirit, we will grow daily in the nine fruit of the Spirit. If our lives are controlled by some other force or people, these fruit will not be evident in our lives.

I have discovered that all nine fruit of the Spirit don't grow at the same time in a person's life. The seeds are there and are germinating, but each one grows at its own rate as the Spirit works in our lives. Our job is not to force growth but to release the power of the Holy Spirit to work on those seeds.

Some of the fruit of the Spirit are more needed at one time than another in our lives. There are times when we need peace more than gentleness. Sometimes we need love more than we need self-control. Few of us would argue that we don't need all the fruit of the Spirit in our lives. They all combine to equip us for living a Spirit-filled life.

The fruit of the Spirit are the affirmation that God is really working in us. They are a yardstick that we can measure our growth by.

## *Affirmation:* Love Remains

*There are three things that remain—faith, hope, and love—and the greatest of these is love.* 1 Corinthians 13:13 TLB

The thirteenth chapter of 1 Corinthians is Paul's expansion of the command that Jesus gave to His disciples on the Mount of Olives. The only difference is that Paul personalizes the love command into his own life. He speaks of the exterior effects of love and concludes with the interior effects it has on his own life.

Paul carves the love decree into permanence by telling us that it will outlast faith and hope. That does not mean that faith and hope are unimportant. It means that love embraces both of them but in the end is superimposed upon them.

In his love letter, Paul talks about the consistent quality of love and the effect it has when operative in a life. He tells us that love is tenacious, enduring, consistent, and powerful. He suggests that there is a quiet strength in love. It needs to make no loud sounds to be evidenced in a life.

Much of the debris of life that surrounds you and me will someday be gone. Things that we value so dearly will decay and disappear. The important will become the irrelevant.

How are you doing in balancing the things that last with the things that will disappear? When you total everything up, will the final answer be *love?*

The test of living is often the test of loving. Take a few minutes right now and ask God to help you sort out the things of love value in your life.

## *Affirmation:* **Through the Fog of Faith**

*What is faith? It is the confident assurance that something we want is going to happen. It is the certainty that what we hope for is waiting for us, even though we cannot see it up ahead.*                                   Hebrews 11:1 TLB

The eleventh chapter of Hebrews is known as the hall of fame of faith. When your own faith is getting weak, it's the place you run to for reassurance. As you read through its testimonies of God's work in others' lives, you cannot help but know and feel God at work today. You quickly discover that the many great things we read about in Scripture came about as a result of people's faith in God to do the extraordinary as well as the ordinary.

Today's affirmation simply defines what faith really is. It is confidence, assurance, and certainty that God will lead us through the fog around us into the clear spaces ahead. Faith doesn't always come with a road map. If it did, there would be no need for trusting God. Faith is like driving through the fog. You know there is a road up ahead; you simply can't see it at the moment. So you drive, trusting your knowledge from other trips.

The eleventh chapter of Hebrews gives us the support from others who have taken the trip of faith. It helps us say, "If they could do it, I can do it!" It is also putting God's track record with them on the line. As the song tells us, "What He's done for others, He'll do for you!"

As you look into the fog of today, what do you see up ahead—problems, stresses, defeats, opportunities, tests? The walk of faith is for the surefooted. Becoming surefooted is trusting God to do what He promises.

## *Affirmation:* **It's All Brand-New**

> *You are living a brand new kind of life that is continually learning more and*
> *more of what is right, and trying constantly to be more and more like Christ*
> *who created this new life within you.*          Colossians 3:10 TLB

Have you ever wished for a brand-new life? Most of us have, especially
when the pressures of the present life crowd in. We look at the travel ads
for tropical islands and fantasize what it would be like to put our feet in
their sands and start all over.

When a person becames a Christian, he begins to live a brand-new life.
That doesn't come about by an instant housecleaning or hurried garage
sale of your life. Becoming brand-new is a long, slow process. It is learning to take the things that once seemed so right out of your life and let
God put in their place the things He knows are right for you.

Many who are new in the faith have an incendiary nature about them.
They want new changes in their lives so rapidly that they simply take a
torch to anything that gets in their way. God never called the new Christian to be a wrecking crew of one. He called us to be people on a journey
with one another, gently letting God take us through processes that will
help us grow to maturity.

The Living Bible version of this verse uses the words *continually* and
*constantly*. These are "hanging in there" words. They do not connote instant reconstruction.

Christ has given us the gift of new life. It is a brand-new kind of life. It
takes a lifetime to get used to. Give your new life some time. Don't rush
it!

## *Affirmation:* **Praising ... No Matter What**

> *I will praise the Lord no matter what happens. I will constantly speak of his*
> *glories and grace.*                              Psalms 34:1 TLB

Have you ever practiced qualified praise? It means picking and choosing the situations in life that you want to praise God for. You get a raise
and you praise the Lord! An unexpected serendipity happens and you
praise the Lord! You get sick with the flu and you—bad-mouth God!
What ever happened to praise the Lord?

Qualified praise is certainly not what David had in mind. David's concept of praise was a strong "anyhow" praise. He did not list the good
things to praise God for and the bad things to boo God for. His simple yet
difficult admonition was to praise the Lord in all situations.

That's hard for me to do. I want to specialize in selected praises when things are going well. I need to learn how to praise the Lord when it seems as though I am swimming upstream against an impossible current. My problem is that I am afraid I will be swept away by the current rather than swept up in the love of God. Those are tough moments of uncertainty for me—but I think I'm learning.

David knew the power of a positive approach to God. He knew that speaking of God's glory and grace fortified his position of praise. David's praise came from looking in the reflective mirror of the power of God. When you know you are surrounded by strength, you can praise God in any and all situations.

David also knew that God, and not the situation, had the last word. We tend to feel that the situation will overrun us and God. But God is the master of every situation.

As you walk today, try praising the Lord in everything that happens to you. You will be surprised at your power!

## *Affirmation:* Seasoner to the World

*"You are the world's seasoning, to make it tolerable. If you lose your flavor, what will happen to the world? And you yourselves will be thrown out and trampled underfoot as worthless. You are the world's light—a city on a hill, glowing in the night for all to see."*　　　　Matthew 5:13, 14 TLB

A famous man died a few months ago. His obituary in the newspaper stated that he was a citizen of the world. Even though he was an American, he belonged to everyone. He had traveled to every corner of the world in his lifetime. He left his mark wherever he went. I was in awe as I read the article and wondered what it would be like to be responsible to the world as one of its premier citizens.

Matthew elevates you and me far beyond the class of this famous person. He classes the Christian as the seasoning of the whole world. We are the catalyst for society that makes it bearable. If we did not fulfill this role that God has entrusted to us, the world would be on a runaway course to oblivion.

Matthew does not leave us with God's dash of spice but tells us that we are also the world's light. We are not only to be sprinkled through society but we also are to illuminate it with the light of God's truth shining through us.

There will be many dark spots in your day that need the light of Christ shining through you. Make sure your batteries aren't dead when you attempt to light up the lives of others.

Salt and light! They are two powerful components that are a part of every Christian. Be aware of what you are today!

## *Affirmation:* **Where God's Power Shows Best**

*Each time he said, "No. But I am with you; that is all you need. My power shows up best in weak people." Now I am glad to boast about how weak I am; I am glad to be a living demonstration of Christ's power, instead of showing off my own power and abilities.*                    2 Corinthians 12:9 TLB

Paul had a troublesome condition that he had asked God to take away. He referred to it as his "thorn in the flesh." There has always been great speculation about what it was. No one knows. After Paul had prayed a third time, God responded to him with the words of affirmation for today.

Paul seemed to feel he could better serve the Lord without his thorny problem. God thought he could serve better with it. He reassured Paul that He was with him and he did not need anything else.

Perhaps you have a thorn you would like to get rid of, but God allows it to remain with you. Have you discovered that you can serve the Lord better with the problem than without it?

God's further word to Paul and to you and me involves power, or should I say our lack of power. We are told that God's power is best demonstrated through the lives of weak people.

Will all the weak people line up, please? Put me at the head of the line!

When you and I run along on our own strength, not much seems to get done. When we admit our weaknesses and let God move through us, a whole lot seems to get done. God doesn't mind how weak we are. He just asks for an open channel to work through.

God's power always shows best when our weakness is in the spotlight!

## *Affirmation:* **God's Big Four**

*For the Lord is always good. He is always loving and kind, and his faithfulness goes on and on to each succeeding generation.*          Psalms 100:5 TLB

We have a store near our home called Big Five Sporting Goods. When ~~ked what the big five was, I got five different answers. It is supposed to ~~ the five big sports, but that depends on how big you think your ~~f you think table tennis is one of the big five, then you will have ~~e something else.

David listed a Big Four for the Lord in Psalm 100. You might be able to list ten or twenty more, but David pretty well described God's greatest attributes.

He first tells us that God is always good. Now we might not always think so when something bad happens. But we have to remember that the nature of God is good. It is not a conditional thing based on what we experience.

Second, David lets us know that God is always loving and kind. That does not mean He stops all unkind and unloving things from happening. God allows things to happen so that His nature might be demonstrated through them.

Finally, David tells us that God follows through with faithfulness. What He says He will do, He does. There are no generation gaps in God's faithfulness to us. Even when we are unfaithful, He hangs in there with us.

God is good, loving, kind, and faithful. When you look around in today's world, you won't find many humans with those virtues. It is good to know that God doesn't change. You can trust Him to be those things to you today!

## *Affirmation:* **The Sharpest Exposure Possible**

*For whatever God says to us is full of living power: it is sharper than the sharpest dagger, cutting swift and deep into our innermost thoughts and desires with all their parts, exposing us for what we really are.*

Hebrews 4:12 TLB

Have you seen the new camera ads on television? Each one seems to promise us a picture with better exposure. One company even claims to have captured some sunlight in its camera. Another claims that it will give you maximum exposure even on the dullest days.

I guess I'm not too good with a camera. My pictures come back from the photo shop either underexposed or overexposed.

God must have a camera with the greatest exposure potential ever. Paul tells us that it shoots right into our hearts and exposes us for what we really are.

That should make you want to go into hiding! It is not too exciting to know that God looks past all our pretense, hype, and phoniness and sees us as we really are. However, He doesn't expose us to embarrass us but to help us see the truth and set us free to really live open lives.

God's exposure tool for looking deep inside you and me is the Word of God. When we read it or study it, we are exposed by its truth and directness. As it cuts a swath through our innermost thoughts and desires, it reminds us of the dentist's drill. It is painful during the drilling, but the end result is that the toothache is taken care of.

Has God been aiming His camera at you lately? Are you constantly dodging around so He can't get a good picture? Stand still a moment. God's exposure only brings about good growth in our lives!

## *Affirmation:* What About You and Your Family?

*"But if you are unwilling to obey the Lord, then decide today whom you will obey. Will it be the gods of your ancestors beyond the Euphrates or the gods of the Amorites here in this land? But as for me and my family, we will serve the Lord."*                                          Joshua 24:15 TLB

One of the strongest statements ever made by Joshua came near the end of his life. He had gone through the ups and downs of leading Israel, and in his final hours presented them with the challenge of serving the true God or false gods.

The challenge of whom to serve is a constant one in all of our lives. Now and then, that choice becomes a very clear one. Do we follow God's directives in a situation, or do we follow our own? Sometimes our choices send us down a totally different road that has far-reaching implications in our lives.

I have met many people who decide not to decide. They merely sit at the point of decision and never move in any direction. Their fear is usually of making the wrong decision.

Joshua was a leader from day one. He never forced decisions on people. He painted a clear picture and then allowed freedom to choose. He also told the people what he would do, regardless of what they would do. He spoke as the leader of Israel, but he also spoke as the leader of his own family. In that capacity, he had a sense of personal responsibility, regardless of what the nation of Israel chose.

What about you and your family? Are you choosing to follow God's way, regardless of where others are headed? Are you willing to take the lead in following God when you have to? It is not easy.

You may have to make some decisions today that will not be popular, if you choose to serve the Lord!

# *Affirmation:* **To Be God's Man!**

*Oh, Timothy, you are God's man. Run from all these evil things and work in-stead at what is right and good, learning to trust him and love others, and to be patient and gentle.*                                    1 Timothy 6:11 TLB

A lady came up to me as I finished a seminar. She smiled at me and said, "I see Christ in you!" Then she quietly turned and walked away. I stood there, rather speechless, and then a strange thought struck me. My head seemed to say, *You are not quite that good yet.* Then I started think-ing of the many reasons this lady's affirmation could not be true. Before long, I had a very long list. It almost made me want to run after the lady and tell her she had the wrong person.

Has anyone ever said that to you? It is a rather scary statement, but also a very biblical one.

Timothy was struggling to follow after God and Paul in the faith. Some days, he did a good job. On other days, he was less than the best. Yet Paul affirmed him with the highest compliment anyone could receive: "You are God's man!"

I can imagine Timothy saying, "Who, me?" He probably thought of all the things he wasn't, rather than the one thing he was.

I think we all do the same thing. Being told we are God's people brings a great sense of responsibility upon us. It is easier not to own the affirmation.

After the affirmation, Paul tells Timothy to run from evil, work at what is right and good, trust God, love others, and be patient and gentle— quite a list. It really tells what makes a person God's man. But you are the man before you are the things that make up the man.

Today, you are God's man in all that you do. (Women are not ex-cepted.) Live out the affirmation and enjoy God's blessing!

# *Affirmation:* **Every Day Is the Father's Day**

*He is like a father to us, tender and sympathetic to those who reverence him.*
                                                   Psalms 103:13 TLB

Fathers' Day is coming! Millions of cards will be sold to accompany the millions of gifts that will be given to fathers across the world. The vast majority of fathers will feel loved in a special way on this day. It is a way to say thanks to our fathers for everything they have been to us.

If your father is no longer alive, you spend the day with memories of your father's love for you. For a moment, you wish he were alive to say one more thank-you.

David had many different views of God. The one we most identify with is the one in today's affirmation. There is an instant understanding of God that comes with being told He is a Father to us. We immediately think of our earthly father and more easily identify with our heavenly Father.

The two attributes that David identifies here about the fatherliness of God are tenderness and sympathy. I think the most valuable things we can receive from a father, after love, are tenderness and sympathy. They are, in fact, composites of love.

When as children we were hurt, bleeding, mauled by the world, it was wonderful to go home to a father's tender love and be healed. Our heavenly Father functions in the same way. Sometimes we forget that, and we view God as judicial and severe. He is loving and cares deeply for us.

Every day is Father's Day with God. He extends His love to us and surrounds us with His gentle care. Do you feel His love for you today?

## *Affirmation:* Sons Are Led

*For all who are led by the Spirit of God are sons of God.*

Romans 8:14 TLB

Taking directions from others is sometimes a difficult task for most of us. Young people struggle to listen to their parents on one hand and make their own choices on the other. Our bosses at work tell us how to do certain things, yet behind their backs, we want to do things our own way. It seems that human nature wants to direct itself.

Taking directions from God is more difficult than taking directions from others. In writing to the Christians at Rome, Paul speaks of the blessing of being led by God and taking our directions from Him. The struggle to be led by God goes back to the Garden of Eden. The roots of the struggle reach from Eden into our lives today. We want to be known as sons of God, but we don't always want to follow the direction that sons should travel in.

How does the Spirit of God lead in your life? How do you know the difference between the spirit and the flesh?

God's leading is always checked against what Scripture teaches. If Scripture does not authenticate direction, it's the wrong direction.

God's leading needs to be shared with Christian friends. God often speaks through them to us about the direction He wants us to go.

God's leading is always committed to prayer. A good rule of thumb is to pray first and move second.

Real sons of God know the leading of God in their lives. Life is no iffy situation. God gives positive direction to those who want to be His children. Sons of God are led by God!

## *Affirmation:* **We Really Are His Children**

*See how very much our heavenly Father loves us, for he allows us to be called his children—think of it—and we really* are! *But since most people don't know God, naturally they don't understand that we are his children.*

1 John 3:1 TLB

Do you want to have some fun today? Here is a little assignment. Go up to at least twenty different people and whisper these words in their ear: "I'm one of God's children!"

I think you will get some interesting reactions. You might even have someone tell you that he wishes he were one, also.

How long has it been since someone reassured you that you were one of God's children? I think I need to be told that about seven times a day. The situations of life constantly seem to be pulling me away from my identity as one of God's children. I think Satan uses this to get me off course and into a place of meaningless wandering. If he can convince me that I have no family ties with God, then he can take over the direction of my life.

Have you listened to the subtleties of Satan telling you that you don't belong to God? Don't listen!

We really are God's children. We are a part of His family and we are surrounded by His love. We desperately need affirmation from the other members of God's family, too. They gently remind us of our family ties and our family responsibilities.

Say out loud, "I really am one of God's children!" And don't worry about who's listening.

## *Affirmation:* **A Ring Around Your Life**

*I can never stop thanking God for all the wonderful gifts he has given you, now that you are Christ's: he has enriched your whole life. He has helped you speak out for him and has given you a full understanding of the truth.*

1 Corinthians 1:4, 5 TLB

Today's affirmation is undoubtedly one of the greatest compliments Paul could give to the Christians in the city of Corinth. Even though their ranks are filled with grumbling and arguing people, Paul still thanks God for the distribution of His gifts to them.

Paul specifically thanks God for three things that He has done for the Corinthian believers. First, God has enriched their entire lives. They are richer now in their spirit than they have ever been. Some of them may feel poorer than they ever were, but Paul assures them this is not the case. God has put something in their lives that did not exist before.

Second, God has empowered them to speak out for His cause. That's never easy. When you and I speak out for God, we find ourselves wanting to apologize in the same breath. It always takes courage to speak out for God. When we open our mouths, He gives us the words.

Finally, Paul tells the believers that God has helped them fully understand the truth. Even though they have disagreements, they come to grips with the basics of what it means to have new life in Christ. For many, this is a reeducation of what they believed before.

When you belong to God, your life is encircled with His love. You are equipped with gifts to serve God and one another. Use those gifts today!

## *Affirmation:* **A Thinking and Watching God**

*Let him have all your worries and cares, for he is always thinking about you and watching everything that concerns you.*                    1 Peter 5:7 TLB

Vacation time is a time to leave all the worries and cares of everyday life behind for a few weeks. Yet, as you go away, you know everything will be there when you get back. Vacation doesn't eliminate your worries. It just files them away for a few weeks.

The only way that you and I get rid of worries permanently is to give them over to God. It is saying to your cares, "I dismiss you from my mind and give you over to the power of God." Then, it's going on with your life and not dredging those worries up again.

The reason Peter tells us to give our worries to God is that He is our caretaker. He is always thinking about us and watching over the things that concern us. You are not making a giant revelation to God when you tell Him about your worries. He already knows they are there because He is thinking way ahead of you.

Sometimes it is hard to believe that God is concerned about the same things we are concerned about. The difference is that we want to take action on them rather than trust the action to God and His wisdom.

The eye of God is focused on you right now. He knows what is going on with you. He is watching and thinking, and He will act if you will allow Him to.

Worry is wanting to own your problems. Trust is giving them over to God for action.

# *Affirmation:* **Today and Tomorrow**

*Your goodness and unfailing kindness shall be with me all of my life, and afterwards I will live with you forever in your home.*          Psalms 23:6 TLB

The Twenty-third Psalm contains more information about the total care of God for His people than any other six verses of Scripture in the Bible. As you read it, you sense God's direct love and involvement with His people. You are aware that He promises direct and complete care for those who belong to Him. It really is a love psalm.

David sums up God's care with words of affirmation for today and tomorrow. He says we will experience God's goodness and kindness throughout our entire lives. Notice that he does not say we will always feel it. He does say it will always be there. Many of us mistake feelings for promise. If we don't feel something, it must not be happening. God's affirmation of His goodness and kindness is enduring regardless of our feeling for it.

David's hope goes beyond this life. God's love and care takes us right into the next life, where we will live forever with God in His home.

You and I live in this world. We contend with its systems and hassles. We learn to be overcomers of its situations. We live surrounded by the knowledge that God is good and kind to us, and His gifts to us equip us to handle whatever comes our way. Our minds and lives are in the present, but our eyes are on the goal of a future in eternity with God.

Welcome here is God's affirmation. Welcome home is God's invitation!

# *Affirmation:* **God Makes Us Victorious**

*How we thank God for all of this! It is he who makes us victorious through Jesus Christ our Lord!*                                    1 Corinthians 15:57 TLB

Death is seldom looked upon as a victory. It is a defeat with a capital *D.* Every possible means is used to keep people from dying. In our world, death is the ultimate failure of life.

Paul wanted to raise the vision of the Early Christians beyond the range of physical death. He wanted them to know that the power of God had conquered death. He wanted their eyesight focused beyond the grave, with its limitations, to God's limitless future for the believer.

The seeds of promise were planted in the hearts of the Early Christians when Paul told them that Christ would one day return and release their bodies from the physical part of death. He did not want them to see death as the end of life. He wanted them to look beyond the grave to what God had promised and reserved for them.

I am not sure that they were as excited about the prospects of eternal life and the Second Coming of Christ as Paul was. If anything, they were probably skeptical. This was new truth that Paul was introducing. It would take some time to get used to.

After Paul had shared the promise of life after death, he gave thanks to God for making all of this possible. He sounded a trumpet of victory that still reverberates today. Perhaps this is why this Scripture is often read at memorial services. It says that death does not get the final victory because Christ has conquered death.

Thank God today that He has given us a victory over death!

## *Affirmation:* You Are My Hiding Place

*You are my hiding place from every storm of life; you even keep me from getting into trouble! You surround me with songs of victory.*   Psalms 32:7 TLB

Have you been caught in any of the storms of life lately? Has it rained on your parade in the past week? Yes! Yes! Yes!

The storms of life can range in intensity from overflowing sewers to broken automobile transmissions to losing a job to losing a friend by death. Their strength to overwhelm us depends upon how vulnerable we are at the time.

When the storms hit, it seems as though Murphy's Law takes over. It never rains a little—it rains a lot!

David got rained on. The storms of life beat on his very existence. He knew he could not stop the storms from coming, but he could find a place to seek refuge. He hid behind God!

Is God big enough to hide behind? Can He really protect you from life's storms? I believe He can. We are the ones who have to seek His refuge.

David said that God kept him from getting into trouble. If you look at David's life, you want to ask the question, "When?" Maybe David meant *more* trouble. He certainly spent some time in trouble up to his ears.

In a final note, David tells us that God surrounds him with songs of victory. Is it easy for you to hear the song of victory over the rumble of the storm of life? Which sounds are you listening to today? I pray that the notes of victory will come through to you!

## *Affirmation:* An Affirmation Out of the Deep

*"I will never worship anyone but you! For how can I thank you enough for all you have done? I will surely fulfill my promises. For my deliverance comes from the Lord alone."*
Jonah 2:9 TLB

Great promises and potent prayers are sometimes made in precarious places. Jonah found himself inside a great fish when he had his moment of reconciliation with God. He had backed himself into the corner of belief when he reestablished his relationship with God.

Sometimes it takes this kind of situation in our own lives to get back in touch with God. We choose our own directions and make our own decisions, and God allows us to back ourselves into a corner. When the light finally goes on in our hearts and minds, we realize that we are off the track and need to get back on it. It happens to all of us.

Jonah assures God that he will never worship anyone but Him. Then he wants to thank God for all He has done. I am not sure if his thanks include being swallowed by a fish. After worship and thanksgiving, Jonah tells God he will fulfill his promises. He said he would go to Nineveh, and now he is ready to go. Finally, he recognizes that the only way he will get out of his present situation is with God's help.

Jonah was caught in a squeeze of his own design. Yet, in the middle of it, he recognized he was wrong. His confession of his wrong led him into a new beginning.

I can just picture some people spotting Jonah on the way to Nineveh a few days later. They may have asked, "Where have you been recently?" I can just hear Jonah's answer: "You wouldn't believe it if I told you!"

Where have you been lately? Sidetracked? Away from God? Get back on the right road!

## *Affirmation:* My Strength and Song

*On that day you will say, "Praise the Lord! He was angry with me, but now he comforts me. See, God has come to save me! I will trust and not be afraid, for the Lord is my strength and song; he is my salvation."*
Isaiah 12:1, 2 TLB

Today's affirmation contains three things we express to the Lord and five things we receive from the Lord. That seems like a pretty fair exchange.

Our expression to God contains praise, trust, and the dismissal of fear. Praise is recognizing God for who He is. It is also an expression of thanks.

Trust is having the confidence that God will do what He says, based on His past record of dealing with us and with all mankind. An absence of fear is usually what happens when trust takes over in a life. There are many things to be afraid of, but God's love casts out fear.

God's response to us starts with His gift of comfort. God is literally saying, *It's all right. You are all right. I will take care of you.*

God also saves us, sometimes from ourselves, sometimes from the things in life that would bury us.

God is our strength, our song, and our salvation. In other words, there is absolutely nothing else I need if I have the Lord. He will give me the strength to live. He will put His song upon my lips, and I will find salvation in none other than the Lord.

Isaiah's words sum up the completeness of God to you and me. We express and He gives to us. There is nothing that God will not give to you today!

## *Affirmation:* **Stretching God**

> *Now glory be to God who by his mighty power at work within us is able to do far more than we would ever dare to ask or even dream of—infinitely beyond our highest prayers, desires, thoughts, or hopes.*       Ephesians 3:20 TLB

I was once asked the question, "What would you do if you knew that you could not fail?" I will have to admit that I had some pretty wild thoughts. How about you? What would you do?

When God is in your life, your potential is unlimited. We are only locked in by our own weakness, fear of failure, or lack of trust. It is sad that so many Christians are limited to small thinking. They must feel that their God is too small to do great things. This certainly is not the God of the Bible. He used simple people to do great things.

Paul presents a God with great potential to the Early Church. He tells those Early Christians that God can do things far beyond what they would ask for or even dream of. He says that God operates on a higher wavelength but that we can tap into that source of power if we choose. God is working within us, seeking to release His great power. We are the limiting factors, not God.

What great things would you like to see God doing in your life? Are you willing to give Him carte blanche to do those things? Are they things that would bring glory to you or to Him?

God loves to be stretched by our thinking and dreaming. He loves to do things that defy description and human explanation.

Start your list today. Set God free in your life!

## *Affirmation:* **Blessings Great and Small**

*But Jesus said, "Let the little children come to me, and don't prevent them. For of such is the Kingdom of Heaven." And he put his hands on their heads and blessed them before he left.*          Matthew 19:14, 15 TLB

Have you ever wanted to push the small, insignificant things out of your life and make way for the big, important things? We all have our own scale of priorities. We decide what should be looked at and what should be overlooked. Sometimes we make the wrong choices.

When the little children flocked to Jesus, the disciples became very rude and disturbed. They saw the children as insignificant distractions to the important ministry of Jesus. They wanted to decide for Jesus what was important and what was irrelevant. Jesus taught them a very valuable lesson that you and I are still learning today.

LET GOD DECIDE WHAT IS IMPORTANT AND WHAT IS IRRELEVANT!

How do you view distractions in your life? Have you ever considered the fact that God may have put some of them in your pathway? Jesus did not tell the children to come back later when He had more time. He took time for them and recognized their importance with a special blessing. They were small people who received a giant blessing.

Small children can easily be swept from our pathways. Small problems can quickly be dismissed from our view. Take a few minutes and look at the collection of the insignificant things in your life. Perhaps you should hug a few of those things to yourself, and bless God for sending them your way today!

## *Affirmation:* **You Are Declared the Winner**

*Dear young friends, you belong to God and have already won your fight with those who are against Christ, because there is someone in your hearts who is stronger than any evil teacher in this wicked world.*          1 John 4:4 TLB

Thirty-five years after Japan signed a peace treaty with the United States, a Japanese soldier was discovered hiding on an island in the South Pacific. When he was told the war was over, he could not believe it. In his mind, and in his life, the war was still raging. Thirty-five years is a long time to invest in a battle that had already been won.

John tells us that those who belong to God have already won the battle with those who are against Christ. That may be hard for you to believe if you are still fighting the battle. We keep coming at the world with our arms flailing and our fists clenched. What would happen if we just folded our arms and said, "Thank You, Lord, for the victory You have already given"?

The battle is over because Christ lives in us. His strength is greater than that of any false teacher. Jesus knew that He had already won the battle over Satan when the forces of His time beat upon Him. That is why He spoke these words of assurance and peace to those around Him. Even His disciples were still fighting their windmills of war. Jesus was out of the battle because He had won and He knew it.

Are you fighting some battles that are already over? You belong to God today. You have already won!

## *Affirmation:* **A Changed Heart**

*"I will give you one heart and a new spirit; I will take from you your hearts of stone and give you tender hearts of love for God, so that you can obey my laws and be my people, and I will be your God."*                    Ezekiel 11:19, 20 TLB

God is in the business of making changes in people. He never leaves anyone the same way He finds him. When we come away from an encounter with God, we are different.

Today's affirmation speaks of God's ability to change hearts of stone into hearts of love. I can almost visualize God chipping away with a hammer and chisel at the hardness of heart in me. I can feel the pain of little chips of stone being replaced by little pockets of love. I desire the change, but I want to avoid the pain that goes along with it.

Israel fought a war of the heart with God. They were cold to God, then they thawed out and responded to Him. Then they forgot the warmth of the thaw and became colder than ever. Kings, prophets, messengers from God, all struggled with the hardness of their hearts.

Very little has changed over the years. God still desires a yielded life and a tender heart from you and me. He desires that we follow Him and be His people. He promises to be our God. Is that enough, or has God left something out?

A recurring theme in the writings of Paul to the Early Church was that they be of one heart and one spirit. He knew that this was the only way they would have unity and purpose. It is still the only way.

Will your prayer today be for a tender heart toward God and what He desires for your life?

# *Affirmation:* **Peace, No Matter What**

> *May the Lord of peace himself give you his peace no matter what happens.*
> *The Lord be with you all.*                              2 Thessalonians 3:16 TLB

I have always admired a person who can keep his calm and composure in tense and emotional situations. I think if I had one prayer left to direct to God, it would be that I would be able to be peaceful in any and all situations that life throws at me. Few of us seem to possess that quality. We are far more explosive than peaceful. Our frayed ends tangle easily with the disturbers of our peace.

What is the difference between our peace and God's peace? Ours is usually conditional, while God's is supernatural. Ours is influenced by situations, while God's peace defies circumstances.

Paul identifies the Lord as the source of peace. He *is* peace. He doesn't have to conjure it up. He asks that the Christians at Thessalonica be recipients of the peace of the Lord, no matter what happens.

No matter what happens—that's a big order. Who knows what can happen? Is God's peace in my life able to fill the big holes when needed—when my children disappoint me—when my friends fail me—when prayer goes unanswered—when I lose my job? It will take a big God with a big load of peace to fill those holes.

God is able. We have peace when we ask for it. It is a gift from God that neutralizes the pressures of life. It is also the confidence of knowing that God is in control.

The Lord be with you today, and may your journey be peaceful!

# *Affirmation:* **A Message From God**

> *Then he said, "This is God's message to Zerubbabel: 'Not by might, nor by*
> *power, but by my Spirit, says the Lord of Hosts—you will succeed because of*
> *my Spirit, though you are few and weak.'"*                    Zechariah 4:6 TLB

Have you talked to an angel lately? If you have, be careful whom you tell. Your sanity might be in question.

Zerubbabel spoke with an angel. The angel's message had to do with the way God gets things done. In reading the words in today's affirmation, we can readily see that God operates differently from the way you and I do.

You and I go about life trying to get our tasks done by our might and power. We work pretty hard some days, and feel drained when evening comes. Our tired muscles and minds tell us it has been a long day.

There is nothing wrong with hard work. What God wants us to understand is that our efforts have to come under the umbrella of the Holy Spirit. It is God's Spirit working through us that really gets the job done properly. Our own strength has limitations. God's power is unlimited.

We all hear stories of self-made men. They started with nothing or little, and made successes of themselves. There are no self-made Christians. If the Holy Spirit does not move through our lives and efforts, the end product will be a giant disappointment.

Sometimes our own efforts are weak. We will succeed because of God's Spirit working in us. Forget your might and power today. Let the Spirit loose in your life!

## *Affirmation:* **Good Steps**

*The steps of good men are directed by the Lord. He delights in each step they take. If they fall it isn't fatal, for the Lord holds them with his hand.*

Psalms 37:23, 24 TLB

This is one of my favorite verses in Scripture. The reason I like it so much is that it makes allowances for my humanity. It sets a standard and a direction for my Christian walk, but it also tells me what will happen if I fall off the walkway.

I meet many people in my travels who have fallen by the wayside of life. They have done some things they are very sorry for, and they still feel remorse and guilt over them. Their wrong steps have led them to believe that they can no longer continue under the direction of the Lord.

David tells us that falling isn't fatal to one's spiritual health. Sometimes it might even help us grow and get stronger. David knew what he was talking about because he took a big fall. He knew the steps of his life were ordered by the Lord, but he took some of his own, and paid the price.

As a young father, I remember reaching out to catch my children when they were just learning to walk. As they fell into my arms, I did not scold them and refuse to let them try walking again. I stood them up and encouraged them to keep trying.

God does the very same thing to you and me. We all fall and stumble around. God reaches out to us with His hands of love and puts us back on the right pathway. He keeps on directing our steps, one day at a time.

God delights in helping us learn to walk! It is a lifetime process!

## *Affirmation:* A Confidence in God

> *But when I am afraid, I will put my confidence in you. Yes, I will trust the promises of God. And since I am trusting him, what can mere man do to me?*
>
> Psalms 56:3, 4 TLB

Where do you put your confidence when you are afraid? Are you ever afraid? I am! Sometimes my fears blot out any trace of confidence I have in anything.

Building confidence is a slow process, whether in people, things, or God. Confidence doesn't come in bunches. It seems to come in gentle wisps. About the time you feel you have a little, it vanishes.

People who look confident aren't always confident. Outward composure doesn't always cover inner exposure. Most of us could use a little more confidence from time to time.

David learned to turn his fears into confident trust in God. He knew that his security for his trust and confidence was found in believing the promises of God.

In a dash of bravery, David asks what man can do to him if his trust is in the Lord. The answer is *nothing!*

What can anyone do to you if you are really trusting in the Lord? Nothing! You can fear what you *think* they can do, but they really can do nothing.

David was a fear squelcher. As he grew strong in trusting God, he encouraged others to do the same.

Go out your door today with these words in your mind: *I've got confidence. God will see me through this day and all my days!*

## *Affirmation:* How God Shields Us

> *What a God he is! How perfect in every way! All his promises prove true. He is a shield for everyone who hides behind him. For who is God except our Lord? Who but he is as a rock?*
>
> Psalms 18:30 TLB

Have you ever run out of superlatives when describing your best friend to someone? You want that person to know how you feel about your friend and what he means to you. David felt that way about God. Although he had his struggles with God, he still affirmed Him to others.

David tells us in this verse that God is five different things. As we look at them, ask yourself if you could describe God to your friends in these terms.

First, God is perfect in every way. That is difficult for us to grasp because our world is filled with imperfections. It is hard to visualize something that is perfect. David says that God has no flaws.

Second, we are told that God stands behind His promises. They are true. When God says something, He does it. Since so many people around us renege on their promises, it may be hard for us to believe God keeps all of His.

Third, God provides a shield for us to hide behind. When the world throws its heavy artillery at us, we need to shield ourselves while we regroup. God provides a secure hiding place for us when we need it.

Fourth, He is our Lord. That's personal, not general. We belong to Him and He belongs to us.

Finally, He is a rock. For me, that represents stability. He doesn't change game plans and agenda from day to day. He is solid and He is there for me—today and tomorrow!

## *Affirmation:* **The Strength of the Word**

*Does not my word burn like fire? asks the Lord. Is it not like a mighty hammer that smashed the rock to pieces?*                    Jeremiah 23:29 TLB

Have you ever read something that burned its message right into your heart? You felt it was written just for you. Sometimes you welcomed the message because it brought healing. Another time, you fought it off because it convicted, stung, and burned right into your soul.

I have had both of these reactions in reading the Scriptures for this devotional journey. What I have concluded is summed up by the Prophet Jeremiah: the Scriptures are both fire and hammer in our lives.

Jeremiah was caught between two worlds when he spoke these words. On one hand, many people were spouting words that they claimed came from God. People were following them, and their teachings caused great confusion. On the other hand, Jeremiah was trying to make known God's real message. His words for today are to help us discern truth from error.

The Word of God will always have a burning effect on our lives. It has a way of cutting through the irrelevancies of life and getting to the core of our problems. We have to be willing to expose ourselves to that Word from God and let the fire do its work. Sometimes that fire has to burn through a lot of garbage before it can do us any good.

A second effect of the Scriptures upon our lives is that of a mighty hammer. The Word often smashes through the walls of resistance and untruth that we have built up over the years. Resistance turned to rubble by the hammer of God's Word will help us build the proper fortification for our lives.

God's Word is strong stuff! Let it work in your life today.

## *Affirmation:* **The Truth in the Word**

*Every word of God proves true. He defends all who come to him for protection.* Proverbs 30:5 TLB

Every parent secretly waits for the day when a son or daughter will come home and utter the words, "Dad, Mom, you were right!" All of the training and advising seems to spill out on deaf ears until that moment of sudden absorption when the words are really heard and acknowledged. We desperately want our words of wisdom to prove to be true in our children's lives. It is not our desire to be proved right. It is our desire to be known as loving to our children.

Allowing the words of God to prove true in our lives is a little tougher than those directed at our children. It may take years of trusting God in certain areas for us to be able to say, "The Word of God has proved itself." We tend to demand immediate results. God seems to be more designed for the long haul. He is not too impressed with instant anything.

One of the ways God's Word proves true in our lives is when we trust Him to be our defender and protector.

Have you felt as if you could use a little defense and protection in your life lately? We spend a lot of time and energy trying to do this for ourselves. We defend ourselves, others, and even God at times. We come to believe that the best protection is a good defense.

God is my defender and protector today. I can prove that His Word is true by allowing Him to be that in my life.

The best defense is always God's! The best protection is to be surrounded by His Word.

## *Affirmation:* **Just Do What You Are Told**

*Again I say, we are telling you about what we ourselves have actually seen and heard, so that you may share the fellowship and the joys we have with the Father and with Jesus Christ his Son. And if you do as I say in this letter, then you, too, will be full of joy, and so will we.* 1 John 1:3, 4 TLB

How many times have you said the words, "Do what I have told you"? We say it most frequently to our children and to those who work under us in our jobs. The implication seems to be that everything will work out if you follow the instructions someone is issuing to you. We have all learned by experience that this is not always true in the human sense.

Is it true in the spiritual sense?

John's witness to the power of Christ is much like Paul's before King Agrippa. John says, "Do as I tell you because I have actually seen and heard the truth and witnessed its effects." He does not give instructions for his own purpose or to prove he knows the inside story.

John's instructions are followed by an invitation to share in fellowship and joy. These are the benefits of following Christ. John invites others to share what he is already experiencing.

Have you invited anyone to share the joy of Christ lately? We often approach people with a "turn or burn" mentality. This is certainly not a loving invitation.

John says, "Come share the joy!" He and his followers are enjoying it and they want others to receive the same benefits.

When people find Christ, we are happy and they are happy. Faith always has reciprocal benefits!

## *Affirmation:* **Singed But Not Burned**

> *When you go through deep waters and great trouble, I will be with you. When you go through rivers of difficulty, you will not drown! When you walk through the fire of oppression, you will not be burned up—the flames will not consume you. For I am the Lord your God....* Isaiah 43:2, 3 TLB

Here's a depressing lineup of problems: deep waters, great trouble, rivers of difficulty, fires of oppression. Does that sound like just one day of your week? One hour of your day? Or perhaps that was last week, and this week you are still wearing the bandages?

It seems to me that blessings come one at a time, while struggles come in great bunches. Isaiah certainly puts a bunch together and doesn't leave anything out. If you read carefully, though, you will not be drawn to the problems and adversities, but you will notice the affirmations of God behind them.

*I will be with you! You will not drown! You will not be burned up! You will not be consumed!*

Write those things in big letters on the blackboard of your life. Isaiah promises us two things: we will have troubles, but we will also have answers! It is easier to see the troubles than the solutions. Troubles distract us and cause self-pity and ultimately depression. Solutions bring joy and celebration.

Which side of the fence are you living on today? Are you living on the problem side or the solution side? You choose your own place.

We will all be singed as we go through the fires in our lives, but God's promise is that we will not be burned up.

## *Affirmation:* **How to Be a Happy Man**

*Happy is the man who doesn't give in and do wrong when he is tempted, for afterwards he will get as his reward the crown of life that God has promised those who love him.*                                      James 1:12 TLB

Have you ever felt like giving in to temptation? Don't try to be pious. Be truthful. All of us have had the thought of giving in to something that presents itself in the form of a temptation. Sincere Christians have no problem with big temptations such as robbing a bank, stealing a Cadillac, or shooting a troublesome relative. We wouldn't ever do something like that. Where we run the gauntlet is through the minority sins such as gossip, jealousy, pride, lying (small lies), and temper tantrums. We should probably add gluttony to the list, too, since eating has become a national Christian pastime.

The Scripture never itemizes temptations. It simply directs us not to give in to *any* temptation, whether large or small in our eyes.

If you want to have a fun day sometime, keep a running list of all the temptations that come your way. Put down the ones you yield to and the ones you resist. Then grade yourself at the end of the day. There is no big earthly reward for resisting temptation, unless it is having peace of mind. Today's affirmation tells us that we will receive the crown of life because our love for God has been affirmed by resisting temptation.

Do you want to be a happier man (woman) today? Slide by the temptations and watch your smile widen with each victory. You will be happier here, and wear a crown up there!

## *Affirmation:* **Pray for Us**

*Finally, dear brothers, as I come to the end of this letter I ask you to pray for us. Pray first that the Lord's message will spread rapidly and triumph wherever it goes, winning converts everywhere as it did when it came to you.*
2 Thessalonians 3:1 TLB

How many people have prayed for you in your lifetime—hundreds, thousands, a handful? It is a warm, loving experience to have people pray for us. Some volunteer to do it when they know we are struggling with something. Sometimes we have to ask people to pray for us when they are not aware of our needs. Many of us try to keep our needs to ourselves, and thus rob others of the joy of praying for us.

Paul was never afraid to ask for prayer. His letters to the Early Church were peppered with requests for prayer. Paul was not the lone ranger of prayer. He openly shared his needs and concerns with others.

As he winds up his letter to the Thessalonian Christians, he specifies what he wants them to pray for. He first says, "Pray for us." We are not sure how many people were included in "us," but Paul was not in the battle for God alone. As he gets more specific, he asks the Early Christians to pray that the Lord's message will spread rapidly, triumph everywhere, and win many new converts. His request was an evangelism special! He wanted others to share what these dear friends of his now enjoyed.

I need God's people praying for me. So do you. We both need to pray that God will use us today to spread His message wherever we go.

## *Affirmation:* **Never Forsaken**

*For if my father and mother should abandon me, you would welcome and comfort me.* Psalms 27:10 TLB

I periodically meet people who do not know who their parents were. Some were raised in orphanages and court homes. They have known surrogate parents all their lives. Some of these parents have been good to them, while others have not. As they get older, many spend years searching for their real parents. A few find them, while many do not.

Being given up for adoption as an infant is never easy to live with as one grows older. There is often anger, misunderstanding, a desire to know why, a need to get even. Giving a child away often sends the lifetime message, "I did not love you!"

The greatest love in the world is God's love for you and me. Close behind it is the love of parents for their children, and children for their parents. It is never an easy love. It goes through a lot of barbed wire as it moves down the pathway of life. Many times it is broken, and many times it is repaired.

David needed to affirm God's love for himself. He wanted to be sure that one love in his life would remain intact, regardless of what he did or who he was.

I pray that you still know and feel the love of your parents. If that relationship is in any way broken, think and pray about mending it today. You will always have God's love. I believe that you will be a richer person if you have both!

## *Affirmation:* **Saved by the Bell**

*We are hunted down, but God never abandons us. We get knocked down, but we get up again and keep going.* 2 Corinthians 4:9 TLB

I was watching a boxing match on television. One of the contestants was taking a tremendous beating. All of a sudden, he hit the canvas. The referee started the count and when he hit eight, the bell rang to end the round. The television commentator exclaimed, "Saved by the bell!" He was, but it didn't matter because the fighter was knocked out cold a minute into the next round.

I have been saved by the bell of God a few hundred times in my life. You probably have, too. We go through a day when it seems as though everyone is punching at us. By the time the day is over, we are hanging on to the ropes for dear life. God rings the bell for us just in time, and we get a chance to catch our breath and clear our eyes. I even get the feeling that God sits us down in the corner once in a while and goes a few rounds for us.

Paul tells the church folk at Corinth that they will be hunted down many times, but they will not be abandoned by God. They will be knocked down, but they will have the power to get up and get going again. You will notice that Paul says, "we." He places himself in the same boat with them. He never talks about the battle from the mountaintop. He lived in the valley with all the other strugglers.

You may feel that you have gone through a struggle recently. Remember that God gives the strength to go on when you would rather collapse. He can save you by the bell!

## *Affirmation:* **The Promise of Returning**

*"For if you turn to the Lord again, your brothers and your children will be treated mercifully by their captors, and they will be able to return to this land. For the Lord your God is full of kindness and mercy and will not continue to turn away his face from you if you return to him."* 2 Chronicles 30:9 TLB

Israel seemed to have a habit of showing God its back. The people were always headed in the opposite direction from the one God wanted them to travel. There was always a plea to turn back to the Lord, accompanied by the promise of what God would do for them if they did.

You and I are not unlike Israel. We get started each day in the right direction with God and then, somehow, we get turned around and headed in the opposite direction. If you are a sensitive and growing Christian, it is usually not hard to right yourself and correct your course. Going the wrong way is very obvious to someone who knows how to go the right way.

What happens when you fail to make that course correction and you spend many days, months, or even years headed the wrong way? Is God still willing to take you back and restore you?

I meet many people who confess to years of wandering away from God. They ask me if God will still take them back. I am quick to answer *yes!*

God established a forgiveness pattern with Israel that is still in operation today. Whether you are gone from God for one hour, one month, one year, or almost an entire lifetime, He still stands ready to take you back.

Kindness and mercy are dispensed to all who return to the Lord. Check your life today. Have you been gone awhile?

## *Affirmation:* Surrounded by His Presence

*"Be strong! Be courageous! Do not be afraid of them! For the Lord your God will be with you. He will neither fail you nor forsake you."*
                                                    Deuteronomy 31:6 TLB

When was the last time someone shared strong words of encouragement with you? Perhaps you were in the midst of a great personal conflict when a friend made your day by sharing words of hope and promise with you. We all need a strong circle of friends around us who will minister to us with words of affirmation and hope.

Joshua was receiving the mantle of leadership from Moses. I am sure it was an awesome moment for Joshua. He probably wondered how he could ever measure up to the record of Moses. It could have been a time of great discouragement for him, but Moses made his day.

I want to reverse the order of priorities in today's verse. Because God is with you and will not fail nor forsake you, you can be strong and courageous and dismiss all fear. If God were not with you, you could not claim His strength. Joshua was aware of Moses' record with God, and God's record with Moses. His assuming leadership was based in part on that history. Moses summed up his many years with God in these few lines.

Because God was with Moses, He would be with Joshua. Because He equipped Moses, He would equip Joshua.

Few of us are strong, courageous, and fearless on our own. We not only need the words of encouragement from others but we also need to rely on what God has done through His servants in the past, and realize that He will still do those things today.

How are you facing today—with an uneasiness and fear, or with the strength of the Lord in your head and heart? Trust in God today. He will not fail you!

## *Affirmation:* **God Is Alive**

*God is alive! Praise him who is the great rock of protection.*

Psalms 18:46 TLB

Do you remember when the front page of *Time* magazine informed us that God was dead? I do. At first it was a shocking exclamation. It was an affront to all that I believed. After the initial shock, I realized that *Time* was not powerful enough to bury God. Nor were the many theologians who supported this theory. It sold lots of magazines, but God refused to play dead.

God must have had one great laugh over that headline. He may have turned to Peter and said, *We'll see about that!*

When was the last time you pronounced God dead—last week, yesterday, or a few moments ago? What made you feel that way?

When the tide of life seems to be headed toward us rather than away from us, it is easy to feel as though we have been deserted by God. The Scriptures carry numerous accounts of people who felt God had deserted them. Many of them started their own self-pity clubs. They felt betrayed, disillusioned, and hopeless.

We want constant reassurance that God is around and operative in our lives. We look for signs of His life in us.

It is easy to believe in God when He is moving mountains in our lives. What about the silent, quiet times when nothing is moving? Those are the hard times when we have to claim the promise that God is alive but is silent, like a rock. That rock protects us but utters no sound.

God is not dead. He is alive and working quietly in your life today!

## *Affirmation:* The Revealer of Mysteries

*"He reveals profound mysteries beyond man's understanding. He knows all
hidden things, for he is light, and darkness is no obstacle to him."*
                                                    Daniel 2:22 TLB

Daniel was in close touch with God. He had to be in order to know the
dream that God had planted in King Nebuchadnezzar's mind. Everyone
else had failed to tell the king what his dream was. Only Daniel had the
wisdom to ask God what the dream was so he could share the interpreta-
tion with the King.

In asking God for His wisdom, Daniel shared his own affirmation of
God's abilities. He acknowledged that God is powerful enough to reveal
things that are far beyond man's understanding. If Daniel had not believed that, it would have been impossible for him to know and interpret
the king's dream. The impossible task that Daniel faced could not be
solved with human wisdom.

How many times have you faced a situation that defied a human answer? Many times! How often have you tried to apply a human answer to
a situation that could only be resolved by a divine answer? Many more!

The supernatural is often just around the corner from the human in
each of us. The flow of life would be smoother for us if we would only
recognize the things beyond our control and invite God to supply His
answer.

Daniel's success was not based upon his human wisdom. It was based
upon his willingness to tap into the mysteries of God. He did it naturally
and with confidence.

When human answers fail, try taking your struggles to the Revealer of
mysteries for the answer!

## *Affirmation:* This Is Your Kingdom

*"Yours is the mighty power and glory and victory and majesty. Everything in
the heavens and earth is yours, O Lord, and this is your kingdom. We adore
you as being in control of everything."*          1 Chronicles 29:11 TLB

The first words a child often speaks are *mama* or *dada.* Close behind
these two very important words comes the word *mine.* I have seen little
children grab their toys when someone else tries to pick them up, and
yell, "Mine!" at the top of their lungs. Somehow, we never forget that
possessive word. We carry it all through life and keep adding things to the
list of what is "mine."

King David had just collected more than $280 million worth of pledged support for the building of the temple. He could have stood back and felt a sense of great pride in his accomplishment. His attitude could have been, "Look at what we have done with our wealth."

David knew where his wealth came from. None of it was really his at all, and he knew it. This knowledge prompted him to affirm the Source of everything we all have. He simply said, "Lord, it is really all Yours, and we are just the caretakers."

A wise man once said, "God always knows whom He can trust with money." I sometimes think that God may not trust me as much as I wish He would.

Who's in charge of what you have? You are probably thinking, *I don't have enough to worry about.* Then who is in charge of the little you *do* have?

You will live easier if you know that everything you have is from the Lord, and He is in control of everything.

## *Affirmation:* **Now That's Status**

*And yet you have made him only a little lower than the angels, and placed a crown of glory and honor upon his head.* Psalms 8:5 TLB

Have you ever had a feeling of insignificance in a certain situation? You attend a banquet and merely fill up one of the chairs at a table. You secretly wish you were at the head table and would be introduced as being someone special. You watch others receiving the VIP treatment and find yourself a little envious.

God strikes an odd balance with mankind from time to time. In one place, Scripture tells us how important we are and how significant in God's creative plan we can become. In other places, Scripture appears to tell us not to take ourselves too seriously.

David attempts to place us in the proper perspective by stating that we are only a little bit lower on the ladder than angels, but God has placed a crown of glory and honor upon our heads. I don't know a lot about angels, but I do know a little about glory and honor. Glory and honor are the result of hard work and faithful living. They are not dispensed to those who don't earn them.

We receive a crown from God when we are faithful to our calling as His people. The crown is not cheap and it is not free. It does not isolate us from others but identifies us as belonging to God.

How are you doing in wearing His crown?

## *Affirmation:* **What Do You Deserve?**

> *He is merciful and tender toward those who don't deserve it; he is slow to get*
> *angry and full of kindness and love.*                     Psalms 103:8 TLB

What's the greatest compliment that someone could pay you? How would you like someone to describe you? We all have our lists and they would be very long. We also know that some people would not say the nicest and kindest things about us.

Today's affirmation is David's compliment to God. How I wish someone could say to me what David said. I would like to be merciful and tender to those who deserve a punch in the nose. I would like to be slow to get angry. In fact, I would like not to get angry at all! I would like to be full of kindness and love for everyone I meet, in all kinds of situations. Dream on!

My only hope of even coming close to seeing some of these things as a reality in my life is to know that they are attributes of God and they can become a part of my life by the Christian growth process.

It is like intravenous feeding in the hospital. You only get the nourishment you need, a drip at a time. It is a slow process, but if you stay connected, you will become stronger.

I can never have these attributes in my life by human willpower or self-motivation. They can come only as a result of the Spirit of God loosing them each day in my life.

We certainly don't deserve God's mercy and tenderness, but He gives them to us anyhow. Those who use us wrongly don't deserve it, but through His love, we can share it with them.

When we are filled with His love and kindness, our potential anger becomes easier to control.

God gives us the good things we may not deserve. They are given so that we can give them to others!

## *Affirmation:* **Real Love**

> *In this act we see what real love is: it is not our love for God, but his love for us*
> *when he sent his Son to satisfy God's anger against our sins.*
>                                                      1 John 4:10 TLB

Love is like a diamond. It needs to be on display to be appreciated. God's love for you and me was put on display when His Son was sent into this world to bring us eternal life and forgiveness for our sins. God could have talked about love, He could have dreamed about love, He could have thought about love. He took affirmative action and demonstrated His love for us.

John tries to verify several important things about love to us. First, he says that the source of love is not our love for God but His love for us. He is the root and source of love. It cannot be conjured up from somewhere else. It cannot be imitated or fabricated. Its origin rests in God.

Second, love is reciprocal. It is only as we receive God's love for us that we can send it back to Him and share it with others.

Love is like an elastic band. The more you stretch it, the more resilient it becomes.

Third, love is atonement. Man had sinned. That is biblical and human history. He deserved condemnation and isolation from God. God is not easily deterred by man's actions. Man's sin had to be dealt with and ultimately was, through Christ's death on the cross. The penalty for sin was paid. Love became the result.

Love is a gift from God to you and me. It is a gift to be passed on to others. Look for a way to demonstrate God's real love in your life today.

## *Affirmation:* Listen to Him

> *Samuel replied, "Has the Lord as much pleasure in your burnt offerings and sacrifices as in your obedience? Obedience is far better than sacrifice. He is much more interested in your listening to him than in your offering the fat of rams to him."* 1 Samuel 15:22 TLB

Why are we always trying to give things to God that He doesn't want? We have a list of things we think God is interested in that we keep trying to push in His direction. We try to make little deals with God, as though He is a friendly local businessman with a corner store. "I will give You two of these, Lord, and I will take one of those!"

Saul was arguing with God through the person of Samuel in today's Scripture. Saul seemed to think God was interested in offerings and the spoils of victory. Samuel was trying to tell him that he was focused on the wrong list. God wasn't that concerned with burnt offerings and sacrifices. God wanted a very rare thing: obedience.

Obedience starts with listening. It is always lost in a sea of words. I think we sometimes try to impress God with our vocabulary. Through our blizzard of words, He is trying to get us to listen to what *He* wants to say, not what we are saying.

The secret to getting good directions is to listen. This is why the Scripture tells us to be still and know who God is.

How much listening have you done lately? Are you bartering and bargaining with God over different things in your life?

Tune up your heart for a listening session today. You may be amazed at what God will say to you!

## *Affirmation:* **The Rain of Forgiveness**

> *"Rejoice, O people of Jerusalem, rejoice in the Lord your God! For the rains he sends are tokens of forgiveness. Once more the autumn rains will come, as well as those of spring."*                                    Joel 2:23 TLB

Have you ever found yourself at a barren time of your life? The blessings that you had once experienced appear to have dried up.

There will be many dry spells in the Christian life. God often has special lessons in growth that we are to learn during those times. God's promise of the dry times is that they will end. They are not intended to do us in, but to help us trust God even more.

Joel's prophecy came to Israel during a dry time. They were questioning their own future. Joel told them to rejoice even before God sent the rain of blessing upon them. It is easy to rejoice after a blessing. It is more difficult to rejoice prior to one.

In Israel's case, the rains were to be a token of God's forgiveness upon their lives. Rain has many symbolisms. It forgives drought, barrenness, famine, heat. Rain is forgiving in a life-enhancing way. Joel assured Israel that this would be no little shower but the long rains of spring and autumn. Spring rains prepare the way for a good harvest in the fall. Fall rains put life back into the soil after the harvest.

God's message to us is that we will not be left alone to shrivel up and blow away during the times of spiritual drought in our lives. His rain will come upon us in a refreshing way when we need it.

Can you rejoice in the dry times that you might be going through right now? If these are times of great blessing for you, soak them up and remember them when the blessings seem to be few and far between.

# *Affirmation:* A New Joy

> *Then he saved us—not because we were good enough to be saved, but because of his kindness and pity—by washing away our sins and giving us the new joy of the indwelling Holy Spirit whom he poured out upon us with wonderful fullness—and all because of what Jesus Christ our Savior did.*
>
> Titus 3:5, 6 TLB

Have you ever heard the expression, "I've been taken to the cleaners"? It usually means that someone has taken very undue advantage of you in some way. In modern terms, you have been ripped off. It's not a very pleasant experience.

Titus tells us that when God gets hold of our lives, we are literally taken to the cleaners. God has washed away the sin from our lives through His heavenly detergents—kindness and pity. He has infused us with the Holy Spirit. Titus says He has poured the Spirit into our lives in full measure. That's a real cleaning experience.

Has God done that for you? If He has, thank Him right now!

There is a second step to the cleaning process. One laundering in God's process brings us into the family of God. We call it conversion. But everything doesn't end there. It starts there. Around our house, it seems as though we are always washing clothes. Day by day, week by week, the washing machine keeps running. It keeps producing clean clothes.

Once we are born into the family of God, we need constant renewing and washing, just as our dirty clothes do. The process never ends. Just as there are always loads of wash waiting by our machines, so you and I stand by God for that daily cleansing we need to keep us going.

God really is in the cleaning business. His indwelling Holy Spirit is the strongest cleaning solvent I know!

# *Affirmation:* Keeping the Glory

> *Since we know that this new glory will never go away, we can preach with great boldness.*
>
> 2 Corinthians 3:12 TLB

As a child in my home church, I remember a man who always prayed that God would give him "holy boldness." I always wondered what this holy boldness was, why he needed it, and why he never received it. Years later, I think I know what he was asking for.

We often share Christ with others in an apologetic way. When asked what we believe and why, it is easier to reply with the lines, "Well, my church teaches. . . ." It's difficult to have that quality of holy boldness that allows us to say, "I believe. . . ."

I have discovered a few things that holy boldness is not. It is not yelling at someone with the good news of the Gospel. I have heard preachers yell and scream at the top of their lungs. That's not being bold, it's being loud. Holy boldness is not trying to jam the good news of God down someone's throat. It is not trying to get people to parrot back answers to your questions so that you can add another notch to your belt.

Holy boldness is having a quiet confidence that God will empower you to speak His words in any and all situations where you have an opportunity. It is speaking those words lovingly and gently. It is taking a risk that you might be misunderstood, but knowing that God can use even that.

What God has placed in your life will never go away. What has happened to you can be shared with others today. May God give you the right kind of boldness that will not be offensive to others. His boldness is always seasoned with love!

## *Affirmation:* **A Prayer**

*Pray for me, too, and ask God to give me the right words as I boldly tell others about the Lord, and as I explain to them that his salvation is for the Gentiles too.*                                    Ephesians 6:19 TLB

How many times have you wished you had the right words to fit a situation? If you are like me, you would say about fifty times a day, at least. Some days, it seems that every time my mouth flies open, my foot gets lodged in it. I have discovered that it is hard to eat your words once you have spoken them.

Paul's prayer has become mine and yours many times. We need God to give us the right words in all the situations we face in life. We need the right words for those we have offended; for those who have offended us. We need loving words for those around us who are hurting and are misunderstood. We need words of wisdom for those who have questions that need answers.

I need the right words as I write this book. How gratifying it is to have a person come up to me and point to words that I have written and say, "I'm glad you said that. It was exactly what I needed to hear."

Paul had a lot to say, but he never lost his concern that his words be words from God. He was so careful in wanting to make the Gospel real and understandable to the Gentiles. Even in prison, he wanted his guards to hear from God through his words.

We will never say all the right things at the right times. More than a few times we will have to apologize for saying the wrong things. God's word to us today is to ask Him for the words we need in all situations. You will probably find yourself short on the right words sometime during this day. Ask God for them!

## *Affirmation:* **A Prayer for Peace**

> *Here are my directions: Pray much for others; plead for God's mercy upon them; give thanks for all he is going to do for them. Pray in this way for kings and all others who are in authority over us, or are in places of high responsibility, so that we can live in peace and quietness, spending our time in godly living and thinking much about the Lord.*                1 Timothy 2:1, 2 TLB

This past Sunday, over eighty thousand people crowded into a football stadium here in Los Angeles to demonstrate against the threat of nuclear war. Their primary concern was that the world should be a peaceful place to live in. Why? Well, for many, so that they could pursue whatever lifestyle they wanted without interruption. For some people, peace is to be used for self-indulgence.

How different from the peace that Timothy tells us to seek. He says that living in peace and quietness will give us the time to pursue godly living and to think about the Lord. I doubt that few people at the rally had this goal at the end of their quest for world peace.

Timothy urges us to pray for others, ask God to be merciful to them, and to give thanks for all He is going to do for them. We are instructed to direct this prayer to those who rule over us: the authorities, the government, the world rulers. The end result of this prayer for our rulers is that we might live in peace.

The Early Christians knew very little about peace, but it did not stop Paul or Timothy from telling them to pursue it.

What would you do with a bushel of peace today? Would you use it for yourself or for the glory of God? I pray that God will give you a portion of peace and quietness today to invest in living for Him.

## *Affirmation:* **An Act of Humility**

> *"And since I, the Lord and Teacher, have washed your feet, you ought to wash each other's feet. I have given you an example to follow: do as I have done to you."*                                    John 13:14, 15 TLB

Feet are definitely not the most beautiful part of the human anatomy. Because we keep them inside shoes and socks most of the time, we don't worry a lot about how they look. One of the most unglorious tasks that

Jesus performed for the disciples was washing their feet. They put up quite a fuss when Jesus brought out the pan and towel. Peter was outraged and told Jesus he would not allow his feet to be washed. Jesus' reply was, "If I don't, you can't be My partner."

What was Jesus trying to communicate through the foot-washing ceremony? It was a common custom in that day to wash the feet of those coming into your home. The roads were dry and dusty or wet and muddy. Sandals were the attire of the day, and dirty feet the result. Servants usually did the washing. What was Jesus trying to prove?

His clear message was that we are all servants to one another. There is no one too good to not perform an act of servanthood. There is to be an equal sharing in the joys and the sorrows, the highs and the lows, the serving and the being served.

How long has it been since you found yourself in the role of servant? How did you feel? Could you rejoice in the opportunity, or did you mumble and complain and try to escape it?

It is never easy to be a servant. Washing feet is not a fun pastime. Remember, you are always at your greatest when you are a servant to someone else!

## *Affirmation:* **Love Is a Building Block**

> *Next is your question about eating food that has been sacrificed to idols. On this question everyone feels that only his answer is the right one! But although being a "know-it-all" makes us feel important, what is really needed to build the church is love.*                                    1 Corinthians 8:1 TLB

The Early Church was full of questions and overfull of controversy. Paul seemed to spend much of his time putting out the fires of dissension. When the question of eating food that had been offered to idols came up, Paul used the opportunity to set the believers straight on what was really important and what was irrelevant.

Have you ever gotten caught in the war of the relevant versus the irrelevant? Why is it that the unimportant things always win out over the important things? About the time you are trying to sort this mess out, some know-it-all pops up and tells you what to do. It seldom helps, and then you have to decide what really counts.

I think Paul must have been chuckling to himself when he answered the current controversy. He told the believers that they could not build a church on the basis of whether it was right or wrong to eat meat offered to idols. He told them they really needed love to build the Corinthian Church.

What do we need to build churches today? A lot of time is spent on fund raising, architecture, membership drives, and programs. Too little time is spent on building a strong love foundation for the church to rest upon.

Well, what do you really need today? Unimportant, time-consuming arguments, or a big touch of the love of God?

## *Affirmation:* Looking for the Wrong Thing

*If we are living now by the Holy Spirit's power, let us follow the Holy Spirit's leading in every part of our lives. Then we won't need to look for honors and popularity, which lead to jealousy and hard feelings.*

Galatians 5:25, 26 TLB

Every June, thousands of varied honors are bestowed upon students across our land. From nursery school to graduate school, the honors are passed out. It is a wonderful time for those receiving the honors, but also a time of disappointment for those who didn't quite make it. It appears that some have to fall short in order for others to succeed.

Paul wanted the Early Christians to know that living the Christian life was not a popularity contest, and the only honor that would be passed out was spending eternity with God. In fact, Paul mentioned that the other side of honor and popularity is jealousy and hard feelings. If you don't believe that, just spend a few minutes with the team that lost the World Series last year.

Many of us are caught in a system of rewards and honors. It is difficult not to take these things too seriously if they do happen to us. We need to treat them as we treat salad at a dinner. It's there, we eat it as a prelude to greater things, but we don't spend a whole lot of time on it.

We are told that the race for the wrong things will not affect our lives if we are led by the Spirit. The Holy Spirit gives us all the power we need and all the direction we will ever desire.

Take a few minutes and do some sorting of the goals in your life today. Are you chasing the wrong things? Life is a constant sorting of priorities. Make sure that yours are in line!

## *Affirmation:* **The Affirmation of Victory**

*Go ahead and prepare for the conflict, but victory comes from God.*
                                                    Proverbs 21:31 TLB

How do we prepare for battles? We face emotional and verbal ones
every day. We spend a great deal of time deciding what to say and what
to do, trying to outthink those who oppose us. We get so used to the process that we find ourselves plotting how to advance one car farther in
heavy traffic. Life often looks like one giant war board as we prepare our
forces for battle.

How much energy have you spent lately on your battle plans? How
much time have you been robbed of as you schemed and plotted? The
theme in so many Old Testament passages deals with battle. Israel was
either going into one, fighting one, or just recovering from one. A clear
note from God sounded in so many of those situations: *The battle is the
Lord's!* In case after case, Israel won over innumerable odds with the
help of the Lord.

Solomon tells us that we can prepare all we want for the conflict, but
any victory we may have will always come from the Lord.

Have you ever felt as though you won the battle yourself? Now and
then we feel as if we did not need the Lord at all. We just breezed in and
won on our own strength. God's response is usually, *We'll see!*

There are many battles we fight that we should give to the Lord. Victory would come a lot sooner if we did.

Will you pray this prayer today? "Lord, I give You my conflicts and
battles. They are Yours. I gratefully receive the victories as a gift from
You!"

## *Affirmation:* **The Maker of All Things**

*The Lord, your Redeemer who made you, says, All things were made by me; I
alone stretched out the heavens. By myself I made the earth and everything in
it.*                                                  Isaiah 44:24 TLB

The other day I saw a beautiful briefcase in a store. I hurried over to
pick it up and admire it. I was impressed with its style, design, and crafted
look. I assumed it was real leather until I saw a little tag on the inside that
said MAN-MADE MATERIALS. What a disappointment. This wasn't the real
thing but a substitute.

I have discovered, as I grow older, that I have a deeper appreciation for
real things. I despise plastics, polyesters, imitations. I realize they are

useful and helpful, so don't get mad at me. You may have a kitchen full of them. I guess I feel there is a conspiracy to trade in the real things in life and get plastic in return.

Isaiah had an appreciation for the things God crafted. He looked around the world and wanted to remind God's people who made it all. We can still look around it today, savor the beauty, and realize that this really is our Father's world. When we realize that God sculpted a mountain, we get a sense of His power and might.

We all need to get out of the city and into the country now and then. What man creates needs to be set aside, and what God created needs to be placed on center stage. It can be too easy to believe that man built it all.

We can stretch our arms into some of the distant spaces of God's creation. We may go where man has never been before, but God was there first.

You and I may be builders, but God is still the Creator. Take a minute to enjoy His work today. Stop and smell the roses!

## *Affirmation:* **God Is Thinking About You**

> *I am poor and needy, yet the Lord is thinking about me right now! O my God, you are my helper. You are my Savior; come quickly, and save me. Please don't delay!*                 Psalms 40:17 TLB

How do you feel when someone sends you a card that simply says, "Thinking of you"? I doubt that you write back and ask your friend what he was thinking about you. It is enough to know that your name crossed someone's mind and he wanted you to know he cares about you. Some days we wonder if anyone even knows we are alive. If we did not enter the door to the world, would anyone come looking for us?

How does it feel to know that God is thinking about you right now? Comforting? Scary? Affirming?

If God could tell you what He is thinking about you, what would He say?

*Slow down. What's your hurry through life?*

*Quit worrying about those hassles and give them to me.*

*I love you even though you don't feel loved.*

He might say these three things and many more. It is good to know that God is thinking about you and me, especially with all the other problems He has in today's world.

The Psalmist tells us that God not only is thinking about us but He is our helper and our Savior as well. He is something to us. He is not a passing thought. He is a present Lord. He doesn't just send us an "I love you." He backs it up by being our protector as well.

Today, you are on the mind of God!

## *Affirmation:* **The Gift of Caring Friends**

*He has given you Paul and Apollos and Peter as your helpers. He has given you the whole world to use, and life and even death are your servants. . . .*
1 Corinthians 3:22 TLB

How would you like to have Paul, Apollos, and Peter as your personal friends and helpers? They certainly were a dynamic trio. With friends like that, you would be a lot stronger in the faith, and more courageous in your walk.

Somehow, the Corinthian believers did not realize the value of this trio. They probably did just what you and I do with our good friends—take them for granted. We seldom realize how important friends are to us until they move to another town.

Whom has God given to you as friends and helpers in your life? The good friends we have are not there by accident. I believe that God has a way of bringing people into our lives to support us and care for us. Sometimes we move through life so fast that we don't allow people time to connect to us and become God's blessing in our lives.

At other times, we want to pick and choose our friends because we know what we like. Well, you may know what you like in people, but God knows what you *need.*

Along with our friends, God has given us the whole world to use and enjoy. We are God's caretakers of friends and world.

Are you open to God's bringing new friends and helpers into your life today? The next person you meet may be by divine direction. Keep your heart open. He may need you just as much as you need him!

## *Affirmation:* **Affirming Our Call**

*"The Spirit of the Lord is upon me; he has appointed me to preach Good News to the poor; he has sent me to heal the brokenhearted and to announce that captives shall be released and the blind shall see, that the downtrodden shall be freed from their oppressors, and that God is ready to give blessings to all who come to him."*
Luke 4:18, 19 TLB

It is easy for Christian growth to become a self-centered pursuit. I meet many Christians who are "inner" centered rather than "outer" centered.

They are consumed with *their* growth, *their* problems, *their* spiritual journey, and what God is doing or not doing in *their* lives. Jesus never dictated a self-centered growth process. His life was "other" and "outer" directed. He never said, "I'm the truth and that's all I need."

Luke recorded Jesus' words as He read from the Prophet Isaiah in the temple. He identified with Isaiah's call and told the crowd that this was exactly what He had come to do. He could have nestled down in a quiet corner of the temple and had a good, contemplative life. He might never have been heard from again, except He had a calling.

Jesus came to preach, heal, proclaim, release, restore, free, and bless people. I doubt that anyone can do that quietly in a corner, away from the mainstream of life.

You and I are called to do the same things Jesus did. They demand reaching out to others. The action is out in the world, not in the filtered silence of the temple.

Will you dare to affirm your call today as one who is also charged to set people free?

## *Affirmation:* **Farming for God**

*"Yes, I am the Vine; you are the branches. Whoever lives in me and I in him shall produce a large crop of fruit. For apart from me you can't do a thing."*
John 15:5 TLB

I grew up on a farm. We grew every kind of fruit and vegetable there is. When I was quite small, I did not have much appreciation for the tremendous crops we had each year. For me, it just meant days of hard summer work, picking, packing, and selling. As I grew older, I realized that farming was a year-round project. It meant pruning, plowing, cultivating, spraying, and harvesting. The harvest never came easily. Farming was a systematized process. Without the groundwork, there was no harvest.

Jesus used many agrarian examples in His ministry. The people understood them because they were a part of their lives.

In today's verse, Jesus sets forth the clear distinction that He is the central part of any plant. Branches grow from the vine, not the vine from the branches. He wants His hearers to know that nothing will happen, growthwise, if He is not recognized as the source of growth. He tells those around Him that they will produce much fruit if they understand the growth process. Then He makes a sharp contrast, telling them that they will produce nothing apart from Him.

Severed branches on a fruit tree will not produce fruit. They will merely die. Even if you cut off a branch that is loaded with buds, it will die. It may live a few days and look very good, but in the end, it will die.

Jesus tells us that we cannot survive and grow apart from Him. We try many times to do it on our own, but we are drawn back to the reality that we have to be connected to Him, the source of our lives. Are you connected to the right Vine today?

## *Affirmation:* **Affirmative Power**

*He replied, "God can do what man can't!"*                    Luke 18:27 TLB

One of the greatest struggles we all have in life is accepting our limitations. Every time I try to run farther than I should, my legs send me a signal that they have reached their limit. I can usually make them go a bit farther, but they do it under great protest. My desire to run a marathon is limited by my legs' desire to cooperate. I can bandage and berate my legs, or I can accept my human limitation and watch others run farther.

It is hard for those who understand limitations to accept the fact that God has no limitations. Jesus summed up His potential with the words in today's text. He simply said that when man comes to his point of limits, God is just getting started.

Can God be limited? Some would say that only our lack of faith in Him limits His power. I am not so sure that is true. I don't believe we harness and render God inoperative by our lack of faith. I believe God can move beyond that and do the great things that will cause our faith to grow. God has to be experienced to be believed.

Much of the time, we are simply afraid that God might do some great thing far beyond our expectations, and we will not be able to handle it. We forget that God will equip us when the need arises.

Do you have a big, all-time list of things you wish God would do? Why are they not getting done? Some of us are afraid of letting God loose in our lives. Once we uncork Him, we won't be able to keep Him in a quiet corner of our lives. He might do some things we can't quite explain.

Can you risk letting God do what you cannot do today?

## *Affirmation:* **An Affirmation of Real Life**

> *I have been crucified with Christ: and I myself no longer live, but Christ lives in me. And the real life I now have within this body is a result of my trusting in the Son of God, who loved me and gave himself for me.* Galatians 2:20 TLB

Have you ever had an identity crisis? Do you ever wonder who you really are? It is easy to get lost in a series of role changes. You graduate from college and if anyone asks who you are, you can identify yourself as a college graduate. When you settle in a career, your identity and your career often merge into one. When you become a parent, another identity struggles to the surface of your life. As you get older, people want to push you into the retiree identity. It is little wonder that many of us struggle with who we really are at different times of our lives.

Paul established his new and permanent identity when he was struck down by God on the Damascus road. It caused him to tell the Galatian Christians that he really knew who he was. He had exchanged the life he once had for the new life Christ had given him. Christ had literally taken up residence in his life and transformed him. I am sure that he still had to correct some people who wanted to call him Saul. With his new identity came a new name. His transformation was a complete one.

Life will take you and me through many changes in identity. The only one that never changes is our relationship to Christ, once we have made the choice to invite Him into our lives. We become persons of the Christ.

God loves you today and you belong to Him. He lives within you!

## *Affirmation:* **Moving and Growing**

> *"The righteous shall move onward and forward; those with pure hearts shall become stronger and stronger."* Job 17:9 TLB

Life for Job was certainly the pits! He had a hard time turning his pits of depression into seeds of growth. Every time he turned around, the voices of his three friends echoed his pessimism. Yet, through his journey of despair, Job periodically sounded forth a barely audible note of hope.

In his reply to Eliphaz the Temanite, Job talks about moving onward and forward, even though he is not sure of how righteous he really is. He talks of growing stronger and stronger, although he is not quite sure when that will happen.

Job sounds a little like you and me. We have the confidence that God is at work within us, but our forward progress is very slow. We would like to be moving at the speed of the proverbial hare, rather than the lumbering tortoise. One thing I am learning about moving more slowly is that I really get to see more of what is around me. Sensitivity is often dulled by fast movement. I can tune in on things if I am moving slower.

Becoming stronger is a slow process. It is like trying to build long-dormant muscles. It takes many days' work for a discernible result. Working on having a pure heart is about as easy as becoming a millionaire overnight. Sometimes I think my only chance of having purity of heart is when I am sleeping.

Purity has a lot to do with our motives. When God is motivating us, our purity becomes a growing thing. If the world is motivating us, watch out!

You will move along and do some growing today. You will go forward and you will become stronger!

## *Affirmation:* **A Special Blessing**

> *If you read this prophecy aloud to the church, you will receive a special bless-ing from the Lord. Those who listen to it being read and do what it says will also be blessed. For the time is near when these things will all come true.*
>
> Revelation 1:3 TLB

What's a special blessing from the Lord? I am not quite sure what it is, but I would be happy to have one anytime. So would you! John tells us that the revelation God gave to him on the island of Patmos was to be shared. God's revelations were not to be carefully guarded secrets. They were to be shared with everyone and to be followed by those who heard them. This is not true of just the revelations of the end times; it is true of all that Scripture says to you and me.

Reading Scripture is always a blessing. It is like looking into God's mirror to find out who we really are and what we should be doing. Reading it is quite simple, but listening to it and taking action upon it is more difficult.

John warned that the things God had revealed to him would come true and that the time was near. Looking back, John's "near" becomes a relative term. Nineteen hundred years later, we are still waiting. It is certainly nearer now than it was then, and all signs prophetically authenticate that.

John promises two blessings in this text. Those who read it will be blessed, and those who do what it says will be blessed. All Scripture falls into that category. The blessings are ours for the taking.

Are you receiving the blessings God promised by living in His Word? Take time today to read a few chapters. You might even read Revelation!

## *Affirmation:* We Will Be Like Him

> *Yes, dear friends, we are already God's children, right now, and we can't even imagine what it is going to be like later on. But we do know this, that when he comes we will be like him, as a result of seeing him as he really is. And everyone who really believes this will try to stay pure because Christ is pure.*
> 1 John 3:2, 3 TLB

Have you ever struggled to be like someone else? We are at best a nation of imitators. Few of us are content to be what we are. Society places people on pedestals, and we try to emulate them in every way. Why else would you use the same shampoo that a famous movie star uses? One shampoo, and we expect to be someone else!

Growing older helps a person accept who he is. Perhaps you realize you have too little time left to try and be someone else. You want to use the time left to be yourself.

John tells us that we don't have to be someone else because we have already reached the top. We are God's children! It can only get better later, when we see Christ in person, because seeing Him will cause us to be more like Him.

What does it mean to you to be a child of God? Is it just a theological fact in your head, or is it a feeling of deep pride in your heart?

You don't have to be like Paul, Peter, or Mark to belong to God. You can be just you. Leave any transformations up to Him.

He will come again. We will see Him as He is. We will be like Him. That certainly beats trying to be like a movie star!

## *Affirmation:* We Are Ambassadors

> *We are Christ's ambassadors. God is using us to speak to you: we beg you, as though Christ himself were here pleading with you, receive the love he offers you—be reconciled to God.*
> 2 Corinthians 5:20 TLB

What does an ambassador do? He represents his country in another country. He is the voice of his country in a strange land. He represents any citizens from his country who may be in that land. It is a position of honor, power, and esteem. Only those who are held in very high regard in their homeland are given this kind of position.

Paul tells the Corinthian believers that we all represent Christ wherever we go. We have been specially selected to be His voice in society. Great responsibility has been placed upon us. He has given us the power and authority to fulfill that position.

Paul looked upon himself as an ambassador. His authority to speak to the churches as Christ's representative was not taken lightly. His message to them was that they receive the love that Christ was offering to them. His desire was that they be reconciled to God; that they share the same union he shared with Christ.

You and I are ambassadors today. It won't get you a special seat at the head table. It won't get you a mansion to live in. But it will give you a joy and confidence in living. You have been specially selected by the Lord of the universe to represent Him to everyone you meet. Your calling card is the Word of God.

The next time you think you are no one special, read Paul's words and unpack your ambassador wardrobe. You come with a message of life to those who need life!

## *Affirmation:* The Light and the Bright

*"O Lord, you are my light! You make my darkness bright. By your power I can crush an army; By your strength I leap over a wall."*
                                                    2 Samuel 22:29, 30 TLB

The twenty-second chapter of 2 Samuel contains David's song to the Lord after a battle. It is one long statement of how David views God's power in his life. If you ever doubt what God is and what He can do, spend some time reading the entire chapter.

In a pivotal part of David's song, he talks about God as the One who turns on the light and eliminates darkness. David recognized that there was such a thing as darkness. He had lived through some big chunks of it in his lifetime. He probably knew that there would be even more, but he also knew the Source of light.

Is the Lord your light right now, today? Are you living through some personal darkness in your life? Perhaps you are even committed to staying in the dark rather than risking God's light burning through your darkness. It is hard to hide when the lights are turned on!

God's light in your life can illuminate some things you would rather keep hidden. All of us have collected a few of those. God's light reveals what they are, and where they are hidden. His concern is not to embarrass us and say, *Look what I found in your life!* His way of love is to set us free from things that hide in dark corners in our lives. As long as they remain out of the light, we will never be free from them.

Will you allow God to light up your life today? Your darkness will be made bright and your heart will be made light.

# *Affirmation:* Living in Joy

*You will live in joy and peace. The mountains and hills, the trees of the field—all the world around you—will rejoice.* Isaiah 55:12 TLB

Have you ever wanted to go on one long vacation for the rest of your life? Vacation means rest and relaxation away from the day-to-day stresses of life. It means spending money for fun, and doing whatever you please. It means staying in bed all day or staying up all night. Vacation is a time of peace and joy that we wish would never conclude.

Do you think this is what Isaiah had in mind when he promised God's people they would live in peace and joy? I think he had more in mind than just a short vacation. He wanted them to live in peace and joy in the midst of stress and strain. Forget waiting until your vacation. Catch the peace and joy right now.

The next formidable question is, How?

A few verses earlier in this chapter, Isaiah tells the people of God that they are to seek Him and call upon Him. That's the secret to having peace and joy in your life. If you are seeking God's best for your life, He will grant it, and with it will come peace and joy as by-products.

Too many of us are in hot pursuit of peace and joy. Our problem is in not recognizing the source. Peace and joy come from within, when we allow Christ to place them in our lives.

Isaiah says that all the world around us will rejoice when we express peace and joy. It's true. People want to celebrate life with those who have found the secret.

The whole world is looking for peace and joy. You, dear Christians, are the possessors of it. Share it today with someone!

# *Affirmation:* Keeper of Peace

*He will keep in perfect peace all those who trust in him, whose thoughts turn often to the Lord!* Isaiah 26:3 TLB

In many strife-torn countries of the world, we have planted contingents of troops known as peacekeepers. Their job is to put down any uprising or stop any attackers. They are to keep the peace intact in the country in which they are stationed. Sometimes it works and sometimes it doesn't.

Christians should be known as peacekeepers. The reason is that we are carriers of peace. Isaiah tells us that God will keep us in perfect peace if we trust in Him. If that trust is truly valid, and that promise is fulfilled, then the peace of Christ will readily be recognized in us.

I enjoy being around peaceful people. There is a sense of quiet confidence and control that they demonstrate. Their peace is usually contagious, and I find myself better for having been in their company.

I don't enjoy being around nonpeaceful types of people. They bring an unsettling quality of life to me, and I am anxious to beat a fast retreat.

Isaiah tells us that one of the ways we can have a sense of peace about us is to keep our thoughts directed toward the Lord. This can be done by listening to Christian music, reading Scripture, praying, or talking with Christian friends. Just the simple process of meditation directs our thoughts toward Him.

Perfect peace is a great goal to work toward. You probably won't get all the way today. Just try to get a little further!

## *Affirmation:* **The Lifted Head**

> *But Lord, you are my shield, my glory, and my only hope. You alone can lift my head, now bowed in shame.*                                    Psalms 3:3 TLB

Have you ever watched people when they are walking? There are some who walk very erect, with head held high. There are others who seem to slouch along, with a carefree attitude. Still others walk with head down, never seeing anything or anyone. How do you walk? Watch yourself in a store window sometime.

I have seen many people walking through life with bowed heads. They probably have every right to do so. Some have had great sorrow and personal tragedy. Perhaps they are afraid to look up, lest something else fall upon them. Others walk with head down so that they will not have to interact with anyone else. Still others walk that way because of personal shame that has invaded their lives. They would probably put bags over their heads if it were fashionable.

David went through a time of shame in his life. His head was so low that he probably bumped it on his knees. Even during this time of great depression, David still recognized that the Lord was his only hope. Sometimes we do not do as well as David. We feel that there is little or no hope for us.

You and I can be thankful that God is in the business of straightening our heads, backs, and necks. He never intended for us to walk in shame. If our wrongdoing has brought us shame, we can confess it and claim God's forgiveness. Forgiveness always lifts bowed heads.

How will you choose to walk today?

## *Affirmation:* Walking, Running, and Flying

*But they that wait upon the Lord shall renew their strength. They shall mount up with wings like eagles; they shall run and not be weary; they shall walk and not faint.* Isaiah 40:31 TLB

How long do you have to wait before the Lord to get the kind of strength Isaiah was talking about? I sometimes wonder about that when I am running downhill in life and am almost out of gas. My heart wants to soar with eagles, but my body wants to be put on hold for a few weeks.

Renewable strength apparently comes in different dosages. One kind tells me that I will be able to walk without fainting. Walking doesn't sound like much of a feat. Most of us feel as if we can walk a little farther in life, unless we are all walked out. Maybe the problems we have been walking through lately have crippled us, and walking is now one step above breathing.

A second kind of strength is the kind that enables me to run. I like that kind because I am a runner. I would like to be able to be strong and run a little farther. Sometimes all I run into are problems. Then my running goes *splat!*

The third kind of strength is the kind that lets us fly with eagles. I am reminded of the little sign that says, HOW CAN YOU SOAR WITH EAGLES WHEN YOU WORK WITH TURKEYS? Good question! There are times when we all need strength to fly a little higher. Few of us will ever get to eagle height, but it is a good goal.

Waiting upon the Lord means renewal for walking, running, and flying. What will be your mode of transportation today?

## *Affirmation:* The Power Source

*"But when the Holy Spirit has come upon you, you will receive power to testify about me with great effect, to the people in Jerusalem, throughout Judea, in Samaria, and to the ends of the earth, about my death and resurrection."* Acts 1:8 TLB

What can you leave behind when you die that will help your children live? I realize that this is not a question most of us want to think about, because it is too gloomy. But the reality is that we will all die and leave some form of legacy to our children, relatives, and friends. Some would hope to leave vast amounts of money so that their heirs would live well. Others would leave prized possessions. Still others would leave a wealth of memories and good instruction.

Jesus had to face the problem of what to leave with the disciples that

would help them go on and fulfill His plans. He left them with the promise of the coming of the Holy Spirit. I am sure they didn't understand
much about it. They were simply told to wait and receive the Spirit in the
Upper Room. They were also told that they would receive the power to
be witnesses everywhere they went.

Power comes in different forms. Sometimes money can buy it, but it
soon fizzles out. Jesus had something in mind that would never fizzle out
in the disciples' lives or in our lives today. The presence of the Holy Spirit
did come, and the result was the establishing of the Early Church. The
power that visited those in the Upper Room that day was awesome. It has
not short-circuited over the last nineteen hundred years. It is still there in
great supply for your life and for mine. All we have to do is ask for it! We
can change our world when we are plugged into the source of power—the
Holy Spirit!

## *Affirmation:* **A Rain of Blessings**

*Yes, the Lord pours down his blessings on the land and it yields its bountiful*
*crops.*                                                      Psalms 85:12 TLB

Have you ever felt that God would run out of blessings? I think some
of us live in fear that God's well will run dry and we will no longer enjoy
His blessings on our life.

God is not stingy in blessing us. David says He pours His blessings on
the land. I am reminded of some of the rainstorms my family and I experienced when we lived in Florida. The natives called them "frog-choking
gully washers." They were downpours with a capital *D.* Streets could become rivers in just a few short minutes. Then the sun would come out and
the storm would move on. God blesses us with those kinds of rains.
Sometimes God's blessings come so fast that we are flooded with them.

I detect some skepticism in you. You are not taking your umbrella out.
You have caught only a few small drops recently, and the big storm
seems to have passed over you.

How's your health? If it's good, that's a blessing. If it's bad, it will give
God a chance to bless you through it. How about your job? If you have
one, that's a blessing. How about finances? If your bills are paid up, that's
a blessing. Oh, you weren't going to count those trivial things as blessings.
Then what are they?

Everything you have is a blessing from God. You, like me, are probably inundated with blessings. You just haven't looked at them in that
light.

When we use the things that God has given to us, He can trust us with more. He won't run out of blessings!

## *Affirmation:* **The Affirmation of Trust**

*"Note this: Wicked men trust themselves alone [as these Chaldeans do], and fail; but the righteous man trusts in me, and lives!"*     Habakkuk 2:4 TLB

The little sign hanging above the cash register in the diner said, IN GOD WE TRUST, ALL OTHERS MUST PAY CASH. A good motto for our times. Trusting in others has become a scary thing.

Several thousand people in my city lost a total of over a million dollars recently in a fraudulent investment scheme. When interviewed, many of them said, "We never investigated them. We trusted them."

Some people trust only themselves. Others trust a few people, while still others trust everyone. Many of us move through our world on the nervous edge of trust.

Habakkuk was a very minor prophet who made a very major statement on trust. He was right on the money when he said that wicked men trust in themselves alone and will fail. Our newspapers and magazines are jammed with stories about people who trusted their own abilities and failed. Some take their own lives so they won't have to face their failures. Others take the lives of those around them who have betrayed them.

Habakkuk also said that righteous men who trust in God will live. They will not just survive; they will live to the fullest. It is a wise person who places his initial trust in the Lord and in his fellowman second. God doesn't send out the wrong signals in leadership. You can trust God to give good directions in all situations.

How is your trust level today? Is it filed neatly under ME or under GOD?

## *Affirmation:* **Affirming Servanthood**

*"The more lowly your service to others, the greater you are. To be the greatest, be a servant."*     Matthew 23:11 TLB

Muhammad Ali was known during his boxing career for proclaiming, before every fight, that he was the greatest. His attempt to intimidate his opponents worked for a long time. Then one day he lost, and he was no longer the greatest. Today he is retired from the ring, and only the echo of his voice remains.

Mother Teresa's picture was in the newspaper recently. She had just given a commencement address at a local college. The article stated that she was the servant of the poor. This humble and lowly servant is in great demand across the world as a speaker. She won the Nobel Prize not long ago. I have yet to hear her proclaim that she is the greatest. Her claim is simply that of a servant. Yet the world pays her tribute and homage wherever she goes.

Being a servant is no easy thing. Christians are called to be servants. How many times we shun that role and want to be served by others. We want to exercise our rights and our status in the human race. People at the top of the ladder are served. They have no time to be servants.

All of us serve somewhere, whether we like it or not. One night you can be the guest speaker at a banquet, while the next, your wife is telling you to take the garbage out. It helps keep a person humble.

To be the greatest, be a servant. Forget the recognition and get on with the serving. Joy comes in serving others!

## *Affirmation:* **How to Be a Success**

> *Early the next morning the army of Judah went out into the wilderness of Tekoa. On the way Jehoshaphat stopped and called them to attention. "Listen to me, O people of Judah and Jerusalem," he said. "Believe in the Lord your God, and you shall have success! Believe his prophets, and everything will be all right."*                                    2 Chronicles 20:20 TLB

The other day I wandered by the "success shelf" in the local bookstore. There were books telling me how to succeed at everything under the sun. One was even directed at telling me how to successfully raise mushrooms. From mushrooms to boardrooms, the waterfront of success was covered. As I walked away, my eye caught another book titled *Dress for Success*. I just shoved my hands down in the pockets of my faded blue jeans and figured I would never make it up the dressing ladder to the top.

King Jehoshaphat had a good word for the army of Israel. He did not pass out military-strategy manuals to his leaders. He did not inspect the spit and polish of their uniforms. He simply told his men to believe in the Lord God and they would have success in battle. Now, that's pretty simple. Does it work today in the battles of life? Try it once. You will be surprised at the results.

Along with the promise of success, the army was instructed to believe in the words of God's prophets. In simple terms, trust God and trust His Word, and you are on your way to success.

Those certainly are not the plans of the world, but God always does things differently anyway.

Today you will have success and everything will be all right if your trust is in the Lord. Leave your footprints in His wet cement of trust!

## Affirmation: **A Great Responsibility**

*"But anyone who is not aware that he is doing wrong will be punished only lightly. Much is required from those to whom much is given, for their responsibility is greater."*                                        Luke 12:48 TLB

Have your children ever complained that one of them has to do more work than the other? You usually respond by saying that so-and-so is older and you expect more from him or her. The reply: "That's not fair."

In your job, you may be getting the load dumped on you because you are older, more experienced, and have greater ability to get the job done. While others stand around and watch, you do the producing. It's just not fair!

Whenever there is a request in your church group for a volunteer and no hands go up, do you usually end up with the job because you always get it done? It's not fair!

God gives gifts for service to all of us. When we use those gifts well, we are called upon repeatedly. It is an affirmation and a compliment to our ability. It can also be an overload.

God's principle is that more is always required from those to whom more has been entrusted. If God has blessed you with great wealth, great responsibility comes with it. If God has blessed you with an important position, the responsibility parallels it. If God has given you the gift of baking brownies, bake them by the truckload!

Are you living up to your responsibilities? Don't moan. Rejoice! They have been lovingly entrusted to you.

## Affirmation: **Affirming God's Work**

*But Jesus told him, "Anyone who lets himself be distracted from the work I plan for him is not fit for the Kingdom of God."*                    Luke 9:62 TLB

Jesus' response in today's Scripture was directed at a man who said he wanted to follow Jesus but first needed permission from those at home. We might feel it was cruel of Jesus not to give the man the opportunity to clear things up at home before he joined Jesus' followers. The point is that the man wanted to find out if others thought it was all right before he took the road of discipleship. If you wait for others' permission to allow you to follow Christ, you may never get there. Asking opinions is usually a pooling of ignorance anyway. When it comes to following Christ, that is a decision that only you can make. It doesn't really matter what others say or think. You stand alone at the point of decision.

Perhaps the man who wanted to follow Jesus thought he would be more popular if he consulted those back at his home. Sometimes we only consult to elevate ourselves and to impress others with potential decisions.

Jesus set a standard for discipleship. Don't be distracted by anything. If anything pulls you away from the work He has planned for you, you will not be fit for the Kingdom. Strong words but honest words.

Every coach of an athletic team says the same thing. We call it sports dedication and accept it.

Are there any distractions in your life that are sidetracking you from God's work? Discipleship demands commitment!

## *Affirmation:* **Affirming Loyalty in Love**

*If you love someone you will be loyal to him no matter what the cost. You will always believe in him, always expect the best of him, and always stand your ground in defending him.*                                    1 Corinthians 13:7 TLB

If I were performing your wedding ceremony this weekend, you would hear these exact words as a part of my ceremony. I can think of no other words that better describe the basic responsibility of love. Most marriages get into trouble when loyalty goes out the window and you stop believing the best about your mate. Loss of expectations follow next, and you soon start attacking your spouse rather than defending him or her. In working with broken marriages over the past ten years, I have witnessed numerous times what happens when this verse is not lived up to.

Loyalty in love always costs something. When a president of our country fell from power, his wife stood faithfully by. The cost was tremendous, but that is the price of real love. Love aims at believing the best about your mate and expecting the best from him or her.

Defending the person you love is not always easy. Sometimes you find yourself defending your child or a very good friend. It may seem easier to join the offense rather than the defense.

Tough love is always an affirmation and reflection of what God's love is to you and me. We struggle with it to make it work. We cry over it to make it real.

Can you affirm your loyalty in love to someone in your life today?

## *Affirmation:* **Hello to Love, Good-bye to Fear**

*There is no fear in love; but perfect love casts our fear, because fear involves punishment, and the one who fears is not perfected in love.* 1 John 4:18 NAS

Have you ever made a list of all your fears? It could run all the way from your fear of getting a speeding ticket to cracking your dentures on peanut brittle. The problem with fears is that they seldom become realities. They are ghosts that hide in the closets of our minds, and only come out when we aren't looking. John was aware that even Christians have fears. He knew that fear could prevent the people of God from living a fulfilled life. He knew that only one thing could eliminate fear from the life of the Christian. That one thing was knowing that God's love was stronger in a believer's life than all the fears he could conjure up.

Have you ever tried to give your fears a dose of love? A common fear is the fear of what will happen tomorrow. How do you deal with that fear?

The Scripture tells me that God is in charge of tomorrow. If I believe that He loves me enough to take me through tomorrow, then there is nothing about it I need to fear. His love will penetrate that fear and remove it from my life.

Some Christians believe they have to have a bag of fears to carry around so that God will have something to do. God has plenty to do. Dump your fears over a cliff and let love be your controller. Perfect love always casts out fear!

## *Affirmation:* **Potholes and Joy Ahead**

*So be truly glad! There is wonderful joy ahead, even though the going is rough for a while down here.*                                          1 Peter 1:6 TLB

I always enjoy flying. At thirty-seven thousand feet the going is always pretty smooth, no matter what the weather is like on the ground. I have flown over blizzards, rainstorms, and heat waves. None of them affect me at that altitude. It is only when I land that I have troubles.

Peter was pretty honest in telling us that the going would be tough for us down here, but there would be wonderful joy ahead. Sometimes we ask, "How far ahead?" When a road sign says, ROUGH ROAD AHEAD, we always want to know how far ahead.

You can't always fly over the rough stuff in life. Every now and then you have to put on your wading boots and slog right along through the middle of it. Our society is great at telling us how to escape almost everything. Yesterday a billboard told me to ESCAPE TO PARADISE. I wanted to get on the next plane, but I had to sit down and write some of this book. Flying away would have been easier!

It is not always easy to fix our eyes on the end of the journey, where the promise of the good times rests. The Early Christians always had one foot in the world, one on the ladder, and a deep desire to move speedily to the Kingdom God was preparing for them. That was the wonderful joy that was ahead. And it still is.

Life is a sprinkling of potholes here and a great deal of joy yet to come. So keep on walking through today. You can be glad that this isn't all there is!

## *Affirmation:* Led to Peace by a Child

> *In that day the wolf and the lamb will lie down together, and the leopard and goats will be at peace. Calves and fat cattle will be safe among lions, and a little child shall lead them all.*                        Isaiah 11:6 TLB

Have you ever wanted to lead a parade? What would it be like to be out front in the Tournament of Roses Parade on New Year's Day? All the world would be watching you and all the exciting parade participants coming along after you. You would be the leader. Such honors seldom fall to most of us. As I watched the parade last year, I thought about leading for a second or two, then I spilled my coffee and came back to reality. I wasn't even a participant. I was only a viewer.

Isaiah tells us of the parade plans God has made. God's parade resembles a circus with a wild-animal contingent, except the wild animals are mingled in with the tame ones. Out front, a young child is leading the whole procession. What does that say to you about how God puts a parade together?

You can say it will be fulfilled prophecy, a miracle, or a demonstration of the kind of peace that God envisions for His people. It will be such a peaceful parade that even a child can lead it.

You and I probably won't get to march in too many parades between now and then. But we can reserve a space right after the lions when God one day brings His peace to all.

In the meantime, you will have to march through the parade of daily happenings in your life. Just make sure you know who is leading the parade!

# *Affirmation:* **Ask for the Secret**

*Ask me and I will tell you some remarkable secrets about what is going to happen here.*                                         Jeremiah 33:3 TLB

Keeping a secret is no easy task. I always wonder how many others have been told to keep the same secret that I have been told to keep. When does a secret lose its "secret" status? Why should there even be secrets?

Jeremiah was in jail when the Lord sent him a message. Jeremiah probably was only interested in when he would get out of jail and get on with his life. The Lord's message was for Jeremiah to ask God about what was going to happen to him and to Israel, and He would reveal some remarkable secrets. Does that sound as if God was playing a game with Jeremiah? Jeremiah could well have said, "Let's quit playing games with secrets. You have my attention. Get me out of here!"

God doesn't play games with you and me. He does expect us to ask Him for things: directions, wisdom in decision making, the right words to speak at the right time.

Many of us know the joy of having a child ask a parent for something special, and the thrill of being able to respond. It is fun to be asked and fun to respond.

I believe God wants us to ask Him for things. He just waits to reveal His plan to us. He has special things in store for our lives. The Scripture tells us that we have not because we ask not.

What would you like to ask God for today? Are you ready for Him to respond to you in some remarkable ways? You just never know what God is up to until you ask!

# *Affirmation:* **The Arsenal of God**

*It is true that I am an ordinary, weak human being, but I don't use human plans and methods to win my battles. I use God's mighty weapons, not those made by men, to knock down the devil's strongholds.*
                                         2 Corinthians 10:3, 4 TLB

Have you ever felt very ordinary and very weak? If you have, you can line up beside Paul. He always recognized his human frailties and weaknesses. Therein lies his secret of success as a follower of God.

Many of us try to handle the weak sides of our humanity by cranking up our motivation machinery. We talk to ourselves and try to think positively. We tell ourselves that things really aren't as bad as they seem. We might even buy a button that says, I'M SPECIAL.

Paul says, "I know who I am and I also know that I cannot use human means to achieve supernatural victories in my life." He knew that the battle was always the Lord's and not his. Most of us are still trying to learn that. We are like David in Saul's armor: formidable in appearance yet inept in operation.

Paul arms himself with weapons from God's arsenal when he faces life's battles. One of the strongest of the weapons is faith. Faith is knowing that God will do what He says He will do. Faith is backed by the history of God's promises in Scripture. Another of God's weapons is His timing. He doesn't do things on our schedule, but follows His own. Another weapon God uses is wisdom. His is far above ours. The wisdom of God may sometimes appear foolish to man, but it works.

Are you willing to let God use His weapons to win the battles in your life? You may be human, but you are connected to a God who is superhuman!

## *Affirmation:* **Affirming Your Trust**

*Do not let this happy trust in the Lord die away, no matter what happens. Remember your reward!*                                    Hebrews 10:35 TLB

Have you ever wanted to park on a happy experience? We all have peaks and valleys in our lives. When a happy peak comes along, we often want to capture it, contain it, and keep it at the center of our lives. But as someone has said, "We all have to come down from the mountain sometime."

Becoming a Christian can be a happy peak experience in your life. You can live in that happiness for a long time. Since Christ is the source of that happiness, it will remain rooted in your life forever. But inevitably things will come along to dispel that happiness.

Paul reminds the Hebrew Christians not to forget how wonderful they felt when they first heard the good news of Christ. He also remembers the great price many of them had to pay for this happiness that had come into their lives. Some of them lost everything they had, and others gave up their lives. It gets more difficult to be happy when those kinds of things come into your life. It is easy to say, "I was happy until. . . ."

Paul was always helping people remember the goodness of the Lord. He kept calling the Early Christians back to the basics. His word for then and for now is don't let your trust in the Lord be a conditional one. Keep your eye fixed on what's ahead, not what's around you.

Is your happy trust in the Lord still in place in your life? Don't let unhappy situations squeeze it out!

## *Affirmation:* A Healthy Affirmation

*And the Lord will guide you continually, and satisfy you with all good things,
and keep you healthy too; and you will be like a well-watered garden, like an
ever-flowing spring.* Isaiah 58:11 TLB

One of our great national preoccupations lies in the area of physical
fitness. We are consumed with the hundreds of methods to exercise our
way to good health. The desire to stay slim or get slim is propounded by
thousands of diet books. We all keep looking for the easy path to better
health. The good-health business is big business.

Good health seems to be a by-product of right living. It does not stand
by itself. It intersects with all the strands of our lives. For Isaiah, a
healthy affirmation contained three things that can be applied to our lives
today.

First and foremost is the guidance of the Lord. When we have clear
guidance and good direction, our minds will be relaxed and at peace, and
our physical bodies will profit as a result.

Second, we will be satisfied with all good things. One of mankind's big
struggles today is to achieve satisfaction. We keep looking over the next
hill for more satisfaction. Only God can bring ultimate satisfaction into
our lives. It comes from within, not without. Satisfaction can come in
very small packages. They can be so small that we overlook them.

Third, good health is the result of good guidance and personal satisfaction. Isaiah doesn't highlight this. He lists it almost as an afterthought.
Perhaps we have the cart before the horse in our society. If we concen-
trated on good living, we would have good health.

Are you experiencing the ever-flowing-spring type of good health in
your life today? The Bible is the best-stocked health food store I know!

## *Affirmation:* Affirmative Speech

*"A good man's speech reveals the rich treasures within him. An evil-hearted
man is filled with venom, and his speech reveals it."* Matthew 12:35 TLB

Have you ever stood in the corner of a room at a party and listened to
people talk? You can learn a lot by listening to the sounds of conversations. You can spot the nervous people, the uptight people, the confident
ones, the happy ones. Speech is the greatest form of self-revelation known
to man. Few of us get into any trouble until we open our mouths.

There are two kinds of communication: peak communication and
maintenance communication. The first kind usually reveals the rich trea-

sures within people, while the other simply fills the air with words about weather, sports, people, and so on.

When was the last time you had a great conversation with someone? You went away enriched, and wished you had more time to spend with that person. Those conversations are few and far between for most of us.

When was the last time you had to listen to a person who was filled with hate and anger? Sometimes just saying hello to such a person unleashes a verbal barrage in your direction. You wonder what you did to cause the ruckus.

What you say to others today will reveal who you are and what is deep within you. Will you be sharing treasures or venom?

## *Affirmation:* An Old Plan for a New Day

*It is God himself who has made us what we are and given us new lives from Christ Jesus; and long ages ago he planned that we should spend these lives in helping others.*                                    Ephesians 2:10 TLB

How much of your time do you give in helping others? Most of us would say, "That's all I do. Everyone is after my time." I think there are two kinds of help we give to others. The first is service help. That usually deals with all the practical things in life. It is picking up your kids after school. It is doing the family laundry. It is maintaining routines and programs that are of benefit to others.

The second kind of help is ministry help. Ministry help is going out of your way to do the extraordinary for others. Some people look at that kind of help as a chore to be done if there is any leftover time. It may mean fixing the plumbing for an elderly lady who is living on a meager pension. It could mean making a late-night hospital call to see a friend who is very ill. Ministry help is love in action.

Ephesians tells us that God planned for us to spend our lives helping others. It was to be normal, not extraordinary. It should not be only in response to a crisis in someone's life. It was to be a daily pattern in living.

I have always noticed how people who live in small, rural towns have plenty of time to help each other. They make an investment in living. Not so in our large metropolises. Time there is self-consumed.

Will you spend some time today in helping someone?

## *Affirmation:* **The Child in You**

> *Jesus called a small child over to him and set the little fellow down among them, and said, "Unless you turn to God from your sins and become as little children, you will never get into the Kingdom of Heaven."*
>
> Matthew 18:2, 3 TLB

Several years ago when my wife and I were in Hawaii, I noticed a number of children flying kites on the beach. With each passing day, my urge to own and fly my own kite increased. Finally, I went to the kite shop, purchased my very own kite, and headed for the beach.

When my kite was launched and flew far overhead, I realized how much fun I had missed since I was a kite-flying child. For a few moments, I was just another kid with a kite on the beach.

What does it mean to become as little children? What did Jesus have in mind? I don't think He was inviting the disciples to go fly a kite. I do think He was inviting them to explore the nature of God with the simplicity of a child. I think He was inviting them to go back in their learning processes to that place where they once were curious about everything, and excited about life. If they could capture that kind of childlikeness as they approached God, they would be well on the way to an exciting faith.

A child is free to say:

> Show me!
> I don't know!
> Teach me!
> Let's play!
> I trust you!

There is a curious mixture of the adult and child in all of us. We want to grow up, but we need to keep the curious and trusting mind of the child alive in us.

Spend a moment with the child in you today. You may even go fly a kite and get closer to God!

## *Affirmation:* **A Quiet Spirit**

> *If the boss is angry with you, don't quit! A quiet spirit will quiet his bad temper.*
>
> Ecclesiastes 10:4 TLB

Has your boss been angry with you lately? Every one of us who works at gainful employment has had the experience of feeling the wrath of our employer. It is not a happy situation but a common one. Our humanity rises to the surface and we want to tell our employer to stick his job in his ear. We want to quit and let him know that we will not be treated that way, whether it is justifiable or not. If you have an angry boss, your place of employment can be a forty-hour prison sentence each week.

Solomon knew about angry employers. He also knew that our desire would be to run away from them. He tells us there is another way, and it is the way of God.

How do you have a quiet spirit toward your employer? A quiet spirit is willing to go beneath the problem and explore the real reason for anger. A quiet spirit is willing to talk things out and admit personal fault. A quiet spirit will not seek revenge but will seek to mend a situation and bring good from it.

The Scriptures tell us that a soft answer turns away wrath. Too few of us believe that. When someone is angry with us, we get angry ourselves.

Our place of employment is our altar of service to the Lord. We spend the significant hours of our lives there. A good relationship with those we work for and with will enhance our Christian witness.

Get out your quiet spirit today and take it to work with you!

## *Affirmation:* **Receiving the Crown**

> *"Stop being afraid of what you are about to suffer—for the devil will soon throw some of you into prison to test you. You will be persecuted for 'ten days.' Remain faithful even when facing death and I will give you the crown of life—an unending, glorious future."*                     Revelation 2:10 TLB

Fear always invades my life when I have to take a test. I don't know why, but I have always wanted to run from tests. Renewing my driver's license every four years is a traumatic experience. Even though I have driven for over thirty-two years, I am always afraid I will flunk my Department of Motor Vehicles ordeal. (I did once!)

Tests are a growth part of all our lives. We may fear them, but we have to take them. John tells us in today's text that the devil is a master tester. As he tested Christ in the wilderness, he continues to throw his tests at us today. What we need to realize is that he can't win. The Scriptures affirm the fact that "greater is He who is in you than he who is in the world" (1 John 4:4 NAS).

Satan can bring up some very strong fears in our lives. He can cause us to fear the past, the present, and the future. We can fear that we will fail Christ and fall to Satan.

John's words are to remain faithful in our testing times, even if we are facing death. In other words, keep standing on what you have stood on up until now—God!

The end result of our standing firm for the Lord in testing times is His promise that we will receive the crown of life and a glorious future.

You and I will end up victorious. We have a great future. Don't let today's testings shake your foundations!

## *Affirmation:* Growing Quietly

*Being punished isn't enjoyable while it is happening—it hurts! But afterwards we can see the result, a quiet growth in grace and character.*

Hebrews 12:11 TLB

Every time I have to discipline my children, I seem to feel worse about it than they do. I take little satisfaction in the knowledge that they are supposed to learn by the process and come out stronger and better in the end. Punishment is hard to mete out and harder to live through. It hurts both parties.

If joy comes in the morning, I hope the results of punishment are not far behind. This is one case where I am more eager for the results than the process.

I have often seen the results of years of testing and processing in older people. They either become hardened and bitter toward life or they let that process mold them into a quiet growth in grace and character. I can hardly wait to get older to share in those results. Grace and character only come by walking through the fires of life. You can't buy them or drum them into your life. You have to *live* in order to get them.

People with quiet grace and character have learned not to take themselves too seriously. They know that God is sovereign and works from the beginning to the end of life. Whatever problems come to them are just a part of the seasoning process of life.

Our backward vision is always twenty-twenty. We look back and tell with pride how something was good for us when we went through it. When we are slogging through it, it can be pretty despairing.

Are grace and character visible in your life? Look for them today!

## *Affirmation:* **Affirmative Planting**

*But remember this—if you give little, you will get little. A farmer who plants just a few seeds will get only a small crop, but if he plants much, he will reap much.*                                         2 Corinthians 9:6 TLB

A farmer who is expecting a good harvest in the fall will not sparingly plant seeds in the spring. I know because I grew up on a farm. When it was planting time, we made sure that we prepared the ground properly and planted the seeds generously. I remember that once I spilled a package of radish seeds. Have you ever tried to pick up seeds that size? I kicked dirt over them and went on down the row. Several weeks later, we had a massive clump of radishes in one place.

The principle of planting seeds carries over into real-life situations. Every day of our lives, you and I are out there sowing seeds. Sometimes they are not always the right kind. Negative seeds grow, too. If you sow dissension, that is what you will reap.

It is always fun to sow the seeds of love. Those seeds have a habit of producing fruit rather rapidly in other lives as well as in our own. Seeds of love should never be sown sparingly. They should be sown in greater abundance than any other seeds.

Our return from the seeds of love is in proportion to the seeds sown. All of us could use just a little bit more love. In order to get it, we have to sow it.

God's richest people are never collectors. They are people who give to others. Collected things only crowd our lives and make our journeys impossible. The more we give, the greater the return.

Make this day a day of giving out more than you receive!

## *Affirmation:* **Marching Orders**

*Then the Lord said to Moses, "Quit praying and get the people moving! Forward, march!"*                                      Exodus 14:15 TLB

The Red Sea was in front of them and the Egyptians were coming up fast from behind them. Moses was trying to capture the moment and extract everything he could from it. It was a one-time, ultimate confrontation between the powers of God and the powers of man.

Some of us would have wanted to build a monument there for all time. Others would just want to get across the sea to the other side as quickly as possible. Moses wasn't quite sure if he wanted to even get his feet wet.

Have you ever been in this kind of situation? Looking back, you see the things you know you must leave behind. Looking ahead, you see one giant barrier to your forward progress. You know God has brought you to this place, and now you are wondering what He is going to do. It is almost like being caught in a giant vise while someone slowly turns the sides in on you.

I think God brings us to that kind of place once in a while just to let us know He is in charge. I think He smiles when He knows that we can't do anything else and we must rely on Him.

As Moses stood at the crossroads of Red Sea Boulevard and Egyptian Alley, God simply told him that praying time was over and action time had arrived: *Get moving. Forward, march!*

I think some of us find it easier to stand around in confusion when God says to get going. The first step out of a tough spot is the step of faith.

What is God telling you today about moving ahead in your life? Is it time to get marching again?

## *Affirmation:* **Eliminate the Negatives**

*"Yes, be bold and strong! Banish fear and doubt! For remember, the Lord your God is with you wherever you go."*　　　　　　　Joshua 1:9 TLB

Can you imagine an NBC reporter interviewing Joshua just after he had assumed the reins of leadership from Moses? The first question would probably be, "Joshua, how do you feel about filling the shoes [oops, sandals] of Moses?"

Joshua's answer: "Fine. The Lord has promised that He will go with me wherever I go. That's all I need to know for now."

It would have been a short interview because Joshua knew that all he could do was trust the Lord, as he had watched Moses do in many situations.

God told Moses that he had to do two things in order to experience good direction from God in his life. The first, be bold and strong, has a lot to do with personal character. Joshua was not expected to just take two pills and have boldness and strength. As he had walked with God, these attributes had been growing in his life. No one noticed them, but they were there when Joshua needed them.

The second thing Joshua was told to do was to banish fear and doubt. That is a little tougher. It has to do with trust. If you know from past experience that God will do what He says, there will be no fear or doubt. The more we trust, the less we doubt.

As you walk out your door today, are you a bundle of fears and frustrations? Or are you able to begin the day with the confidence that God is with you wherever you go? He is!

## *Affirmation:* **A Cleansing Affirmation**

*Come, let's talk this over! says the Lord; no matter how deep the stain of your*
*sins, I can take it out and make you as clean as freshly fallen snow. Even if*
*you are stained as red as crimson, I can make you white as wool!*

Isaiah 1:18 TLB

Have you ever had something come back from the dry cleaner with a
spot still on it? We all have. Dry cleaners are not flawless. We take the
article back and sometimes are told that there is no way the spot can be
removed. It has ingrained itself into the fabric to such an extent that it is
now permanent. And it usually happens to our favorite sweater!

Some of us get spots on our lives that refuse to be removed. Some we
inflict upon ourselves. Others are put there by different people and situations. We try to hide these spots from other people. Sometimes it's like
trying to hide a pimple on the end of your nose. You can't pretend that
you are blowing your nose all day long. Pretty soon, someone points to
your nose and you say, "I know, I know!"

God has the best spot remover in town. No matter how deep the stain
that causes the spot, He can take it out. Do you believe that? Then why
continue to carry your spots around? Maybe you would feel lost without
them. You wouldn't have anything to blame your failures on.

When you and I come to God, we come with all our spots, blemishes,
and marred countenances. He lovingly removes them, permanently. They
don't return. They are gone forever.

Let God remove any spots on your life today!

## *Affirmation:* **In Training**

*Let God train you, for he is doing what any loving father does for his children.*
*Whoever heard of a son who was never corrected?*          Hebrews 12:7 TLB

Have you ever been to an athletic training camp? Everything that is
done there is geared to helping athletes prepare for competition. Each
spring, baseball teams head for warm climates to prepare for the coming
season. Training facilities are designed with the most modern equipment
available. Each athlete is expected to be trained to his optimum potential.
When camp breaks and the season begins in earnest, the athlete is expected to be in condition and play to the best of his ability.

What would a training camp for Christians look like—comfortable
pews, stained-glass windows, quiet organ sounds, soothing sermon, cook-

ies and coffee in the fellowship hall? Sounds more like a nursing home than a training camp. I find it interesting that the Scripture talks about the Christian life as a battle, and we are the warriors preparing for that battle. No wonder we aren't taken seriously by society. We make big sounds that are followed by little or no action.

How does God train His people? He takes them through trials, struggles, hassles, hurts, and heartaches. It's like running the high hurdles. You fall and get all skinned and scraped, but you get back up and keep running.

You and I are in training. Life is the camp. God is the master trainer!

## *Affirmation:* **Never Wasted**

*So, my dear brothers, since future victory is sure, be strong and steady, always abounding in the Lord's work, for you know that nothing you do for the Lord is ever wasted as it would be if there were no resurrection.*

1 Corinthians 15:58 TLB

Wasting time seems to be a hobby for some people. No matter when and where you find them, they aren't doing a whole lot. Some people create a lot of dust but don't get much done. Time management seems to be an executive preoccupation. There are numerous books on the subject, all telling us how to squeeze more juice from a minute. Corporate executives are trained to waste no time because time is money.

How do you know when you are wasting time? We all can think of something we should be doing when we are not doing it. We can feel great waves of guilt sweeping over us if we don't get certain things done.

Even Christians get hooked on how they use their time for the Lord. Some are trying to do too much, while others are doing too little. It appears to be a very confused army!

Nothing you do for the Lord is ever wasted. That's what Paul told the Early Church. It may seem insignificant to you, but it is not wasted. That's good to know, because I sometimes feel I am not getting a whole lot done for God. All I can do is offer Him my best and count on Him to use it to His glory.

Whatever you do for God today will not be wasted!

## *Affirmation:* When Looking Ahead Counts

*Look straight ahead; don't even turn your head to look. Watch your step.*
*Stick to the path and be safe.*                    Proverbs 4:25, 26 TLB

It sounds as though Solomon has gone into highway construction.
These are the kinds of signs we expect to see on the interstate highways.
They are caution signs that will keep us out of trouble. But Solomon was
not talking about the freeways. He was talking about how to deal with
prostitutes.

Most Christians that I know would skip over these verses because they
would admit this was certainly no problem to them. Perhaps physical
prostitutes cause no threat to you, but what about the other forms of
prostitution? We can prostitute ourselves in numerous ways in life. Prostitution is the wrong use of something to gain a reward.

We can use our God-given gifts improperly. We can take honest desires and turn them into dishonest ones. We can believe that we know as
much about something as God does. We can sell our souls to the devil.

There are plenty of things that we should not be looking at in life. Just
a quick side-glance can lead to distraction and disaster. We are cautioned
to look straight ahead, watch our steps, and stick to the right path. That's
good advice wherever we walk in life.

Most people who get sidetracked don't plan on its happening. It sneaks
up on you when your attention is diverted. Some friends of mine have left
their Christian faith because they got sidetracked. They didn't plan on it,
but it happened.

Watch where you are going today. Prostitutes may not be your problem, but other things might be!

## *Affirmation:* Where to Look for Bread

*Jesus replied, "I am the Bread of Life. No one coming to me will ever be hun-*
*gry again. Those believing in me will never thirst."*

John 6:35 TLB

Someone has said that half the world could live on what Americans
throw into their garbage cans. We live in a land of abundance, while the
other half of the world starves. It is no fun to be hungry. Most of us have
only experienced missing a meal now and then. We complain that we are
so hungry we could eat a horse. How little we know what it is really like
to be hungry. I don't know because I am not sure I have ever truly been
hungry.

Jesus came into a hungry world. The people weren't physically starving, as many are today. They were spiritually hungry and looking for reason and purpose in their lives. It was to them that Jesus addressed Himself when He said He was the ultimate answer to spiritual hunger. He announced that He was the Bread of Life. Few understood what He was talking about. They probably scratched their heads and walked away, thinking that His comments were interesting but rather puzzling.

Jesus also announced that He was a permanent spring of water and that those who drank from Him would never thirst again. Even fewer understood the meaning of that.

What did Jesus accomplish by saying this? He affirmed that He was on earth to meet people's needs, both spiritually and physically. His ministry affirmed that He did both.

Where are you looking for bread and water? Don't look in the wrong places or your hunger and thirst will never be met. Look to Jesus!

## *Affirmation:* Turning in Evil for Good

> *But Joseph told them, "Don't be afraid of me. Am I God, to judge and punish you? As far as I am concerned, God turned into good what you meant for evil, for he brought me to this high position I have today so that I could save the lives of many people."*   Genesis 50:19, 20 TLB

When was the last time God turned a disaster in your life into a diamond? When you were going through the disaster, were you aware that it would become a diamond? Probably not! Your feelings were echoed in the words, "Get me out of here!"

I have had numerous people come up to me during my ministry and tell me they would not be the people they now were if they had not gone through their particular crisis. That doesn't mean that a major crisis or disaster is a good thing. It simply means that God can bring good out of it.

As far as Joseph's brothers were concerned, they had taken care of him permanently by selling him off into slavery. Joseph didn't check out on God during that time, and God didn't check out on Joseph. Both of them allowed the time to be used for a later good result. This is why Joseph could say that God turned an evil thing into a good thing. If he had not been placed in the pit, he would not have climbed to the pinnacle. It was when he got to the pinnacle that he could help the most people.

God can take you from a pitiful situation and bring blessing to you and to others. Just because you can't see how doesn't mean it can't be done. Leave the "how" to God.

Climbing any ladder starts with the bottom rung!

## *Affirmation:* **Who Gets the Glory?**

*For everything comes from God alone. Everything lives by his power, and everything is for his glory. To him be glory evermore.*   Romans 11:36 TLB

I remember my daughter's asking me for money one day when she was very young. I said I didn't have any at the moment, and she responded by saying, "Let's go to the bank and get some!" For a long time she thought the local bank just handed out money to anyone who drove up. When she realized that you have to put money in in order to take it out, life taught its first cruel lesson.

Banks are pretty important in our lives, and it is easy to believe that everything good comes from them because they are connected with money.

A Christian really starts growing up when he realizes that everything comes from God. He is beyond banking, government, nations, and a universe. He is the source of everything. That's easy to forget in a consumer-oriented society. We go to the supermarket so much that we look upon it as the provider of our daily bread. We forget that the supermarket rests in God's hand of provision, too.

God is the source, God is the power, and everything reflects His glory. It takes a long time for God to get that through to us. When we acknowledge it, we won't rely on our own feeble power but will feel free to tap into His power for our lives.

Are you plugged into a dead outlet today? Plug into the Lord. He is your source. He gets the glory!

## *Affirmation:* **Are You Famous for Your Faith?**

*Men of God in days of old were famous for their faith.*   Hebrews 11:2 TLB

How many people in your church are known for their faith? I think I would have a struggle to name 5 out of 500. Now that doesn't mean that the other 495 have no faith. It means that they aren't known for their faith. They might be known for other things that are important.

How do you become known for your faith? Do you have to read one hundred books on faith? Do you have to get a Ph.D. in faith from a local seminary or university? Is it caught or taught?

When you look at the heroes in the hall of fame of faith in the Book of Hebrews, you discover that many of them were not very important people. Their acts of faith made them well known.

Faith, simply defined, is the ability to trust God for what man deems impossible. Impossibilities wipe out most of us right at the start.

Is faith an outdated commodity in the twentieth century? Have we become too realistic and practical to accept the mystical?

When an act of faith brings godly results, why are we so stunned? God certainly hasn't changed over the centuries. It must mean that we have changed, and the challenge to our faith has been dulled.

Who will be famous for their faith in our time? It could be you or me, if we are willing to put our faith on the firing line.

## *Affirmation:* **Anything?**

*"If I can?" Jesus asked. "Anything is possible if you have faith." The father instantly replied, "I do have faith; oh, help me to have more!"*

Mark 9:23 TLB

A young boy possessed of a demon was brought to Jesus for healing. The disciples had already tried to heal him and failed. His father had probably built up a wall of doubts when he finally got the child to Jesus. His comment to Jesus was, "Oh, have mercy upon us and do something if you can!" Jesus seemed to be startled when He reiterated the question: "If I can?"

His affirmation to the father came in the words, "Anything is possible if you have faith." Some of the responsibility for healing was placed back on the father of the small boy. If his attitude had been one of disbelief and skepticism, little would have happened.

The father's response was that he did have faith and he wanted to have a whole lot more. Now that sounds a little like me. I have just a little, usually, and wish I could have a lot more. You probably feel the same way.

Faith is always a growing thing. It takes time and goes through a stretching process. When I see little things accomplished through my faith in Christ, I am ready for bigger things. Faith is a mountain that grows.

How would you evaluate your faith right now? Do you have a tiny bit or a lot? Faith is not to be stored up—it is to be used. It is God's muscle in our lives. An unused muscle atrophies. A used muscle becomes stronger. Stretch your faith today!

## *Affirmation:* **Death Brings Forth Life**

*Jesus replied that the time had come for him to return to his glory in heaven, and that "I must fall and die like a kernel of wheat that falls into the furrows of the earth. Unless I die I will be alone—a single seed. But my death will produce many new wheat kernels—a plentiful harvest of new lives."*

John 12:23, 24 TLB

Any seed must die in order to create new life. Sometimes that sounds like an unfair principle, especially to the seed. God has so ordered the process of life and death, and He lived out that process as an example to all of us.

One of the strongest growth principles in the Christian life is that we have to slowly die to ourselves in order for Christ to live through us. That usually is a lifelong process for most of us. We die by degrees, and the process is painful.

Jesus' death on Calvary certainly produced a mighty band of new believers. Read the Book of Acts and you will discover the real results of Jesus' death and Resurrection.

You and I are the new wheat kernels that the death of Christ has produced. Our mission in life is to carry on that process, not by our deaths, but by our living for Christ.

Is your life producing a harvest of new lives? It is easy to forget that we are seeds. We die to self, Christ lives in us, and others find new life because of His life in us.

## *Affirmation:* **A Short Missionary Journey**

*"Heal the sick, raise the dead, cure the lepers, and cast out demons. Give as freely as you have received!"*                                    Matthew 10:8 TLB

Jesus had a special in-house training program for the disciples. He mapped out a short missionary journey for them to see how they would respond to the needs of people. As he spelled out His instructions in the tenth chapter of Matthew, it became apparent that this was to be a testing time for the followers of Jesus.

The first thing He told them was to announce what they were all about. Then He told them what to do. Next, He told them what to take along, or rather, what not to take along. Then He told them where to stay and how to act. Finally, He told them how to handle rejection. That all sounds like a first-aid kit for a spiritual journey in the twentieth century, except for the healing part. Some people don't believe that God can do those things in this century.

Jesus didn't just want to prove who He was. He wanted people to know that He loved them. His healing ministry exemplified that, in so many ways. Healing is love in action.

Jesus told the disciples to give as freely as they had received. That's really the key to an effective faith. You and I have to give ourselves away if we are going to gain anything in our lives.

Is it easier for you to give or to receive? Practice some giving away today. Your missionary journey may not be a short one, but it is an important one!

## *Affirmation:* Who Chose Whom?

*"You didn't choose me! I chose you! I appointed you to go and produce lovely fruit always, so that no matter what you ask for from the Father, using my name, he will give it to you."*                               John 15:16 TLB

Have you ever been the last one chosen for a team? Not a very happy experience, is it? I can remember my sandlot baseball days. When I started out playing ball, no one wanted me on the team. I was either chosen last or completely ignored. It didn't help my self-esteem much. It is always more fun to be picked first.

In an inner-circle meeting with the disciples on the Mount of Olives, Jesus lets them know that they were chosen. He tells them that they did not choose Him. I doubt that too many would have chosen to follow an itinerant carpenter whose only claim to fame was that He was the Son of God.

Jesus did the choosing and the appointing of the disciples. Their task was to be productive. Jesus gave them an affirmation to go along with their calling. He said that the mention of His Father's name would bring them excellent results in getting what they asked for. And it did. What they accomplished in the Early Church was prefaced by, "In the name of the Father."

God has chosen you and me. Unlikely prospects that we are, we are chosen to follow Him. We, too, are to produce fruit. We, too, can ask things in the name of the heavenly Father, and we will receive them.

Nothing has changed—just the date on the calendar!

## *Affirmation:* Multiplying the Insignificant

*Then Andrew, Simon Peter's brother, spoke up. "There's a youngster here with five barley loaves and a couple of fish! But what good is that with all this mob?"*                               John 6:8, 9 TLB

Can the few insignificant gifts you might have tucked away in your life be multiplied many times by the Spirit of God? Many of us consider our gifts too few and too small to be of any great consequence to the people around us. We tend to ignore them, hide them, apologize for them, and never seek to cultivate them.

A small lunch for one, tucked under a little boy's arm, was far short of a catered dinner for five thousand—until Jesus took possession of it. When He touched it, it became a feast for the multitudes. It was no longer average, unnoticed, common. It became the center of a celebration and the heart of a miracle.

You and I are the possessors of many quiet, ordinary gifts that lie untouched in a corner of our lives. Gifts need to be gently touched and blessed by the love of God in order to be used for the joy and benefit of others.

Think for a few moments about the gifts that lie undiscovered in your life: the gifts of sensitivity, caring, patience, compassion, love, peace, joy. Some of your gifts may look about as exciting as five loaves and two fishes—until you offer them to God and He blesses them.

God has a way of affirming what appears to be ordinary in our lives and bringing about extraordinary results.

What's in that brown bag under your arm?

## *Affirmation:* **A Few Last Words**

*I close my letter with these last words: Be happy. Grow in Christ. Pay attention to what I have said. Live in harmony and peace. And may the God of love and peace be with you. Greet each other warmly in the Lord. All the Christians here send you their best regards. May the grace of our Lord Jesus Christ be with you all. May God's love and the Holy Spirit's friendship be yours.*

2 Corinthians 13:11–14 TLB

We close *Every Single Day* with the final words that Paul shared with the Corinthian Christians. After struggling through many problems and trials with them, Paul shared the strong affirmation of what Christ's love was really all about. His words to the Early Christians are words for today. We can add little to them. We can only encourage you to follow them.

Every single day you live is the Lord's. He is at work in you, perfecting His plan.

*May God's love and the Holy Spirit's friendship be yours!*